Marta Dyczok

Ukraine Calling

A Kaleidoscope from Hromadske Radio 2016–2019

With a foreword by Andriy Kulykov

Assistance by Oksana Smerechuk, Caitilín O'Hare, and Larysa Iarovenko

UKRAINIAN VOICES

Collected by Andreas Umland

1 *Mychailo Wynnyckyj*
Ukraine's Maidan, Russia's War
A Chronicle and Analysis of the Revolution of Dignity
With a foreword by Serhii Plokhy
ISBN 978-3-8382-1327-9

2 *Olexander Hryb*
Understanding Contemporary Ukrainian and Russian Nationalism
The Post-Soviet Cossack Revival and Ukraine's National Security
With a foreword by Vitali Vitaliev
ISBN 978-3-8382-1377-4

3 *Marko Bojcun*
Towards a Political Economy of Ukraine
Selected Essays 1990–2015
With a foreword by John-Paul Himka
ISBN 978-3-8382-1368-2

4 *Volodymyr Yermolenko (ed.)*
Ukraine in Histories and Stories
Essays by Ukrainian Intellectuals
With a preface by Peter Pomerantsev
ISBN 978-3-8382-1456-6

5 *Mykola Riabchuk*
At the Fence of Metternich's Garden
Essays on Europe, Ukraine, and Europeanization
ISBN 978-3-8382-1484-9

The book series "Ukrainian Voices" publishes English- and German-language monographs, edited volumes, document collections, and anthologies of articles authored and composed by Ukrainian politicians, intellectuals, activists, officials, researchers, and diplomats. The series' aim is to introduce Western and other audiences to Ukrainian explorations, deliberations and interpretations of historic and current, domestic, and international affairs. The purpose of these books is to make non-Ukrainian readers familiar with how some prominent Ukrainians approach, view and assess their country's development and position in the world. The series was founded and the volumes are collected by Andreas Umland, Dr. phil. (FU Berlin), Ph. D. (Cambridge), Associate Professor of Politics at the Kyiv-Mohyla Academy and Senior Expert at the Ukrainian Institute for the Future in Kyiv.

Marta Dyczok

UKRAINE CALLING

A Kaleidoscope from Hromadske Radio 2016–2019

With a foreword by Andriy Kulykov

Assistance by Oksana Smerechuk, Caitilín O'Hare, and Larysa Iarovenko

ibidem
Verlag

Bibliographic information published by the Deutsche Nationalbibliothek
Die Deutsche Nationalbibliothek lists this publication in the Deutsche Nationalbibliografie; detailed bibliographic data are available in the Internet at http://dnb.d-nb.de.

Bibliografische Information der Deutschen Nationalbibliothek
Die Deutsche Nationalbibliothek verzeichnet diese Publikation in der Deutschen Nationalbibliografie; detaillierte bibliografische Daten sind im Internet über http://dnb.d-nb.de abrufbar.

ISBN-13: 978-3-8382-1472-6

Printed in the United States of America

Contents

Andriy Kulykov
Foreword. This is the Book I Need 9

Marta Dyczok
Introduction 11

Mykhailo Samus, Hanna Hopko, Andreas Umland
"NATO's Warsaw Summit and Ukraine" 17

Chrystia Freeland, Volodymyr Groysman, Andriy Shevchenko, Mychailo Wynnyckyi
"Canada and Ukraine: Shared Values and Real Economic Opportunities" 29

Andriy Kulykov, Kateryna Smagliy and Paul Niland
"The Killing of Journalist Pavel Sheremet in Kyiv: In-Depth Commentary" 39

Dennis Lozinsky, Daniel Bilak and Frank Sysyn
"What Role Does Religion Play in a Hybrid War?" 53

Olexiy Haran and Brian Whitmore
"Is War the New Normal in Ukraine?" 65

Volodymyr Ohryzko, Brian Mefford, Michael Getto and Jairo O. Nascimento
"War, Sports and Politics" 75

Oleksander Tkachenko and Serhii Plohkii
"Shadow of the 1991 Moscow Coup Today" 83

Serhiy Holovatyj and Bohdan Nahaylo
"Ukraine: 25 Years of Independence, a Thousand Years of History" 91

Olena Bilan, Cameo by Boris Johnson
"IMF Loans & Economic Challenges: Western Sunrise in Ukraine" 105

Timothy Snyder
"Ukraine Commemorated the 75th Anniversary of the Babyn Yar Tragedy" 113

Nestor Gayowsky
"Ukraine, Canada & a Satellite Phone: How History Happened in 1991" 121

Serhii Plohkii
"Read This Book with a Martini. Shaken, Not Stirred" 131

Yevhen Fedchenko
"How Ukraine Was the Testing Lab for Russia's Information War against the United States" 139

Daniel Drezner
"What Can Ukraine Expect from Trump: Temporary Insanity or a Permanent Shift?" 145

Hennadiy Afanasiev
"I Participated in a Pro-ukrainian Protest against Russian Occupation" 153

Ihor Poshyvailo
"Celebrating Ukrainian Easter: Not Rabbits and Chocolate but Paska and Pysanky" 161

Olesia Ostrovska-Liuta
"Laughter and Strength Featured at Kyiv's Book Arsenal" 171

Peter Solomon
"Who Judges the Judges? Peter Solomon on Successes & Challenges of Legal Reform in Ukraine" 181

Ulana Suprun
"Putting an End to the 'Wild West Pharmo-Mafia' in Ukraine" 193

Pablo Mateu
"Assisting Ukraine's Uprooted – UNHCR and Partners in Action" 207

Pavlo Mamontov
"Wounded Warrior Now Competing in Invictus Games" 217

Volodymyr Kulyk
"Why All the Fuss? Ukraine's New Education Law" 223

Andrey Kurkov
"We Don't Need a New Maidan" 233

General Sir Rupert Smith, Sir William Jeffrey and George Anderson
"Conflict Resolution in Donbas: No Magic Formula, Political Process Is Needed" 245

Brian Whitmore
"There Has to Be an 'or Else.' Washington Analyst Whitmore on War, Ukraine, Russia, Hybrid Containment, and More" 261

Michael Bociurkiw and Kateryna Kruk
"Was It All Worth It? Babchenko's Case and the Credibility of Ukrainian Authorities" 275

Oleksandr Danyliuk
"Everything Was Agreed in Advance" 289

Michel Terestchenko
"The Good, the Bad, and the Very Ugly. Michel Terestchenko on Ukraine Regional Politics" 301

Jaroslav Skira
"Resurrection of Christianity in Ukraine. Prof. Jaroslav Skira on Religion and Politics, and Newly Created Orthodox Church of Ukraine" 311

Olga Onuch
"Ukraine 2019 Rada Election. Olga Onuch on Results and Implications" 325

Foreword

This is the Book I Need

I need this book because it helps me not to err in my memories of very important years in Ukrainian history. My recollections of those years are very personal and thus may be misleading. I need yardsticks to measure the validity of what I imagine I remember against what was happening there and then as perceived by other people. Compare, and you have a better chance of keeping a true picture in mind.

Dr. Marta Dyczok produced a series of radio shows that reflected the most pressing issues of Ukraine's life in those years. They combined topicality, and moreover, urgency. Her pod/broadcasts were interviews with important speakers, sometimes already accomplished opinion leaders, and sometimes, those who would gain part of the necessary experience for being influencers from talking to her. The show covered a set of issues of paramount importance to Europe (and some would say, for the world), as Ukraine stood up against the open aggression of Russia, the country whose rulers are bent on regaining a degree of the regional and global dominance it used to have so recently.

For us at *Hromadske Radio,* Dr. Dyczok's voluntary contribution to our work was a bright example of solidarity with Ukraine's cause, proof that what we have been striving for was also of importance for a person from a totally different country; sometimes, it would seem, from a totally different world. What Dr. Dyczok did, by devising and running her radio show, was evidence of the fact that we do not live in parallel worlds, however different they are: our worlds do cross, they interact and overlap, and shape each other, even if this takes a long, long time.

What did this effort mean for Dr. Dyczok? One thing I can say for sure: this was in no way a materially rewarding experience. Being financed by grants and having to resort to lengthy periods of unpaid work more than once, we could never offer Dr. Dyczok a salary or any other remuneration worthy of the time and effort she applied to planning, recording, and then making her material fit for broadcast or for putting it online as podcasts. As Canada in general has shown a strong measure of solidarity with Ukraine and provided tangible help to our country, so did Dr. Dyczok. Of course, it is naive to presume that a country acts in this or that way in relation to another country out of pure idealistic considerations. There have to be common interests. However, an individual is a different organism than a country, and a person may act first and start to think about explaining their motives later. I doubt if Dr. Dyczok has ever thought of the need to explain why she launched and then led this series of radio shows. She probably just heard Ukraine calling, and responded to this call by doing what was appropriate in the moment. In her turn, by making this series, Dr. Dyczok called out to many people so that they could form their ideas about what was going on in Ukraine.

I need this book to remind me sometimes that Ukrainians are not alone in their opposition to aggression. I need this book to be sure that there are ways to attract attention and empathy to what we are going through. I need this book to have proof that people from other countries are capable of sharing this world with us.

Apart from reading this book, do find Dr. Dyczok's podcasts and listen to them. Enjoy their versatility, and think about why this academic scholar wanted her shows to feature a Ukrainian melody every time. Maybe it is easier to make an educated guess after you have listened to "Ukraine Calling." Listening will give you a deeper appreciation of what is written in this book, as what is said and how it is said is often so meaningfully different from any written text.

The motto of *Hromadske Radio* is: *Slukhaite. Dumaite.* Listen. Think. It was a bit different for Dr. Dyczok. I have the impression that for her it was: Listen. Think. Share!

Andriy Kulykov
Co-founder and Chairperson, *Hromadske Radio*
Kyiv, Ukraine

Introduction

This book is like a time capsule. It's a selection of in-depth interviews about Ukraine that aired between 2016-2019 on a show I created for *Hromadske Radio* (Community Radio Ukraine).

In early 2016 people kept asking me, "What is going on in Ukraine?" My best friend. My dentist. My favourite librarian. My students. Various media outlets. Russia's undeclared war against Ukraine was continuing and the story was in news headlines. But few English language sources explained the details and the bigger picture. I kept thinking it would be great if I could direct people to a reliable source instead of repeating things over and over, so I decided to create one.

A group of people I know in Kyiv had formed an independent radio station, *Hromadske Radio,* and I had done some English language podcasts for them. It occurred to me that this quality media outlet would be a natural place for such a project. I approached the Co-founder Andriy Kulykov and Editor-in-Chief Kyrylo Loukerenko. The concept was to create a weekly English language show that would provide an overview of the main headlines, in-depth interviews on a main issue, a look at the country's cultural scene, and some music. They loved the idea. So I decided to devote my summer to the project. Andriy came up with a name for the show, "Ukraine Calling," and Kyrylo found designers to make the logo.

I had worked as a journalist for the *Guardian* and *Radio Canada International* in the early 1990s but had no idea how to create, produce, and host a weekly radio podcast. So, I reached out to my friend Brian Whitmore who had created the very successful *Power Vertical Podcast* at *RFE/RL*. And he coached me. One piece of advice was. "Start with a big story." The NATO Warsaw Summit was coming up, so I chose that to be the subject of the first episode and it aired on 9 July 2016.

It was very exciting but also a bit overwhelming, since at first it was just me working on the show. And the sound engineer Andriy Izdryk. He was a bit quirky but highly professional. As we were editing the second episode, we came to the phone interview I had recorded with Chrystia Freeland, then Canada's Foreign Trade Minister. Izdryk said, "The sound quality is poor. We can't use it." I was flabbergasted. "But it's Chrystia Freeland!" I said. "The sound quality is poor," he repeated calmly. I insisted, so we took it to Kyrylo. He initially agreed with Izdryk, but after some convincing on my part, agreed that a short segment of the interview could be used. It aired and you'll find it in this book. Izdryk worked on all the episodes, except for the few times he was on vacation. In addition to being an amazing sound engineer, he is one of the coolest people I've met.

Another thing Brian mentioned was that a signature jingle for the show was important. Kyrylo sent me a link to the *Hromadske Radio* music data base, but I couldn't find anything I liked. I wrote to my musician friend Foma (Serhiy Fomenko) and asked if he had something I could use. He sent a few clips. I chose one. And by the third episode we opened the show with our new signature jingle.

Then, in early August, Larysa Iarovenko wrote to me. "Great job with *Hromadske Radio*. Please let me know if you need any help, I would volunteer." We had worked together when she was the administrator of the Petro Jacyk Program at the University of Toronto. In 2016 she was living in England and we'd stayed in touch. I replied, "Wow, yes, please!" She wrote back, "What do you need help with?" "Everything!" was my answer. "OK, what do you need help with most?" the sensible Larysa asked. "Transcribing." And that's how she became the show's first transcriber. Larysa would eventually lead a transcribing team and, more importantly, became the heart and soul of the show, helping me with all aspects of the show throughout its history.

With each episode Ukraine Calling's audience grew. But as the end of the summer neared, I grew worried about the future. Soon I would have to go back to my university and resume teaching. I had not found anyone to continue the show and was afraid the project would die. On my last evening in Kyiv I was having dinner with a friend on a terrace in downtown Kyiv and telling her how sad I was feeling that this project would not continue. Then Marko Suprun walked by. He waved and I invited him to join us. "Why so sad?"

he asked. I explained. "I'll do it!" he said. "Really?" I was incredulous. But he said, "Sure." And, just like that, Marko saved the project. He became the show's new host.

And that's how it was for the entire three years the show existed. People just volunteered or agreed to help. When in the autumn Marko became busy and couldn't host every week, Bohdan Nahaylo stepped up and offered to help when needed. I had interviewed the former *RFE/RL* executive for the eighth episode, and he did many excellent shows for Ukraine Calling. Later Oksana Smerechuk did the same. She had initially volunteered to help transcribing, then gave me a wonderful interview about Christmas traditions. When I heard her great radio voice, I invited her to become one of the hosts. And so we had four alternating hosts, since in addition to producing the show, I continued to host when I could. A few times when we were in a crunch, the *Hromadske Radio* people stepped in and helped out. One week, when no one was available to host, Andriy Kulykov proposed an interview he'd done with military experts. Another time when we suddenly lost the host in the last minute, Kyrylo did the interviews.

The rest of the team also grew through serendipity. I was invited to deliver a lecture about Ukraine's media at Cambridge University, England in October 2016, and mentioned Ukraine Calling. Afterwards, PhD student Maria Terentieva approached me and asked if she could help. The same thing happened after I delivered the Mohyla Lecture at Saskatchewan University and that's how Nicole King joined the team. A number of my own students also volunteered to help with various parts of the show, Caroline Gawlik, Maksym Sviezhentsev and his wife Ilona Sviezhentseva, Malika Nazurova, Leah Wagner, and I started using episodes in my teaching. Later a friend of a friend, Caitilín O'Hare, offered to join the transcribing team. She not only did a great job but later put together the first draft of all the interviews which I used to prepare this book.

And so the Ukraine Calling team became this transatlantic team of volunteers working in different countries, different continents, and different time zones. Every week, when my teaching, writing, meetings, and other work was done, I would start thinking about the theme for the next week's show. I'd reach out to see who was available to do what and we would start working on the various sections. By mid-week, whoever volunteered to host would have done the interview, and the sound file would be sent to Larysa, who would divide the work among the transcribing team. In the meantime, the people responsible for the news headlines and cultural overview would be preparing their sections, and I would be selecting the music for the week. Then I would find someone to record the introduction, news, culture and music sections. The various audio parts would then be sent to Izdryk for compilation, I would assemble the text and send it to Kyrylo. In addition to running the programming for the entire *Hromadske Radio* station, every week he would pull the show together and post it on the website. That was the moment we all waited for! To see the show posted online and listen how it had turned out.

There were times when none of the hosts in Kyiv could conduct the feature interviews, so I tried to figure out how I could. It occurred to me that universities have radio stations with recording studios. I found the one at mine, which is the student run *94.9 CHRW Radio Western*. I made an appointment with the station manager, Timothy Glasgow, told him about Ukraine Calling and asked if he might consider helping out and allow me to use their studio to record interviews. He enthusiastically agreed and asked what kind of recording software *Hromadske Radio* uses. Of course I had no idea so, connected him with Izdryk in Kyiv and was intrigued to see how sound engineers communicate. A number of the interviews in this volume were recorded in that studio.

Others also joined the team at various times, including Alexander Konovalov, Irena Chalupa, Anna Kirishun, Dmitry Smiyan, Tanya Bednarczyk, Rich Raycraft, Adam Courts, Ira Solomko, and Alex Wishart. My heartfelt thanks go out to each and every one of these people who helped make the show happen. Also to all the people who took the time out of their busy schedules to give interviews for the show. And to Dmytro Konovalov, who came up with the idea of publishing this volume.

As an historian, I am acutely aware of the importance of primary sources, how narratives get distorted when they are missing. I'm also very aware of the ephemeral nature of radio and that things can disappear from the internet. So I started working on the idea of publishing a selection of Ukraine Calling episodes in a book format, to preserve them. It was challenging to find a publisher for this type of book, but when I contacted Dr. Andreas Umland, who was a guest in the first episode, he enthusiastically agreed.

All 124 episodes couldn't fit into this book, since the transcript of the interviews alone was over 500,000 words. Some difficult choices had to be made. My thanks to Oksana, Caitilín, and Larysa for helping me narrow things down and work on preparing the manuscript. The news and culture sections have been omitted, the selected interviews have been edited, and in some cases abridged. Should you be so inclined, you can find the full shows by clicking on the links provided. And for anyone who wants to see/hear/read all the episodes they're available on the *Hromadske Radio* website: https://hromadske.radio/en/podcasts/ukraine-calling

Thanks for listening!

Marta Dyczok
Western University
London, Canada

Episode 1

"NATO's Warsaw Summit and Ukraine"

with Mykhailo Samus, Hanna Hopko and Andreas Umland
9 July 2016

https://hromadske.radio/en/podcasts/ukraine-calling/nato-s-warsaw-summit-and-ukraine

NATO's Warsaw Summit was all over the news in early July 2016. As leaders of the world's most powerful military alliance prepared to meet in Poland, many in Ukraine were wondering how the meeting would affect them. To get some deeper insight into the NATO-Ukraine relationship and the Warsaw Summit, Marta Dyczok spoke with a number of experts.

Marta Dyczok: Our first guest is Mr. Mykhailo Samus, Deputy Director for International Affairs at the Centre for Army, Conversion, and Disarmament Studies, in Kyiv. Thank you for joining us. The NATO-Ukraine relationship is often discussed in terms of what NATO can do for Ukraine or what Ukraine should do to improve relations with NATO. Is there another way of looking at this relationship, particularly in light of what's been happening in Ukraine over the past two years?

Mykhailo Samus: Yes, we could find another way, and it looks like Ukraine and NATO are trying to find it. For example, during the Summit in Warsaw, the question of creating a NATO centre for hybrid warfare could be discussed with Ukraine. And possibly in Ukraine we will have a new centre, and NATO will try to find new knowledge about hybrid warfare from Ukraine's experience. Because Ukraine is a unique country now in Europe and the Euro-Atlantic space. It is participating in real conventional war and a new type of hybrid war with Russia. To have such an enemy in warfare is a very unique kind of experience. And I would say, not only after the end of the Cold War but even since the Second World War, no country in Europe has had such an experience. If you remember the issues about using the Multiplier Launcher Rocket System (MLRS), GRAD for example, it's an extremely powerful weapon which Russia uses against the military and civilians in Ukraine. I think that there wasn't use of these weapons since the Second World War.

Dyczok: So NATO can learn from Ukraine's experience?

Samus: Yes. I spoke with many American and other experts and analysts, and they said that they are now trying to find as much real information as possible from the battlefield, what might be new for the armed forces of NATO countries. For example, I spoke with the President of the Potomac Foundation, Mr. Karber. He told me that their analyses showed that NATO is not ready for such a war. And Ukraine can show them how to fight with Russians. Now NATO can study how Ukrainians fight every day, every minute with Russians, and that could prepare them for the next potential conflict with Russia in other regions like the Baltic States and the Black Sea Region.

Dyczok: So that's a very different perspective than usual, where NATO teaches Ukraine, and that leads me to my next question. Ukraine has been participating in joint military exercises with NATO since the mid 1990s. Has this had any impact on the development of Ukraine's military?

Samus: Sure. If you remember, the first attempt of Ukraine's leadership to change the Ukrainian Armed Forces towards NATO standards was after the first Maidan in 2005, 2006, 2007, with Minister of Defence, Anatoly Hrytsenko, and at that time the new reforms started. And of course, during these joint exercises the Ukrainian Armed Forces got a lot of knowledge about how to improve, for example, communications, command and control systems, how to deal with new procedures in headquarters. So these are the main questions. Because if Ukraine is trying to be closer to NATO, the main question is how to operate together. But as Ukrainian leadership changed, so did the geopolitical models of a strategic course toward NATO, towards neutrality, towards Russia. That meant that the Armed Forces were always under the influence of our own changes in the political system and the political opinions of the leadership. So some experience was lost before 2014, and the Ukrainian Armed Forces weren't prepared for war with Russia. Not because of bad joint exercises with NATO partners, but because of a bad situation in Ukraine and its leadership.

Dyczok: Do you think that Ukraine's government has done enough to secure support from NATO and other international actors in the war that's happening on its territory?

Samus: I would *not* say that the main goal of Ukraine now and Ukraine's leadership and Armed Forces is to join NATO. The main goal and main tasks are to defend Ukraine and build an effective defence security system, to defend Ukraine from aggression from the Russian Federation.

Dyczok: But surely Ukraine needs help with that?

Samus: Yes, and because of this we could have different instruments. One of the most effective, theoretically, would be NATO. And we have a lot of support from NATO. But in reality, NATO is pretty weak on the political side and political point of view. That's why Ukraine's leadership and Ukrainian Armed Forces, as I know, tried to ask to require a lot of help from NATO side. But I'm sure NATO could do more for Ukraine to be better prepared to defend its country from Russian aggression.

Dyczok: But does Ukraine do enough to try and secure that need? You said that NATO could be doing more, but has Ukraine done enough to reach out and meet the criteria that NATO is setting out for Ukraine?

Samus: I think yes. First of all, NATO is not an organization that gives help. It's an organization set up to defend its Members from threats, not defend Ukraine because Ukraine is not a member. This is a stereotypical myth that NATO has to help Ukraine. Ukraine is a partner, Ukraine is a close neighbour of NATO and of course, since Russia destroyed all the rules of international law and order, NATO could help Ukraine. And actually, NATO is helping Ukraine. But if you're talking about defence, Ukraine used to do it by itself. It did not rely much on someone else to come and fight for Ukrainian soldiers. Even if we're talking about weapons, Javelins, or anti-tank systems, something like that, NATO won't give Ukraine anything of this nature because NATO as an organization doesn't care about it. It is not an issue for NATO as an organization. About concrete weapons we [Ukraine] need to talk to partners. Concrete actors like the United States, Canada, or Belgium, or the Czech Republic. Only through bilateral communication with Ukraine and other partners.

Dyczok: The Warsaw Summit is in part about firming up NATO's eastern border. About self-defence, Poland, the Baltic States. What is likely to change for Ukraine as the result of this summit?

Samus: It is very important that NATO is finally trying to defend its eastern border, because before Russian aggression against Ukraine, NATO didn't have any operational plans on how to deal with, for example, a Russian brigade getting Estonian or Lithuanian territory. Now I know that NATO is pretty serious about it, the United States is sending in troops on rotation. New troops to the Baltic States, new troops to Poland. Some discussions go well beyond the Warsaw Summit, discussions on the Black Sea, like the creation of some group. It's very important for Ukraine because Ukraine could participate in all of these structures, in all of these initiatives. Even the existence of this group in the Black Sea will have an influence on Russia, because Russia will need to react. And secondly, Russia understands that NATO is trying to stay in this region and trying to deter Russia from here.

Dyczok: Our second guest is Hanna Hopko, Chairperson of the Committee on Foreign Relations in Ukraine's Parliament. Ms. Hanna Hopko, could you please tell our listeners why is the NATO

Warsaw Summit important for Ukraine? What is Ukraine hoping to walk away with?

Hanna Hopko: Thank you so much for asking these important questions. After the Alliance's last Summit in September in 2014 in Wales, our President raised the issue of the war in east Ukraine and we built a coalition to fight Russian troops on Ukrainian territory. It's important for Ukraine to have the support of NATO and NATO Members to stop Russians and also to see a sustainable ceasefire, to withdraw heavy artillery and military troops from Ukrainian territory. Also, to push the Russians to allow OSCE and other international organizations to have access to the Occupied Territories. And also, we rely on NATO support to return Donbas and Crimea. It is also important to raise energy security issues, because this is the issue of independence. Besides energy security and security itself, it's also important because Ukraine could bring to the NATO community our experience of fighting this hybrid war, that Russia is using as an instrument to grab territories and break international law.

Dyczok: Public opinion in Ukraine continues to be divided on the issue of NATO. Recent public opinion polls have shown that even after the annexation of Crimea and Russia's triggering war in Eastern Ukraine, less than 50% of the population of Ukraine would vote for membership in NATO. Ukraine's President Poroshenko regularly makes strong statements about the need for partnership with NATO and moving forward on that relationship. You chair the Parliamentary Committee on Foreign Relations. What is the opinion on that Committee? Is there unity on that Committee? Are political elites united on this question?

Hopko: There is a tendency for the growth in public support for Ukraine becoming a member of the NATO community. This is because of the threat and the Russian war in Eastern Ukraine and also after the criminal and illegal annexation of Crimea. People have begun to understand that we have a threat from Russia, and this is why NATO could be our ally, to help prevent and stop [the war], and to guarantee peace in Ukraine. But also, I think that we have to be very clear that before we demand NATO membership, we have to increase our capacity and we have to reform our security and defence sector to meet NATO standards. This is some homework for our Parliament and our government. And in our Committee we have support, all members are in strongly in favour of moving towards European and transatlantic integration of Ukraine, understanding that this will provide us with better support, better defence and this is the step for the future.

Dyczok: Do you think that Ukraine has done enough to prepare itself, whether for NATO membership, or a closer relationship, and do you feel that NATO has done enough for Ukraine?

Hopko: It's important for the Ukrainian government and Ukrainian Parliament to speed up the process of reforming the defence and security sectors. Also, to pass a law on cyber security and involve more partnerships with United States, Canada, UK, and other countries to make our army more professional. And here there are a lot of opportunities to work closely and more intensely with our neighbours like Romania, Poland, and also with the Baltic States and Bulgaria. Those countries, who are [new] members of the NATO community could also add to our improving of standards, and also, they could benefit from our soldiers, who are fighting Russian troops daily, and they are getting experience in this hybrid war. So they could share this experience. But I think this is from both sides. Ukraine has to be more proactive in reform and in fighting corruption. In the military section, Minister of Defence, working [on promoting] new people and new faces with new experience in the General Staff, Minister of Defence, the Ukrainian Army. This is really important. For NATO, besides the increase in the budget to protect countries in the eastern flank, they could support Ukrainians through NATO funds, focusing on information and hybrid warfare, focusing on logistics training to increase our preparedness in case of escalation of the conflict, and to be ready for a rapid response.

Dyczok: Thank you, and the last question is: NATO leaders are also preparing to meet with Russia's leaders at the Summit and after the Summit. What is Ukraine's response to that?

Hopko: [NATO Secretary General] Stoltenberg expressed his strong position in support of Ukraine, he talked about Russian troops when Russia was denying that its troops were on Ukrainian territories. So on the political side we have seen a lot of support. From their side, NATO is pushing Russia to comply with international standards and international obligations and to implement their part of the Minsk Agreements. This is a very important issue. We know about their Deterrence in the East strategy, and their Soft Power Deterrence through intelligence, through other opportunities. I think that this type of dialogue is the way to send Russia a clear message, that Russia is the one who initiated and who started a criminal annexation of Crimea, and this happened after the Georgia situation. So now it's Russia's obligation to leave Ukrainian territories, to stop the fighting and shelling. This is the only way to explain to the Russians that without the steps from their side, it will be impossible. We may not like these meetings, NATO and Russia and their Commissions, but still we understand that through this type of dialogue, it's important to keep Russia understanding that NATO is increasing their capacity to defend the Baltic States, Poland, through the modernization of security and defence sector, investing more in cyber security. And as we can see and analyse in comparison to previous summits, now we see more NATO attention to the east of Europe, and this is really important.

Dyczok: NATO is preparing to defend itself. That is wonderful for NATO members, but there's a war happening on the territory of this country. Ukraine is not a NATO member, so they have no obligation to defend it. But it must be difficult to watch that they are defending themselves and yet not really helping Ukraine.

Hopko: Yes, but Ukraine could benefit the NATO community because Russia is testing. There are hybrid technologies on

Ukrainian territories. Also, through the partnership that NATO members, like Romania, they have a brigade, and Ukrainian soldiers could be part of common training. In Bulgaria, the same. Because we are facing the Black Sea Region, we also have to keep in mind that Russia might test and might use the Crimean Peninsula for nuclear weapons. And this is a threat for NATO members like Turkey and Bulgaria, and we have to keep in mind that we have to develop this general strategy of how to prevent potential threats in the Black Sea Region. This is the opportunity for Ukraine to seek cooperation with NATO members in the Black Sea Region to strengthen our capacity and for our army to protect ourselves.

Dyczok: Our third interview is with Dr. Andreas Umland, a German Political Scientist, a Professor at the National University o Kyiv-Mohyla Academy. He has a unique perspective since he is from Germany, he is an expert on European politics, but he works in Kyiv. Thank you very much for joining us. The question I wanted to start with is, given all the challenges with international security and stability, how important is Ukraine on the larger agenda?

Andreas Umland: Thanks for inviting me Marta. I think that's a main problem that Ukraine currently has. I think that at least among the political and intellectual elites in Europe there is now a better understanding that the fate of Ukraine is not just important for Ukraine, but also in a way linked to the European project and the future of the post-Soviet era. But Ukraine is now also competing with a lot of other issues. Brexit has added yet another important theme to what European bureaucrats and Western diplomats and politicians have to worry about. The main challenge for Ukraine is to keep itself on the agenda. I think in principle there is an understanding in Germany among politicians in the Bundestag, among diplomats, among journalists, that Ukraine is a key topic, but in the public and mass media especially, there are now so many competing topics. The refugee crisis, the financial crisis. Greece as a peculiar problem of the EU and the relationship to Turkey. And now also Brexit. In that situation, Ukrainian diplomats and journalists and friends of Ukraine have to work hard to keep Ukraine in the headlines so that people don't forget about it.

Dyczok: You mentioned the challenges facing Europe. One of the big ones is unity. Brexit is simply the last big story that has challenged the whole concept of European Union unity. Are we seeing similar things within NATO? NATO is making very strong public statements, "We will do this, we are united, we are going to protect and defend ourselves and all our Allies." But behind the scenes, is there unity among the NATO membership, or do we see similar cracks?

Umland: I would say that the situation in NATO is somewhat better than in the EU. That's simply because the costs for NATO are not linked to certain economic sanctions and the cost that may entail for certain business groups and lobbying groups in NATO. So at least on the official level, we see much more unity in NATO now than in the EU where there is a lot of discussion now which strategy is best in regard to Russia. And there are certain countries like Greece, Cyprus, Hungary, that are relatively pro-Russian. I think that on the NATO level this doesn't come that much to the fore. Also, I think that situation is different in NATO in that the US is a dominating player in NATO, and the countries are therefore behaving in a different way. But I think in the long run for Ukraine, the EU might be more important than NATO. Because at least as long as Ukraine has a confrontation with Russia, it will not be able to provide security assurances. There might be lots of help in selected areas, and there might be lots of cooperation and so on, but I think that the chance to really get integrated into the West is, for now at least, the European Union and not NATO. The Association Agreement in a way illustrates that. And therefore at the end of the day, Ukraine has to concentrate on its foreign relations, let's say, more on the European Union rather than on NATO.

Dyczok: Do you see any possibilities for the reorganization of defence alliances beyond NATO?

Umland: Yes. I think this is the only solution for at least a provisional period that countries like Georgia, Moldova, and Ukraine have. I think the best chance to get some security structure, some embeddedness in the international sphere, is now to work towards this well-known concept of an Intermarium, an alliance of the countries between the Baltic and the Black Seas. This is an old concept from the interwar period and it has been discussed a lot already. And now since the annexation of Crimea and the covert intervention in the Donbas, I think that is has come to the fore again. Currently, the idea of a Black Sea-Baltic Sea alliance of the countries from let's say, Lithuania to Georgia, maybe even including Azerbaijan, is not something that is on the agenda. Currently it is not something that is hotly discussed. But if the current situation continues, if on the one side, the Russian regime will not change and Moscow policy stays the same, and on the other hand, NATO and the EU are not going to give any serious security assurances to Moldova, Georgia and Ukraine, then I think that in two or three years we will actually have this discussion about an Intermarium, about a temporary security alliance between the countries in Eastern Europe. Basically, a coalition of those countries willing, within NATO and outside NATO, that are maybe ready to join in a bloc or a joint agreement, join forces in their information war, in their trade war and hybrid conflicts with Russia.

Dyczok: Dialogue, discussion, that is what's going to be happening at the NATO Warsaw Summit. One of the items that has been on the agenda is dialogue with Russia. How effective are NATO's strategies of deterrence to facilitate further dialogue with Russia? What's that relationship like? How effective can dialogue be with a military alliance?

Umland: Well, I think that it has to go hand in hand, because I think that this language of deterrence, of unity, and of resoluteness, that's exactly how one should talk with Russia. I think the idea that we can build up on some common European identity or some civilizational dialogue and all these ideas, they are not getting very far. NATO and the EU have to be resolute and united and deterring and then they can expect that Moscow will take the West seriously. Currently I think that that can still be improved. There have to be clearer signals to Moscow, that this period of appeasement is over. The appeasement that we have seen over the Transnistria conflict, South Ossetia, Abkhazia, and even partly Crimea, and the sanctions that were introduced after Crimea's annexation were rather moderate, I would say. This period is over, and the more people understand that in Moscow, the better the chances will be to get some solutions.

Dyczok: Let's talk about outcomes. What can Ukraine realistically expect from this Warsaw Summit? A lot of expectations, a lot of new aid packages will be announced with great fanfare. But realistically, what will change for Ukraine after this summit? Crimea is occupied. There is war in the east. What will this summit give to Ukraine?

Umland: Well I think immediately it will be only additional cooperation and additional aid that will not change the situation in principle. But I think the more these discussions are going on, the more the nature of the problem will become obvious. At least that's what I hope from the different members of NATO, the diplomats and militaries of NATO. And then I think in the midterm, what we could expect is maybe some understanding. At the end of the day, countries like Georgia, Ukraine, and Moldova need some international embeddedness, they need a security structure. I think that if in Washington, in Berlin and in Brussels, and London and Paris, the political and diplomatic leaderships are comfortable with the conclusion that they need to do something about these countries, although they are not going to take them in. Neither into NATO nor the EU. Soon what I think they could do is to give a green light to countries like Poland, Romania, and maybe even Turkey to cooperate closer in the military sphere with Georgia, Moldova, and Ukraine. Maybe allow them, these East European countries like Turkey, to give security assurances to the countries that are currently in this grey zone. In fact, we already have a model for that. In 2010, Turkey signed a Treaty of Strategic Partnership of

Mutual Aid with Azerbaijan. In spite of this neutral name of the treaty, it's in fact a military security arrangement. Article 5 of this Treaty says that the two countries, meaning Turkey and Azerbaijan, will give military aid in case of an attack on Azerbaijan. So this red line, if you want, has already been crossed. What now can come out of this NATO Summit and in general with the discussion in NATO, is that NATO will give assurances to the Baltic countries, to Poland, Romania, to Turkey, that they can go forward, that they can provide these countries that are currently in the grey zone with security assurances and that these zones and NATO members will be defended physically by the US in the case that they will be in a conflict with Russia. That would be the main thing. What Washington and NATO would have to do, is basically is tell the East European countries you can go ahead, you can help Ukraine, Moldova and Georgia. Our agreement stays. Our Article 5 of the Washington Treaty stays, so you are secure. We will not provide security assurances to Ukraine for instance, but you can do so, and we will support you on that.

"Canada and Ukraine: Shared Values and Real Economic Opportunities"

with Chrystia Freeland, Volodymyr Groysman, Andriy Shevchenko and Mychailo Wynnyckyi
15 July 2016

https://hromadske.radio/en/podcasts/ukraine-calling/canada-and-ukraine-shared-values-and-real-economic-opportunities

Canada and Ukraine signed a Free Trade Agreement this week, on 11 July 2016, in Kyiv. To explain why it is important for both countries, Marta Dyczok spoke with a number of the key actors and analysts.

Marta Dyczok: We reached Canada's International Trade Minister Chrystia Freeland by phone in Lviv. She was instrumental in preparing the Canada-Ukraine Free Trade Agreement and traveled with Prime Minister Trudeau to Ukraine where the Agreement was signed this Monday, July 11th. Thank you so much for taking the time to talk to *Hromadske Radio*.

Chrystia Freeland: It's great to talk to *Hromadske* and it's great to talk to you, Marta.

Dyczok: Thank you. Ukraine's Prime Minister Groysman, explained the benefits of the Canada-Ukraine Free Trade Agreement for Ukraine in an interview he gave exclusively to *Hromadske Radio*, that we'll hear later in the show. Minister Freeland, can you tell our listeners why Canada is interested in a free trade agreement with Ukraine?

Freeland: We are interested for two reasons. The first is strategic. As you know very well Marta, Canada has a long and very warm relationship with Ukraine. And that relationship is built partly on the very close-knit ties. But it's also built on our real understanding of the shared values between Canada and Ukraine. Particularly today, where Ukraine is facing this double burden of Russian annexation of part of its territory, and Russia aggression against another, and needing to continue economic reform. So, for us, this Free Trade Agreement, it's first of all deepening our strategic partnership and supporting Ukraine. We really believe that an essential part of Ukraine's fight right now is on the economic front. By opening up more economic opportunities for Ukraine, that's a very powerful form of support.

But secondly, we see real economic opportunities in Ukraine. We see opportunities in the agricultural sector, we see opportunities in the IT sector, we see opportunity in services, education, and we see opportunities in aerospace, which is an area of strength for both Canada and Ukraine. Evidence of the fact that this is really emerging potentially as a moment of real economic opportunity in Ukraine, is that after our Business Forum, which we held in Toronto in the middle of June, since then we have already had half a dozen agreements signed between companies that got together then. And then just this week, on the occasion that of the signing of our Free Trade Agreement, we signed three more agreements. One, with Bombardier in the train sector, one in the agricultural innovation sector, and one in the educational sector. It is important to note that all these activities are happening even before the Agreement has come into force yet. Now the Agreement has been signed, it still needs to be ratified by both our parliaments. So, I think there are some real economic opportunities.

Dyczok: Ukraine's Prime Minister Groysman gave *Hromadske Radio* an exclusive comment on the Agreement.

Volodymyr Groysman: The world today is a global village, but I think that the potential of Canada's economy and Ukraine's economy is not sufficiently utilised in our bilateral relations. Creating a free trade zone opens up reciprocity and investment opens up markets. This is job creation, closer economic ties. And I would say that this Agreement opens up a new phase in our bilateral relations.

This was a shared initiative. Many people in the Canadian Government and the Ukrainian Government worked towards making this happen. Minister Freeland, the Government of Arseniy Yatseniuk. I joined in at the final stages of negotiations. Our Ministry of Economic Development and Natalya Mykolska, the Deputy Minister and many Ukrainians. This was a collective effort which produced results. Agriculture, metallurgy, and other areas where we can develop trade. I think this is just the beginning. We just signed the Agreement, and now we will make it work. This is a free trade agreement with Canada. Canada has this type of agreement with the EU. We have a similar agreement with the EU, so now we have this global reach.

Dyczok: Ukraine's Ambassador to Canada, Andriy Shevchenko, shared his perspective. When you became Ambassador, the Conservative Party was in power. Shortly afterwards there was an election and the Liberal Party won the election. We now have a new Prime Minister, Justin Trudeau of the Liberal Party. In the time that you have been Ambassador, have you seen any changes in Canada's policy towards Ukraine?

Andriy Shevchenko: With the new government, I think we see some differences in style, and we see some differences in the priorities of the government. But overall, Ukraine is very privileged to get support from Canada no matter which party is in power. I think the message of the new government in that sense is very clear, that Canada supports Ukraine's independence and territorial integrity.

Dyczok: You accompanied Prime Minister Justin Trudeau on his visit to Ukraine this week. He had a number of important meetings. One of the things was the signing of the Canada-Ukraine Free Trade Agreement. Given the slight differences in corporate culture between the two countries, what challenges do you see in making this agreement effective?

Shevchenko: I'll talk about the Free Trade Agreement in a moment, but first I want to say that my priority for the visit was to make the new Prime Minister of Canada falls in love with Ukraine, just like I have fallen in love with his wonderful country. In that sense, it was quite a successful visit. Now about the Free Trade Agreement. To make a long story short, in the next 7 years we will get rid of 99% of the tariffs between our two countries. Most of them will be gone immediately after the Treaty is ratified by the two Parliaments. And with business, I think we should find new appropriate words for Canadian businesses to explain that they should give Ukraine a chance and give the Ukrainian market a second look. Some Canadian companies already have experience dealing with Ukraine, unfortunately not always good experiences. But there are so many changes in this country. I think the business environment is obviously improving, and our job is to make sure that Canadian businesses see those changes.

Dyczok: The Trudeau visit comes on the heels of the Warsaw Summit. And there is a lot of discussion in Ukraine about the fact that war is continuing and Ukraine is looking for international support. What were they hoping for, and what do you see that happened?

Shevchenko: I am really satisfied that he (Trudeau) had the chance to go to the Yavoriv Training Base. By the way, it is the largest military training base that is equipped according to NATO standards in Europe, and I think that we can get better use of that training base.

Dyczok: Sorry to interrupt, for our listeners who don't know what the Yavoriv Base is, can you please explain what it is and what Canada's relationship with that is?

Shevchenko: It is a military training base in Western Ukraine, very close to our border with Poland. At the moment, we have Canadian officers there, all together maybe 200 officers, who are helping to train Ukrainian officers. Even as we speak, they are helping us to make our army stronger. When Trudeau spoke to the Canadian officers, they told him extraordinary stories of their friendships and relationships with the Ukrainian soldiers. They told him stories that they heard from the Ukrainian soldiers. They talked about the heroism of the Ukrainian soldiers. Also, they told the Prime Minister that they learned a lot from Ukrainian soldiers on specific military issues. Well, at the end of the day, Ukraine is now fighting a war against the second largest military of the world. It's a conventional war with tanks, artillery, with trenches, something that many armies around the world don't even think about anymore.

Dyczok: It's like World War I all over again.

Shevchenko: Exactly. That's what the Canadian soldiers told the Prime Minister. We used to see this in films and read about it in books. And now we know that if we deal with such an aggressive power as Russia, we should be prepared to fight that kind of war. It's also about the hybrid war which Russia is fighting against us. So I think that it was very important that the Canadian Prime Minister had the chance to talk to these people and get this knowledge from them. And I really hope that he will find the words to bring this message back to Canada, to his Government and to the Canadian public. They should know how much we appreciate their help. They should know in Canada, they should be very proud of their soldiers for what they do here.

Dyczok: Our next guest is Dr. Mychailo Wynnyckyi, who was born in Canada, has a PhD in Economics and Sociology from Cambridge University in England, and has been living and working in Ukraine for the past 15 years. So he knows both Canada and Ukraine from the inside like very few people do, and has the analytical skills to help us understand this relationship. Professor Wynnyckyj, thank you very much for joining us.

Mychailo Wynnyckyi: With that slew of compliments, how could I have possibly not come today!

Dyczok: Canada and Ukraine. They are very different countries. But they have one thing in common. They both live next door to a very powerful neighbour that in many ways defines their politics, economics, and their reality in some ways. A Canadian Professor a number of years ago described this as asymmetrical relationships. Canada-US, Ukraine-Russia have these asymmetrical relationships that define them, and this is perhaps the basis for cooperation and for understanding. Canada and Ukraine have just signed a new trade deal this week. Is this perhaps, looking at that relationship, that the two middle powers working together because they understand the world in a very similar way?

Wynnyckyj: I think we can easily get into a trap that the Kremlin wants us to get into. The trap is this discourse of geopolitics and I think that that is a really problematic trap. Just because someone at some point talked about middle powers. Well, middle powers is really an idea that comes from the 1960s after the Second World War, when countries were trying to define themselves. You have two superpowers and then middle powers. I don't think it's relevant. And quite frankly, there are a lot of things that make Canada and Ukraine very similar, but I don't think geopolitics is one of them. Because the asymmetrical relationship concept ignores that fact that Ukraine is next door to a very large economic power called the European Union, where Canada does not have an alternative economy next to it geopolitically besides the States. So, I really don't buy the comparison.

I do think however, that from a very simple economic perspective, Canada and Ukraine have a lot of similarities. If we look at the structure of GDP, the structure of the economy, if you take away Alberta, the oil sands, and you take away the fisheries, what you're left with is the core of the Canadian economy which is very similar to the Ukrainian economy. It's agriculture and it's services. This is what the Canadian economy is all about. And interestingly enough, the Canadian economy has traditionally been a small-medium business economy, as opposed to the United States which has been a large corporation economy. And if we look at what Ukraine is turning into now, in the post-Maidan reality without Donbas, it is very much becoming a small-medium business type of economy. So I think there are an awful lot of economic similarities.

But more importantly, this is something we don't talk about enough. If you make a comparison worldwide between Ukraine and a country, and then the Ukrainian relationship with Canada, and another country's relationship with another large power, another economy, we need to talk about Israel and the United States and Ukraine and Canada. The Ukrainian-Canadian diaspora is the equivalent in terms of the economic and political power in Canada, to the Jewish diaspora in the United States. We have a massive resource in this country which is very often under-utilized. And I think that when Prime Minister Trudeau was here, he was very clear about the fact that there are 1.3 million Canadians of Ukrainian descent and that is a very significant constituency. And he was very clear in his speech, for example, he has two Cabinet Ministers who are of Ukrainian descent. That really means a lot both politically and economically. And I think the future of Ukraine is very similar to that of Israel. Israel had forty years of being in a perpetual war, with a very strong friend behind it. And I think that the Ukrainian relationship with Canada and Ukraine's future is unfortunately a long-term military prospect. I think Ukraine is lucky to have a very strong friend in Canada and a lot of political clout amongst Ukrainians in Canada.

Dyczok: Well, you've sort of answered my second question which was, how important is Canada to Ukraine? Because there is a lot of talk about strategic partnerships, special partnerships. Canada was the first country to recognise Ukraine's independence 25 years ago…

Wynnyckyj: By the way, you have to be careful with that one. The Poles get really angry with that one. The telegram from Poland came like thirty seconds before the Canadian one did.

Dyczok: The first Western country, yes indeed, thank you for that. But in terms of real cooperation, has there been really a lot of cooperation between the two countries? Last week when the NATO Summit was starting, the talk here in Kyiv was about the United States and Germany, not about Canada.

Wynnyckyj: I think we have a problem with public perceptions on both sides. The Ukrainian public perception is that we need to be friends with a Strategic Partner called the United States. But unfortunately, from a US standpoint, Ukraine is just another conflict somewhere in the world. Or just another problem country. It happens to be in Europe, it happens to not be on the priority list.

For Canada, Ukraine is on the high priority list because of the Ukrainian diaspora, and also, I think it's important that that relationship in fact is very strong militarily. Canada has 200 military advisers in Ukraine in Yavoriv. The United States has 200 military advisors in Ukraine. Let's look at the military might of these two countries. The commitment from Canada of 200 advisors is massive compared to what the military might of Canada is, whereas the US commitment is pretty symbolic, let's put it that way.

The Canadian side is a bit reserved, they're not necessarily talking about it enough. I mean it's very symbolic that Prime Minister Trudeau did go to Yavoriv last week, he was supporting the Canadian troops and made a point of that. The Canadian Prime Minister chose to come to Ukraine on his first international visit beyond the United States.

Obviously, there was a NATO Summit, but he could have gone to Germany, he could have gone to Brussels, he could have gone to South America, he could have gone to Asia! He chose to come to Ukraine. And I think that's a very important symbolic act. Obviously, his first trip was to the United States. Okay, well that's the asymmetrical relationship if you like. But I think that when you're talking about NAFTA and a free trade zone and the largest unguarded border in the world, I think that that was a logical step.

But the fact is that his first international trip beyond North America was Ukraine. I think that's an important symbolic gesture. Now I do think that the implication of your question is correct, that the Ukrainian side is under-appreciating that special relationship, that Ukraine could have potentially have even stronger ties with Canada.

Dyczok: This week the Canadian-Ukrainian Free Trade Agreement was signed here in Kyiv by Prime Minister Trudeau and Ukraine's President Poroshenko. You have been teaching at the Kyiv Mohyla Business School for a number of years. Free trade agreements are wonderful documents. How realistic is the actual implementation of this document? Do you see that it will be successful given the somewhat different corporate cultures in the two countries?

Wynnyckyj: You're being very polite about the corporate cultures, you're really asking about corruption problems, etc. Look, at the end of the day, something has happened that is very important. Normally, free trade agreements are signed when there is already a very strong trade relationship between two countries. In this particular case we've gone ahead of the game. We've signed a free trade agreement with the hopes that the small and medium business sector of Ukraine will take advantage and Canadian small and medium business sector will take advantage. Canada and Ukraine are competitors in the agricultural sector. Ukraine is the number two exporter of grains in the world, Canada is number one exporter of grains in the world. So, there's not going to be a lot of cooperation in agriculture specifically. Perhaps in investment there might be, in other areas like IT, services, the foundation is already there, and I think there is a lot of potential.

The issue is that the Ukrainian business community, and the structure of Ukraine's economy is in a state of massive flux at the moment. We are moving away from an economy of financial industrial groups controlled by ten families, and already this is one of the things I get really irked about when I hear Western analysts talking about that fact the Ukraine remains an oligarchic economy. Show me the oligarchs! The oligarchs that we have are bankrupted, or if they're not bankrupt, they're on the verge of it. They have had really massive losses over the last couple of years. The exception is [Ihor] Kolomoisky of course. But that's another story.

The point is that if you look at the structure of the Ukrainian economy today it's massively changing into a small-medium business economy. Teaching at Kyiv Mohyla Business School there is one thing I've learned, and that is that the learning potential of Ukrainian businesses owners and Ukrainian managers. They learn very, very quickly when there are opportunities. What the Canadian government has done at this point is, obviously there is the symbolic act of supporting Ukraine, but one of the most important things that has been done is to open the door to provide an opportunity. Knowing what I know about Ukrainian entrepreneurs, they're going to jump on it. And I hope that Canadian entrepreneurs jump on the opportunity as well.

"The Killing of Journalist Pavel Sheremet in Kyiv: In-Depth Commentary"

with Andriy Kulykov, Kateryna Smagliy and Paul Niland
22 July 2016

https://hromadske.radio/en/podcasts/ukraine-calling/killing-of-journalist-pavel-sheremet-in-kyiv-in-depth-commentary

Journalist Pavel Sheremet was killed by a car bomb in the centre of Kyiv as he was driving to work on Wednesday morning, 20 July 2016.

Marta Dyczok: We have in studio with us today three people to look at what happened, why it happened, and what it means. Andriy Kulykov is a journalist. He is one of the founders of *Hromadske Radio*, he is the Chairperson of *Hromadske Radio* and knew Pavlo Sheremet personally. Kateryna Smagliy is the Director of the Kennan Institute here in the Kyiv office. Paul Niland is a journalist, an entrepreneur, a publisher, and a commentator. Thank you very much for coming in to talk about this rather difficult subject.

I'd like to start with Mr. Kulykov. You knew Pavlo Sheremet as a colleague, as a friend, and you did what turned out to be the very last interview Pavlo Sheremet ever gave, the day before he was killed. Andriy, you knew Pavlo Sheremet, could you tell our listeners what Pavlo was like as a journalist, as a colleague, and in your opinion, why was he targeted? This was not a random act of terrorism. This was a targeted killing.

Andriy Kulykov: Pavlo or Pavel, as the Belorussian form of his name is, was a very forthcoming person. He was the kind of person that did not like to hide his feelings and emotions. He coped with them rather well when it came to his writings and most of what he wrote was well-substantiated and was not the result of emotions but rather an attempt to analyze what was going on.

He was a person that came to Ukraine because he was first denied the right to properly work in his native Belarus, and then in Russia where he went from Belarus. I rarely saw a person who would come to Ukraine and so fully accept this country. And rarely have I seen a person that was so fully accepted by many, many people in the country. Although he stayed a citizen of Russia, I think that Pavlo lived the life of a Ukrainian and tragically, he died the death of a Ukrainian. Why was he targeted? Well, first of all, he was rather well known. I would not say he enjoyed nationwide popularity with every Ukrainian…

Dyczok: I don't think any journalist apart from very few do.

Kulykov: OK. But he was a person to whom many of the thinking strata would turn their attention. Not that they necessarily liked what he wrote or what he said, he was also a very interesting radio personality, of course. To kill such a person means to draw attention to what they intend to do. What they intended to do is another question. Whoever did this, I think the final aim was to scare or to intimidate Ukrainian journalists, apart from, or simultaneously, trying to further destabilize the situation in the country.

And one more thing. To kill Pavlo Sheremet was very important because he was a success story. He was a success story although he had to leave two countries, because of his professional morals, because he wanted to find a free country. And after Belarus and after Russia, he finds a place for himself in Ukraine, which strives to be democratic, and his life and work here was proof that Ukraine at least wants to become a democratic country. So to kill such a person…

Dyczok: Is demonstrative.

Kulykov: Yes. It meant to show, "Don't go there, they do not treat journalists properly. Ukraine is dangerous for decent people."

Dyczok: That leads me to what I wanted to ask Ms. Smagliy about. You are a long-time observer, a commentator on Ukrainian politics. What does the response of the Ukrainian authorities tell us about what's happening in Ukraine today? We saw the Head of Ukraine's National Police on the crime site almost immediately, saying, "I'm going to get to the bottom of this." Within hours of the killing, Ukraine's President Poroshenko was calling together his security advisors and, in a televised statement, saying, "We do not condone this killing, we are going to get to the bottom of this, and I assign each of you personally to get your best people working on this." This is quite the contrast from 2000, when another journalist disappeared, and his headless corpse appeared. What does the reaction of the Ukrainian authorities tell us about what's going on in this country?

Kateryna Smagliy: I think we can observe that there is both an internal and external context to this brutal murder. As you have noted, the Ukrainian authorities tried to link this killing to the possible external influence on Ukraine. That was what President Poroshenko said, and that was kind of indirectly reconfirmed by Prosecutor General Lutsenko. And to some extent, we can see the parallels with the murder of Gongadze. Because just as in 2000 when Georgiy disappeared, Ukraine was on a track to success. Ukraine had a lot of Western partners, relations with the West were on the upswing, President Clinton visited this country three times, in 1994, 1995, and then just three months before Georgiy disappeared in June 2000. And clearly our northern neighbours do not want Ukraine to succeed, to tighten its bonds with NATO and the EU. And they needed to demonstrate once again that this is a criminal state where journalists are murdered, a failed state basically. So today, when Ukraine is once again demonstrating that it is a successful country, full of promise and full of potential, and we just had a successful visit by the Canadian Prime Minister Trudeau, when the Free Trade Agreement with Canada was signed, when our Vice Prime Minister for European Integration Klympush suddenly announces Ukraine may have the visa liberalisation regime with the EU, Ukraine sends too many positive signals. Yes, we have a lot of problems that we publicly discuss, but still there is this promise of success. So there is a parallel, so you need to cut the success story short.

The second parallel is that they need to create some destabilization within Ukraine. Because when Gongadze disappeared the Ukraine Without Kuchma movement started. And today there are some social motivations which can push Ukrainians to fight against the Poroshenko government because of rising utility tariffs, because people are dissatisfied with the pace of reform. We already see that people and journalists who are now in parliament, like Serhiy Leshchenko have already founded a new movement, the Democratic Alliance. We saw the anti-corruption campaign led by Saakashivili. So, yes indeed, there is growing opposition to the Poroshenko government, so the murder of such a figure as Pavlo Sheremet who was the common-law husband of the founder and owner of *Ukrayinska Pravda*, Olena Prytula, can again push changes to be stronger, and finally…

Dyczok: Sorry to interrupt, just a reminder to listeners, Pavlo Sheremet, was a journalist working for *Ukrayinska Pravda*, which is owned by Olena Prytula, and Serhiy Leshchenko, who you've just referred to, also came from that publication.

Smagliy: Yes, and I fully agree with Andriy Kulykov, who had used this term already, Ukraine is a "failed state" and we could observe that…

Dyczok: Sorry Ukraine is a failed state?

Smagliy: That the murder of Pavlo Sheremet could be presented by some circles in Russia and Russian journalists as an indication that Ukraine is a failed state because journalists are killed here in broad daylight. And, by the way, a lot of Russian commentators and journalists have immediately jumped in, literally minutes after the murder, and started using the murder to create this narrative to say, "Look Ukraine is a country where the government is corrupt, where the government does not care for its own people but is killing people in the east. It is a country where a journalist that once abandoned Russia and Belarus in hopes that he will find a free, democratic Ukraine, basically his dreams have not been fulfilled because journalists here are being murdered." So we see this narrative, which serves as an indication that Russia and Russian Secret Services and Russian FSB agents, who, as we know, are still present in this country, could indeed stand behind the murder.

Dyczok: But there's a lot of dissatisfaction within this country, and what you've referred to is this, "There hasn't been enough change" that's coming from within the country and that leads me to what I wanted to ask Paul about. You published a very interesting piece in the *Kyiv Post* this week where you speculate what Ukraine would have been like had the Euromaidan revolution failed and Yanukovych is still in power. You're really responding to that narrative that nothing has changed, and everything is bad, everything is getting worse. In view of what just happened, would you change your view on the fact that things have actually changed in this country?

Paul Niland: No, I'm not changing my view on that. But I'll come back to some of the things that I said then, but to carry on for just a moment talking about the motive behind Pavel. One of the most important things I've seen since the awful event is that straight away the authorities have said they want to involve outside investigative authorities, the FBI and Europol. For me that's the most important indication that this is not a murder that is going to be somehow covered up by the vested interests that exist in Ukraine. The fact that they're willing to open up, the fact that they're willing to consider it the same way as MH17, the fact that the Ukrainian authorities are going to say look you deal with it, because they know they have little credibility themselves and they have little credibility for many reasons including what happened to Gongadze and so on.

But another point I wanted to come back on, is something that you said Andriy. You said that Pavel felt Ukrainian here. I want you to know, and I want the people listening to the show as well, that that's not just because there was some kind of Slavic bond there, that he's Belarusian and then a Russian citizen and so it's all these Slavs together. I know many people, European people, many Scandinavian people, people who've been here for a long time, who also very much feel like they've bonded here and they're a part now of this Ukrainian project going forward. I'm a part of that and I've lived here for a very long time, and I wrote the piece that you referred to, Marta, because I was standing on a Saturday afternoon and I was challenged to do so by a friend. He said ,"You write some serious stuff. Why don't you have a laugh, why don't you do something that will make people stand up and pay attention, and use that as the base." What if the revolution had failed? Where would we be today? The kind of repressions we would be suffering today… I joked about Serhiy Kurchenko's 30th birthday, and you know for a man who was worth 7.4 billion according to his own Forbes magazine, it's like they're gloating at us, right? Kurchenko was this guy who came from nowhere as a 27 year old, within the space of twelve months he had amassed a fortune of 2.4 billion dollars. And yes, there's a lot of people who are of the opinion Ukraine hasn't changed, nothing has changed. It's wrong. There are lots of people who are of the opinion as you just said, Katya, that the reforms have been too slow. That 's absolutely right, there does need to be more, but if we hadn't succeeded on Maidan, things would be very, very different here…

Kulykov: You've gone completely native.

Niland: Yes.

Kulykov: To say, if *we* hadn't succeeded…

Niland: Yes. But that's what I say. That's how I feel, and many of my friends say the same. I remember a comment from a Danish friend of mine on Facebook saying, you know, we are all a part of this. And yeah, I say *we*. I was at the site of Pavel Sheremet's murder and I know you were there putting flowers down as well.

Dyczok: I was there, Andriy was there, I don't know Katya if you had a chance to visit.

Niland: I put flowers down and then a TV camera came over and was asking me what I thought, and I said, "как это может быть в наш красивый Киев?" or, "How can it be in our beautiful Kyiv?" So yes, I say we, I say ours, I'm Ukrainian.

Kulykov: I still think that by pointing so quickly and without doubt to Russia, our authorities tried to sort of distract people's attention from the possibility that there still may be a Ukrainian part in this. When we mention the murder of Georgiy Gongadze, and we speak of Pavel Sheremet's death, do we know, do we remember, how many journalists were killed in Ukraine over twenty-five years? Sixty-five, I was told today at the First National TV Channel. Sixty-five, and I think that it would be absurd to say that all of them or even most of them died because of outside interference.

Niland: It would be absurd.

Kulykov: Before we cross the T's and dot the I's, or before the law enforcement bodies pronounce the verdict, I think we should keep our minds open, as they should, to all theories. And another thing that really troubles me, while many people say that this is a good sign, is what Khatia Dekanoidze, the Chief of the National Police, said. She said that the investigation of this should be a matter of honour for us. Why?

Dyczok: It should be a matter of honour for every killing.

Kulykov: Yes.

Dyczok: This is a horrific killing, it is a targeted assassination, but every death needs to be investigated. I want to know what role journalism has to play in this? The police will be doing their investigation, but there's investigative journalism. Is there a role here to play for journalists? Andriy you said this was meant to intimidate journalists, but perhaps this could be a way of invigorating journalists to do more investigative journalism, not just about offshore companies, but about all sorts of things.

Niland: I think that should be the response. I think the response from journalists should be not be to be intimidated but to write more. We don't know what Pavel was working on. We don't know whether there was some anti-corruption investigation, something like that he was about to break. But I think that everyone that's putting information into the public sphere should re-determine themselves. They should not be intimidated and not change the path that they're on. You mentioned early on that it was a directed killing and it was a terrorist act, but it's like any other terrorist act, what do you do? You can't give in to the terrorists, you can't change your behaviour, you can't succumb to what their demands are and give up. What did Pavel do? He never gave up his morals, like you said Andriy, he refused to, and we should do the same and more.

Smagliy: Yes, I fully agree. Today Canadian historian Taras Kuzio published a very powerful piece where he calls on President Poroshenko to continue all the promises that were given by former President Yushchenko and the Council of Europe, where he promised that the Gongadze case would be fully disclosed and those who not only committed this crime, but also those who ordered this crime, would be brought to justice. Ukrainian society and the international community kind of have their ideas of who could have ordered this crime, those people are still around. They even participate in the Minsk process, and former President Yushchenko and current President Poroshenko, who at the time of Yushchenko served as the Chief of Ukraine's National Security and Defence Council, they still are very silent about opening all the details of that case. That is why the parallels are there. And why Katya Gorchinska and other journalists who were colleagues of Pavlo Sheremet call on President Poroshenko and demand full transparency and an open discussion with regard to how the authorities react these days to all this investigative journalism pieces that have been produced now en masse. We have so many investigative journalists in the country who produce TV shows, radio programs, and publications almost daily.

Dyczok: And there's no accountability, or not enough accountability.

Smagliy: There's not enough enforcement. The legal system simply doesn't work. So this is the key problem. And I remember that a week ago when the International Renaissance Foundation, this is the Soros Foundation in Ukraine, held a small expert meeting with Pavlo Sheremet present. Yevhen Bystrytsky has posted the words which Pavlo said during this meeting and he asked a few rhetorical questions.

Dyczok: Like what?

Smagliy: Well I can quote, "What exactly are we concerned about? Are we talking about clots blocking the reform process or about the fact that it is necessary to extinguish the fire? Or are we scared of the revenge of the opposition, the pro-Russian forces, or greater social radicalization? We as a society must understand what we are afraid of. So where is the enemy? Where is the enemy? Is it external or internal?"

And Pavel said, in his opinion, the enemy was internal, because the enemy was injustice, the old system of corrupt politicians that still exist as a tight group, who still cover for themselves and who block any real, not surface, reforms. So he said he saw no changes, he saw no real breakthroughs. And his last words were, "What we see now is that the old social consensus fell to its hands and knees," because there is a civil society in Ukraine which we all know is very strong. But in addition to this five percent of civic activists who still fight very hard for the Euromaidan ideals, we have ninety-five percent of this country, which is tired of reforms. People who are not ready to stand up for their rights, and who basically see a country where there is so little justice, where politicians themselves cover up for the injustice. So what is the incentive for them to fight for this country and to defend the leaders who they elected a few years ago on so many sacrifices that had already been made?

Dyczok: Andriy, you wanted to jump in here.

Kulykov: Yes, Kateryna's mention of former President Yushchenko reminds me that some of the most famous criminal cases in Ukraine's history remain either not investigated or many people believe that they haven't been investigated to the end. The killing of Gongadze that Kateryna mentioned is one of those where many people say that although the actual perpetrators were seized, the people who commissioned the killing are still unexposed. And the alleged poisoning of Mr. Yushchenko when he was a Presidential candidate, is still an enigma for many, many people. And I hear that there is still a chance, and a very sad chance if this happens, that Pavel Sheremet's killing may go un-investigated and unpunished.

Dyczok: Well, I think we all hope that journalists contribute to that. There are many elements to an investigation. Paul, you had something you wanted to comment on.

Niland: We're looking at all cases and historical cases, and the opportunities in the years since the Gongadze killing for people to bury evidence, for people to cover up what their roles are, for witnesses to be put out of commission. It's more difficult, obviously, to come up with some answer there, but it's essential for such a high-profile case as Gongadze. But far more recently than that, I wrote an article at the beginning of this year and it appeared in the days in the wake of the resignation of the former Economy Minister. Shortly after Aivaras resigned, I think it was two days later, all of a sudden, there was a breakthrough in the Euromaidan killings and there was a picture of President Poroshenko sitting with the then Prosecutor General Shokin and the head of the SBU and they said, "We found the weapons." Then the SBU, later that day, released photographs of the weapons.

Kulykov: You should explain to listeners what the SBU is. It's not as well known as the FSB.

Niland: Sorry, the Ukrainian Internal Security Services. Thanks for pointing that out. So the Ukrainian Security Forces released these photographs of these weapons that they'd found, and when I saw these photographs, I rarely lose my temper, but I went mad, because the photographs clearly showed leaves on the trees. Now Aivaras resigned in January, right?

Dyczok: So they had the evidence?

Niland: They had the evidence back in the summer, and they'd clearly sat on it, waiting for a politically convenient moment for when they needed to change the subject all of a sudden. So two days after what was a very high profile resignation, and it wasn't just the resignation, it was the reasons that Aivaras gave in his resignation speech.

Dyczok: And remind our listeners what were the reasons for his resignation?

Niland: The reason why Aivaras resigned is because he claimed there's still an investigation going on here. I know he spoke to the National Anti-Corruption Bureau about his allegations, that a certain Mr. Kononenko, a Member of Parliament and a person quite close to President Poroshenko, put pressure on him to appoint certain people to key positions in state-owned enterprises. And I believe it was a key success that the reformers of the previous government, as they were leaving, one of the last things they managed to push through, was to get several employees, foreign specialists, to come in to head up these certain state-owned enterprises. And it was a demonstration of actually no, you actually can't get away with that anymore. But for me the investigation into what happened in the shootings on the 20th of February of 2014, when there's video footage, there is video footage from behind the police lines, and we can see faces. We can see people who are not wearing masks, and the snipers were wearing masks. But a sniper, when they put on their gear and take their weapon, it's a very specialized weapon and they're very individualized weapons. We can see faces of people who were behind police lines. I do not believe that we cannot identify those people. There's no record of who was around the Presidential Administration on Bankova Street on 20th of February? That's just wrong.

So yes, there are many investigations, and maybe the historical ones we stand less of a chance of coming up with justice in those cases. But Maidan can't be messed with. A hundred people gave their lives and again, what if Yanukovych hadn't gone? The opening of that article that I wrote there, said that the hundred people that gave their lives died in vain, and the last insult to their memory was when Instituts'ka Street was reopened for traffic and the memorials to them were swept away. So I was writing that, but actually what I was talking about when I wrote that the memorials were being swept away, were the memorials to Boris Nemtsov, up in Moscow. There were a few parallels with the situation with other people to the North. But the Maidan investigation has stalled, and it was deliberately manipulated, and that's unacceptable.

Kulykov: When I was listening to Paul, I thought, we started with a killing of just one person. And there are so many things that may be connected to it. I think that both Kateryna and Paul are very right in pointing out the necessity of involvement. And you said it, how journalists can speed up or help the investigation. Many, many people should be involved in different ways. Not messing with the investigation but providing whatever kind of evidence they can. And on the day of the murder, there was a small rally to commemorate Pavel Sheremet on the Maidan. I think that the two hundred who took part is absolutely insufficient. Well there are reasons, of course, many people still did not know. They were working, they were not paying attention to even the hottest and the most tragic news. But this conversation will be put online on the day when there will be another ceremony for Pavel Sheremet in downtown Kyiv. And I strongly believe that many, many more people will come to this. Not a happy note, but it does provide…

Dyczok: Optimism. This is a horrific killing and we will continue to follow the story of uncovering who did it, and why it happened, and the consequences. Thank you very much for your comments, your insight, and I hope to see you all again on Ukraine Calling.

"What Role Does Religion Play in a Hybrid War?"

with Dennis Lozinsky, Daniel Bilak and Frank Sysyn
29 July 2016

https://hromadske.radio/en/podcasts/ukraine-calling/what-role-does-religion-play-in-a-hybrid-war

Two orthodox pilgrim marches happened in Kyiv this week.

Marta Dyczok: We reached Dennis Lozinsky, Staff Member of the Department of External Relations of the Ukrainian Orthodox Church, Moscow Patriarchate, by phone. Mr. Lozinsky, thank you for speaking to us. Can you please explain to our listeners why your church organized a pilgrimage march in Kyiv this week?

Dennis Lozinsky: Thank you for having me. To start, I'd like to mention that it is not a pilgrimage but rather it was a Holy Cross procession. It has a very ancient tradition behind it. It is a form of prayer that has been practiced in the Orthodox Christian Church for over a millennium. In fact, it takes its origin from the late fourth century. And since that time, it has become popular and quite widespread over the Christian world. The procession is organized with different purposes, although all of them are united under one goal. And that is to gather together and raise a prayer to God in a joined voice. In most cases the procession is a prayer to God for something extraordinary and highly important that touches all the people of society. In history, we can find a lot of instances where the Holy Cross procession was carried out in the time of natural disaster and wars. And always the purpose of the procession is only one aim; a joined, whole-hearted prayer. And not a demonstration of a prayer, but in some ways a demonstration, joined and praying together, because we all go under God and everything is in His hands.

We can see that there hasn't been anything new happening lately here in Ukraine, such a procession are pretty normal and widespread, a prayer over all the Christian Orthodox world. And of course, here in Ukraine, in Kyivan Rus', Christians have been using this form of prayer for centuries. So the Holy Cross procession that we have we have finished lately, gathered together thousands of Ukrainians. We have information about over 80,000 people who participated in the procession in different places of the truth. People united by one faith, one hope and one desire to stop war in Ukraine, giving their heart to pray to God for His mercy to bring peace to our Motherland Ukraine, love and mutual understanding in our hearts and minds.

Dyczok: Our next guest is Daniel Bilak, a Canadian lawyer, who has been living and working in Ukraine for 25 years, and also advising Orthodox Churches on Autocephaly during his time here in Kyiv. Thank you very much for joining us. Mr. Bilak, this week there ware two pilgrimage marches in the centre of Kyiv. City streets were closed off, there was a lot of extra security. Could you explain to our listeners why there were two pilgrimage marches?

Daniel Bilak: Well for historical reasons, we have essentially at least three main Orthodox Churches in Ukraine. The Ukrainian Orthodox Church Moscow Patriarchate, which is tied to the Russian Orthodox Church; the Ukrainian Orthodox Church Kyiv Patriarchate, which is not recognised by other Orthodox churches, whereas the Moscow Patriarchate is; and the Ukrainian Autocephalous Orthodox Church, which has now become a very small part of the complexity which is the Ukrainian Orthodoxy today. This is all about showing Ukrainians who has support and who doesn't. We have gone through an enormous transformation in this country in the Orthodox Church since Independence, when the single Orthodox Church in the country was tied to the Russian Orthodox Church. There was a split in 1992, which created the Ukrainian Orthodox Church and Kyiv Patriarchate, which became the Ukrainian patriotic, if you like, branch. It held its liturgies in Ukrainian, its sermons in Ukrainian, and became much more tied up with the whole identity politics in the country. Which is something we are still struggling with in Ukraine.

The Moscow Patriarchate had two pilgrimage marches, actually, one starting in Kharkiv and marching on Kyiv, the other starting in Ternopil, at the Pochayiv Lavra Monastery in Ternopilska Oblast. They were designed to show Ukrainians across the country the strength and the popularity of the Ukrainian Orthodox Church, Moscow Patriarchate.

Today's pilgrimage by the Ukrainian Orthodox Church Kyiv Patriarchate is traditionally held on July 28th, which marks the anniversary of the baptism of Kyivan Rus by Prince Volodymyr the Great. That usually attracts a very large crowd.

Dyczok: So, these are symbolic?

Bilak: They are very, very different messages. One of them is all about canonicity and belonging to the Orthodox world and the connection to the Moscow Patriarchate. And the other one is about the reassertion and the validation of the Ukrainian identity in a religious sense. These are very important issues, especially today, when Ukraine finds itself in a very serious conflict with Russia, war with Russia, where those churches have seemed to be taking sides.

Dyczok: Were you able to go to either of the marches, and if you were there, could you explain, were they different, and if they were, how were they different?

Bilak: I felt the march of the Moscow Patriarchate because I had to take the Metro in. I usually drive into Kyiv in the morning.

Dyczok: Let me just explain what Mr. Bilak is referring to. Many of the streets in central Kyiv were blocked off during the march of the Moscow Patriarchate and thousands of extra police were put on the streets to safeguard security. There were fears of provocations and people were expecting that there might be some violence. I actually went to the one on the 27th, because its in my neighbourhood, and there was no violence. So there was a lot of police presence, and a lot of people who weren't actually marching. They were driving up in SUVs and buses. But people who work in the city centre had to take public transit to work.

Bilak: Yes, coming back to your question, I did not partake in the Moscow Patriarchate march. I saw the walk because the march passes right by my office.

The last two years have fundamentally altered the calculus. Both the political and the religious calculus surrounding these two Orthodox Churches. The Moscow Patriarchate counts numbers of churches, hence this building spree that has been on for the last 25 years to build as many churches across the country as possible. What a lot of people don't appreciate is that the Russian Orthodox Church, which sort of underpins the Moscow Patriarchate, claims to be the largest church in Orthodoxy by number of parishes. That is very true. But what is not appreciated is that more than half of those churches are in Ukraine. This is why the number of church buildings actually counts. Whereas because of the relative positions taken by the churches in this conflict, with the Moscow Patriarchate remaining highly visibly neutral in the conflict. But the Kyiv Patriarchate provided sanctuary to the students on the night of November 30th (when they were beaten by the Berkut at St. Michaels by the Golden Dome, during the Euromaidan) has been front and centre of saying, "We need our own church, we support Ukraine, we support the Army." At its own expense it has been providing chaplains to the Army. So, they are very different, in feel and perception, and the population which really didn't understand, to a large extent, the difference between the different churches. It was all Orthodox. They were all called Ukrainian Orthodox Church. They didn't think about the Patriarchate part.

However, this issue is very important, because today people do understand the difference, because of the positions that the priests and the bishops have had to take and were forced to take by events. If you look at the opinion polls and the surveys, they show almost 60% in favour of the Kyiv Patriarchate.

Dyczok: Which is a huge change from ten years ago.

Bilak: Well, in fact, it's almost a reversal to the numbers, which is a sea change in terms of perspective. This of course is what's driving today. The President too has been very open about this. He views this as a national security issue. The two marches are very different, and they reflect the underlying values of the two churches as well.

The pilgrimage march of the Moscow Patriarchate was very much for the believers of the Moscow Patriarchate. It was a show of strength, it was a show of numbers, to say we are still large enough and in charge as we historically have been. Continuity.

Whereas the official proceedings today, dovetailed as well, I think, with the Kyiv Patriarchate's overall approach, which is very ecumenical. Patriarch Filaret has an excellent relationship Patriarch Sviatoslav of the Ukrainian-Greek Catholic Church. And an excellent relationship with the Chief Rabbi and the Chief Imam of Ukraine. And they all work together in the All Ukrainian Council of Churches.

Dyczok: And I believe they were all there today.

Bilak: They were all there today. Moscow Patriarchate is very much of, this is our territory, you must all be Orthodox, if you're not Orthodox, then you must know your place and don't make too much noise. You look at the laws that Putin has just passed in Russia, which are profoundly disturbing in terms of freedom of expression and freedom of religion, and freedom of religious expression as well. The Kyiv Patriarchate, because it has an outward-looking view, is much more ecumenical, is much more European in its approach. It's Occidentalist as opposed to Orientalist. This is where we get to the crux of the matter. It's making the explicit point that our Orthodoxy, Ukrainian Orthodoxy, comes from Constantinople. It doesn't come from Moscow. This is the subtext of the two marches. This is where the whole issue of Autocephaly comes in, which is independence of a church. Unlike Catholicism, Roman Catholicism, Orthodoxy is somewhat decentralised. You have the Patriarch of Constantinople who was the first among equals. But historically, each country has its own Orthodox Church. But Ukraine did not for many years.

Dyczok: Basically, what does the Ukrainian Orthodox Church, the Kyiv Patriarchate, want? Independence?

Bilak: They want an independent Ukrainian local church.

Dyczok: Where would that leave the Moscow Patriarchate?

Bilak: It's unlikely at this stage that we will have a single unified church, because Moscow would never allow that. Moscow will never relinquish its claim to the Ukrainian lands because that means that Moscow will lose most of its authority in Orthodoxy. It will be about the size of the Romanian Church.

Dyczok: The fact that both marches were held very peaceably was something that a lot of people were pleasantly surprised about. There was all this speculation in advance, all this extra police presence on the streets, setting up metal detectors. What do you think that says about a country that is at war, that has this complex tense issue and yet it goes very smoothly and peacefully?

Bilak: I think it shows several things. I think it shows, foremost, that people are concerned about a lot of other things other than pilgrimage marches. They were well received. I think it was more of an irritation in some places, but people joined in. Ukraine is a pretty tolerant place. Notwithstanding, the religious conflicts over the past 25 years have been about property as much as they have been about canonicity.

Dyczok: There have been incidents in the past that have been violent.

Bilak: But remember, there are a lot of provocateurs as well. Perhaps on both sides.

Dyczok: And that is probably what people were afraid of for this week.

Bilak: Well, there apparently were some provocations by so-called Ukrainian nationalists against the Moscow Patriarchate march, but by and large, the Government and the President should be given a lot of credit for bending over backwards to ensure that they could march. That both churches could march. The President has been very clear on his position that he wants to see Autocephaly for the Ukrainian Church and that he'd like to see it on the basis of the Kyiv Patriarchate. He respected the rights of his citizens to express their own views.

Dyczok: Our final guest is Professor Frank Sysyn, Director of the Petro Jacyk Centre for Historical Research at the University of Alberta. Prof. Sysyn joins us by telephone from Toronto. Thank you very much for finding the time to talk to us. Could you help our listeners understand why is religion such an important battlefield between Ukraine and Russia historically?

Frank Sysyn: Religion is an important part of this battlefield because religion is also interconnected with identity, with historical traditions. And above all, with an ongoing dispute or difficulty, as to whether there are two differing religious traditions on the territory of contemporary Ukraine and Russia, or are they one tradition? And above all, should they be one church, and a one-way civilizational zone? Which we might call from the Russian perspective, Ruskii mir, that is the Russian world.

Now why do I say that this is a long-term difficulty? Because the church that was begun in Byzantium that came to the city of Kyiv, developed an ecclesiastical structure, or church, over a huge territory of eastern Europe. In the Middle Ages, over many kinds of peoples, and languages. It did it through a language and culture that was Church Slavonic, neither Russian nor Ukrainian. In fact, Church Slavonic is closest to the South Slavic languages, contemporary Bulgarian or Macedonian. And that religious culture that existed in the Middle Ages is in many ways the formation of both modern Ukrainian and modern Russian culture.

But from the very beginning, this huge church that is created based out of Kyiv, is much too big in its territory to be effectively administered. And from the Middle Ages, from the beginning on, there were tendencies to divide that entity up. And what we can say is that by the 15th century, two very differing religious traditions developed. One, in Kyiv and the areas of Ukraine, particularly in Western Ukraine, a tradition that saw itself as closely related to the ancient Kyiv tradition.

Then in many ways a new offshoot in the North, based on the territories of Suzdal, the territories now around Moscow. These entities then broke off into separate churches in the 15th century. They were both Orthodox Churches but for over 200 years they were in differing states, they had different cultural traditions. And above all the Orthodox church in Ukraine based on the Slavonic culture, was also interconnected with the Western Christian world with many new tendencies and thought processes that did not really influence the Russian church of this period.

And then after the political act of 1654, when Hetman Khmelnytsky swore allegiance to the Tsar, there was a tendency to try and impose the rule of the newly created Patriarchate of Moscow (which was only created in 1589) over the Metropolitan See of Kyiv. And that in 1686, is enacted in an Act, which many in the Ukrainian Church today view as un-canonical and created what was the Imperial Russian Orthodox Church. That was the church of the Imperial tradition, greatly transformed in the times of Peter I, almost created into a non-Orthodox church as the Patriarch is abolished. That continued all the way to 1917 and the breakdown of the Russian Empire. And much of the 20th century religious history of this territory, has been one in which a movement to form a specific Ukrainian Orthodox Church has attempted to set up its independence from the Russian Orthodox Church.

So, in many ways, the Ukrainian church issue in the Eastern world is already over a century old. That is describing in a modern period, the former Ukrainian Orthodox Church. But in many ways, culturally, civilisationally, one of the important aspects is, does one see an organic Ukrainian religious tradition coming out of Kyivan Rus, having its own specificity, or does one see it as part of a Russian Church, which in many ways has taken over for many of the aspects of the Russian state and political culture.

Those two processes contend to this day, and are now extremely influential at a time when one has its independent Ukrainian church, and independent Ukrainian state, but one which in many ways Russia has not fully accepted as an independent Ukrainian state, and in which religious institutions, which have revived greatly in Ukraine after the period of Soviet persecution, have become very important in influencing culture and society in Ukraine.

Dyczok: What role does the church and the religious conflict play in the military conflict, the hybrid war that's going on in Ukraine?

Sysyn: What we can say is that in many ways the Patriarchate of Moscow, which cooperates closely with the Russian government, has what might be called soft power. It is what is in many ways the last great imperial institution and still tries to exercise its influence over the former territory of the Soviet Union, and even farther beyond it. And therefore, once an ideology of the so-called Russian world, that is the concept that Russia also had a say over the fate of territories in which there were Russian speakers or that were formerly part of the Russian Empire or the Soviet Union, once that ideology was created, in many ways in tandem between the Russian church and the Russian state, it was set on a collision course with a Ukraine which wanted to be a European state, a fully sovereign state, and one in which the Ukrainian sate was also interested in the preservation of Ukrainian culture as well as the rights of all its minorities.

One aspect of Russian foreign policy (and policy of the Russian Orthodox Church) has been to do everything it can to ensure that a Ukrainian Orthodox Church not be set up, which is fully recognised by the Orthodox world, that is canonical and hence, that's caused the current split in Ukraine. This is not an unusual circumstance. The creating in new states or newly formed states, of autocephalous, independent orthodox churches and traditions, has often been much disputed in which the so-called mother church struggled against it. Indeed, in the 19th century when the Russian Orthodox Church became autocephalous, it wasn't recognised for a good 140 or 150 years. Similar things happened in Bulgaria. What we are now seeing is a working out of this process. It's not only in Ukraine that this occurs. This occurs today for example between the Serbian Church and the Church of Macedonia. So these are very difficult ecclesiastical problems and how one forms an independent Orthodox church, recognised as a full member of the Orthodox community.

The reason that it has become so difficult is because the Russian state does not want to really recognise Ukrainian sovereignty. It wants to block all aspects of a sovereign church in Ukraine. The other side of this, is that there are considerable size of groups in Ukraine, particularly in the hierarchy of what once was the Russian Orthodox Church and now is the Ukrainian Orthodox Church that is under the Moscow Patriarchate, that really do not accept as well Ukrainian sovereignty or Ukraine as an independent state with a relationship with Russia as with any other independent state. These also involve cultural traditions, that is the kind of traditions that they see themselves as part of. That reluctance has created a crisis in Ukraine in religious culture, in Ukrainian culture generally. And we now we have seen it emerge in a time of conflict between Ukraine and Russia in many ways.

First of all, in the reports we have had, that in the church in the areas of Donbas and Crimea, at least clergy from the church, who have intervened on the side of separatists or of Russia in these conflicts. Even more important for all of Ukraine, at the moment the Ukrainian Orthodox Church as in the prayers it puts out, wants to portray in many ways this conflict as a civil war internally in Ukraine. That is adopting the line of the Russian government that there is not a Russia intervening in Ukrainian affairs, and as well as we have recently seen with the March of Peace that was established by this church to come on the day of St. Volodymyr, this in many ways would call for peace but that peace is being called for by on one side. On the Ukrainian side. We see no such movement in the Russian church in Russia to attempt to convince the Russian government that to stop this intervention.

Dyczok: Professor Sysyn you're a historian. I'm wondering if I can get you to comment a little bit on the geopolitics. Constantinople, to remind our listeners, is located in Turkey. And Turkey has in the last little while, started a sort of rapprochement with Russia. How will this affect the religious issue?

Sysyn: The Constantinople Patriarchate, still now in Istanbul, is a much reduced, small group of believers but it has still the Patriarch there, and that has been the strength of that church. That is the Primate of all Orthodoxy. The Constantinople Patriarchy has considerable constituencies, for example in north America. Now the issue is, will the Turkish government intervene in these affairs? The Turkish government has in many ways used the Christian believers, both the Orthodox and the Armenian Apostolic believers, as a pawn in international relations. It has given them more autonomy in periods in which it has wanted to move closer to Europe and to join the European Community. Obviously, if it turns away from this, it will respond very differently. The decisions made by the Turkish government to its relations to above all Moscow, and because of that also with Kyiv, will, I think, influence government policy and affairs. But I think Constantinople Patriarchate and Patriarch Bartholomew, now must think in broader international terms and constituencies when informing these policies. So yes, all of these are part of an international political game as well. There is no question the Russian government will try and prevail on the Turkish government to influence Constantinople and how it acts. The question is how Constantinople will proceed and, of course, if Turkey turns towards Ukraine one might see a differing policy. I think the internal church affairs are much more important than what the Turkish government will do at the moment in these affairs. I really do think that we have reached a point where it will partially be resolved within Ukraine. Until now I think the grey issue in Ukraine has been, a large constituency, by all polls and surveys we have of believers, are ready to go over to the Kyiv Patriarchate. The clergy was much more reluctant to make this decision, and above all the bishops of the Ukrainian Orthodox Church. So, we have a real dissension between a population now in

Ukraine, which would seemingly favour an independent Ukrainian church; a clergy much more reluctant; as well as bishops who still seem to think in the conceptualization of the Russian world. There are various constituencies within the Ukrainian Orthodox Church, the Moscow Patriarchate, but the fact that its Metropolitan, has for example recently tried to halt holding religious services in Ukrainian, or at least that this would not spread a movement, as we saw the unwillingness of them to stand to honour those who died in the struggle for Ukraine and that all of Ukraine saw, shows that church hierarchy is extremely conservative and many would argue, is still very tied to Moscow and to the Kremlin. That is both to the Russian Orthodox Church but also to the Russian government.

"Is War the New Normal in Ukraine?"

with Olexiy Haran and Brian Whitmore
5 August 2016

https://hromadske.radio/en/podcasts/ukraine-calling/is-war-the-new-normal-in-ukraine; https://soundcloud.com/hromadske-radio/is-war-the-new-normal-in

US Presidential Candidate Donald Trump made even more waves than usual in an ABC TV interview when he suggested that he might 'look at' recognizing Russia's annexation of Crimea.

Marta Dyczok: Thank you both for joining us. I'd like to start with Professor Haran. Professor at the National University of the Kyiv Mohyla Academy, and Research Director, Democratic Initiatives Foundation. You know that last Sunday Donald Trump, said, "The people of Crimea, from what I've heard, would rather be with Russia than where they were." He also said that Russian President Putin is not in Ukraine, and when corrected by journalist George Stephanopoulos, "Well, he's already there, isn't he?" Trump said, "OK—well, he's there in a certain way. But I'm not there. You have Obama there. And frankly, that whole part of the world is a mess under Obama with all the strength that you're talking about and all of the power of NATO and all of this. In the meantime, he's going away. He takes Crimea." Seemingly blaming Obama for Russia's annexation of Crimea. What did you make of this? What does this mean for Ukraine?

Olexiy Haran: Well first of all, it's one of many statements by Trump. Regarding Mexicans, Muslims, transatlantic partnerships, the ability or inability of NATO to defend other countries. So he has already many statements, how can I put this diplomatically, which are not really correct. But definitely what he said about Crimea is a shock for Ukrainians. Because it shows that either Trump does not understand international relations, he doesn't know what has already happened in Crimea, or he's very cynical. He knows but he doesn't want to recognise it. And there was an article about his adviser Manafort, who was previously adviser to Yanukovych (the former president of Ukraine who was very corrupt, a person who wanted to become a dictator, and was finally ousted as a result of the massive Maidan protests in Ukraine). And now Manafort is advising Trump. There was an article in the *New York Times* about that. This is a shocking statement a lot of Ukrainian media and experts are discussing it. So again, I think this is not wise, I'm using a very diplomatic expression, not wise. I think it demonstrates that Trump simply doesn't grasp international relations and also the international obligations of the United States. And the importance of Eastern Europe in general for American security.

Dyczok: And there was that delegation of French parliamentarians that visited Crimea. This all got me thinking, is this the new normal? Crimea has been annexed; war is continuing in Eastern Ukraine. And I'd like to turn to Mr. Whitmore here. *RFE/RL Power Vertical* creator. Politicians are making statements on the other side of the Atlantic. Here in Ukraine the war is continuing. You produced a very interesting series of podcasts that caught my attention, you called the war in Ukraine, "The Invisible War." That was last July, when there was the highest number of casualties. Since 2015, the war is almost not appearing in international media. What does this mean? Is the war the new normal? What are the implications of this?

Brian Whitmore: Yes, Marta, I think that's part of it. I called it, "The Invisible War," and in today's *Daily Vertical* I called it, "The War Without End." I'll explain why I think that in a minute. July was indeed the deadliest month in the Donbas in a year in terms of both civilian casualties and troops killed in action. Now part of this is cyclical. Summer, as we know, is fighting season, and the fighting tends to spike in the summer. Part of it is that the peace process is completely stalled. And part of it is that you have a lot of armed men in the occupied parts of the Donbas who have no life to go back to. Without the war they have nothing.

But the real reason I think this is happening, and this is going to continue to happen, and why I think this is a war without end, is that in a broader sense there is no way to reconcile the two sides in this. Russia is not going to accept any settlement that does not give Russia a de facto veto over Ukraine's future political direction. And the authorities in Kyiv, not to mention the Ukrainian people, sensibly and reasonably, I think, aren't going to accept any settlement that does give Moscow a veto over Ukraine's future.

And when you cut through all the minutia of Minsk, this is what you have. You have these two irreconcilable positions. One of them the Russian position, quite unreasonable, I think, and the Ukrainian position I think quite more than reasonable. But this is why the Minsk process was flawed from the get-go. And this is why Minsk is for all intents and purposes, dead in the water. It's a war without end for this reason.

One other thing I would add is that the war in Donbas, is it's really Moscow's only leverage over Kyiv. They can't rely on a lot of the other levers they used to rely on pre-war to influence Ukraine. They went all in on the war and without the war they really have nothing. So in a sense it's in Moscow's interests to keep this simmering at a low boil unless they get what they want, which Kyiv is not going to give to them. And if the war ended on any other terms, other than the unreasonable demands that Moscow is making, then Moscow would stand to lose all its leverage. Therefore I just don't see a way out. I wish that were not the case. But I believe that is the case. And it's not good. And it's particularly not good for the people who are living along the front lines in the Donbas.

Dyczok: Professor Haran, same question to you. Have Ukrainians become used to the fact of war, getting on with their daily lives, and hoping their sons, brothers, husbands, don't get called up?

Haran: Actually, this is a very difficult question to answer because on the one hand Ukrainians do not want to recognise that the occupied parts of the Donbas will not return to Ukraine on Ukrainian terms. Ukrainians do not want these territories to be reintegrated under Russia's conditions. Because as Brian rightly said, it would give a lot of leverage over Ukrainian affairs to Russian hands. On the other hand, psychologically, yes, maybe people live under these conditions and they have adapted to this. So life in Kyiv looks peaceful. Some people watch this happening in a very distant region. If you look at the map of Ukraine, you will see that the territory which is controlled by pro-Russian proxies is marginal. Only 3% of Ukrainian territory.

So if you want to disprove the allegations that this is a civil war just look at the map. Look at the map and everything will be clear. I think what the way out can be on the one hand a strong Ukrainian Army which can seal this front-line zone. On the other hand, I definitely believe that Western sanctions should be in place. And we know that this is not easy because the EU sectoral sanctions are [in place] until January 31st of next year, but then we don't know what will happen. And Russia is trying to divide the EU. So I believe there are a lot of questions.

But what I think is important for Ukraine, we may even keep this conflict as a frozen conflict but to try and concentrate on reforms in the rest of Ukraine. Because I believe this is part of Putin's scenario, as Brian rightly said, to use it to destabilize Ukraine's economic and political situation. Perhaps one of the ways out would be just to recognise that we cannot control the territories, try to seal this front line. Definitely we need improvement of capacity of the Ukrainian Army. And here I think western support would also be crucial, not only in supplying some systems, military systems, but also in helping to reform the Ukrainian Army. And then for Kyiv to concentrate on reforms within Ukraine. This would be the best answer to Putin and what he's doing in Donbas.

Whitmore: I think Olexiy hits the nail on the head here, quite frankly. Ukraine needs to focus on what it can control. Ukraine cannot control what's going on in the occupied parts of the Donbas right now because Russia's just not going to give that territory back. If Ukraine made a military push to take it back, all Russia would do is surge troops across the border like they've done in the past and push Ukraine back. So there's really little Ukraine can do right now. You're stuck with this stalemate now.

But what Ukraine can do is concentrate on reforming its economy and reforming its political system and turning the vast majority of Ukraine that the Ukrainian authorities do control into a success story. And that would be the best answer to Mr. Putin. And I think sooner or later the people in the occupied parts of the Donbas will think twice about which side of that line they want to live on. I know which side any sane person would want to live even now. And if you have a Ukraine which reforms itself and becomes a successful, viable, European state, well the choice is a no-brainer.

Haran: And we need an adequate Western reaction to what's going on, definitely not the Trump reaction.

Dyczok: What would be an adequate reaction? You've mentioned sanctions. The Minsk process, has this failed, as Brian pointed out?

Haran: The best way, actually, would be to de-couple sanctions from the Minsk process, which is dead. And if we remember, sanctions were introduced even before the Minsk 1 agreement. They were introduced because of MH17 [the Malaysian airliner that was shot down over Donbas on 17 July 2014], because Russian troops appeared in Donbas, That's the main story. So I think the sanctions should be kept because of that.

We don't need any talk about so-called elections in the occupied areas. You know it's impossible to have free and fair elections there. But again, the real question is, whether the West will be united on that, because we see differences within the EU, and actually the American position was very important in keeping EU sanctions. So that's why we're looking with such attention to the Presidential campaign in the United States. Because the American position and understanding of what's going on the ground is really important for keeping sanctions.

Whitmore: Well, I would say, as a political analyst, I'm quite confident that when all the votes are counted, that the American president's going to be someone who's friendly to Ukraine. I'll just leave it at that.

But I agree with you, Olexiy, that we need to get away from the modalities of Minsk. All these discussions about sequencing, and whether the elections happen first, or Russia gives the border back first, this is exactly the conversation Moscow wants. They can keep having this conversation about this minutia and these modalities where the larger macro issue is, let's face it, that Russia invaded Ukraine, is ignored. And Russia is able to point the finger that Ukraine hasn't fulfilled Minsk because they haven't had elections in a war zone. So the first thing we need to do is get away from the entire Minsk process because it's a failure. It was a flawed deal from the start, it served the purpose of stopping the fighting at the time, but it was clear to anybody who knew anything about this conflict that it was not going to work. We've got to get away from Minsk.

In terms of the sanctions, I think you're absolutely right, decouple the sanctions from Minsk. I'm of the opinion that the sanctions should be made semi-permanent. I'm of the opinion that Moscow is waging a kinetic and non-kinetic war against the West. The kinetic part's happening in Ukraine, the non-kinetic part is happening with all sorts of other things, other things they're doing in the West such as hacking the Democratic National Committee's e-mail servers, for example. But I think we should be focusing on a non-kinetic containment. Sanctions are a big part of that, so I think you're absolutely right about that.

Dyczok: Sorry to interrupt, Brian, you use this wonderful word kinetic. Can you explain to our listeners what you mean by that?

Whitmore: Kinetic is where you're using force, and non-kinetic is when you're not using overt force. I could use a different word if you want.

Dyczok: No, no, that's a great word, I just wasn't sure that everyone understood it, so thank you for explaining. Olexiy is nodding his head here, saying aha, yes, that's exactly the lines that he was going on, did you want to jump in here Olexiy?

Haran: Yes, I fully agree with Brian, the problem is unfortunately with the readiness of Western politicians, first and foremost European politicians, to strongly resist what Putin is doing. And unfortunately, we know that some politicians in Europe, follow the "understanding Putin, we need to take Russia's security concerns into account," line and so on. So a lot will depend on what will happen in the presidential elections in France, and parliamentary elections in Germany. And, again, the presidential election in the United States.

So, unfortunately, what Putin is doing is following the tactic of every dictator against democracy. He's trying to use democratic rules in these countries to undermine democratic procedures, and in order to undermine their ability to resist. That's what happened on the eve of World War II, the tactics that were used by Stalin and by Hitler. And a lot will depend on the readiness of European politicians, and on public opinion as well. Because Putin is trying to manipulate public opinion.

Dyczok: And seemingly successfully, in some ways.

Haran: In some ways yes. And again, I fully agree with Brian, and I'm happy that you agree with me that we need to de-couple sanctions from the Minsk process. But the question is, whether these cautious, pragmatic, European politicians would like to do that. Because they are afraid to provoke Putin, to escalate the conflict. So frankly, unfortunately, I don't think that they are ready to do that. So we, especially Ukraine, we need to play with this Minsk process, as one analyst said, "Minsk is a theatre, everyone is playing his role." And for Ukraine it's important to continue to play the role, "yes, we are in favour, we don't want to violate. We need the Minsk agreements to be fully implemented, we need to keep it." Unless the West would be ready for more decisive steps.

Whitmore: And in the current season, I agree with you Olexiy. I don't see the West being ready for more decisive steps. I think you pinpointed it precisely, the parliamentary elections in Germany and the presidential elections in France are the key things to watch. I'm actually pretty confident that those two elections will turn out well for Ukraine.

Haran: Brian, I'm knocking on wood!

Whitmore: We're always knocking on wood, that's one of the mottos of my life. But I think right now the best thing Ukraine could hope for is a frozen conflict in the Donbas, to be honest.

Haran: Yes, I agree with that.

Whitmore: I don't think you're going to get it. I think you're going to get a simmering conflict. I think you're going to get a conflict that's going at a low boil like it is right now, as opposed to the classic frozen conflicts in Georgia's Abkhazia region, South Ossetia regions, and Moldova's Transnistria region, where those conflicts truly are frozen. But I think Moscow learned a lesson from that whole experience. When the conflict became frozen in Georgia, what happened in the rest of Georgia? Well, they turned completely pro-Western. Because the pro-Moscow parts of the country were in these frozen conflict zones. And I think they understand, correctly, that the exact same thing's going to happen in Ukraine. So they're going to try and keep this thing going and simmering at a low boil. They're going to keep trying to divide Europe and play to these Putin 'understanders' in order to get sanctions lifted. It was a close call last time around when the commission [PACE] voted on sanctions although they did manage to get it through. We'll see what happens in January. But I don't think, at least until this round of elections is over, I don't see the conversation changing, turning towards de-coupling the sanctions from Minsk. I would like to see that but honestly don't see it happening.

Dyczok: So we have a huge task facing Ukraine and prospects for peace somewhere on the horizon.

Whitmore: And I would say the huge task for Ukraine is to focus on what it can control. And what it can control is get moving with the reforms. And turn the part of Ukraine that they do control, the vast majority of Ukraine, into a success story. That's the best answer to Mr. Putin.

Dyczok: Olexiy?

Haran: I fully agree.

Dyczok: Thank you very much, and hopefully next time we meet there will be more positive news to report.

Haran: The positive news, I'm always saying, is that Ukraine is resisting Putin. The Ukrainian Army is resisting the strongest army in Europe. Ukraine survived despite all of Putin's plans. So that's a reason for optimism.

Whitmore: And I would add to that, yes, I think it's pretty remarkable, that Ukraine basically fought Russia to a draw in a war. That's pretty remarkable. But in order to preserve that remarkable victory Ukraine now has to win the war of governance. Ukraine has to turn itself into a successful, prosperous, European state. And unless it does that, that victory, of fighting the largest army in the world to a draw, would have been in vain.

Dyczok: Well, the task is now with the politicians in Ukraine, and other parts of the world.

"War, Sports and Politics"

with Volodymyr Ohryzko, Brian Mefford, Michael Getto and Jairo O. Nascimento
12 August 2016

https://hromadske.radio/en/podcasts/ukraine-calling/war-sports-and-politics

The 2016 Olympic Games began in Rio this week and Russia ramped up the heat on Ukraine.

Marta Dyczok: Volodymyr Ohryzko was Ukraine's Foreign Minister in 2008 when Russian tanks rolled into Georgia during the Beijing Olympics. So he has an insider's perspective of how these crises are handled. We reached Mr. Ohryzko in Kyiv by phone. This week Russia once again ramped up the rhetoric and aggression against Ukraine and Crimea during the Olympic Games. This is not the first time that Russia has chosen to act aggressively towards a neighbouring state during Olympic Games. What's the significance of the timing of this?

Volodymyr Ohryzko: It is really a very stable way of Russian thinking and the Russian way of doing foreign policy. I do not think that we should talk only about similarities with what happened in 2008. This is really the standard manner of Russian foreign policy: to be aggressive, to be unpredictable, and to create problems for neighbours, and, in fact, for itself.

I would say that today we are in a very different situation. First of all, because we have a completely new international environment. Remember in 2008 Western countries came back to business as usual very quickly, probably in two-three months. Now we have a very strong Western position saying to Russia directly, "Stop your aggression or sanctions will continue." I do not think we should compare these two situations because Russia is much weaker, the West is much stronger, and Ukraine is at least trying be militarily strong as well.

Dyczok: That was my next question. You as an insider saw how the crisis was resolved in Georgia. What should Ukraine be doing in response to the latest statements coming out of the Kremlin?

Ohryzko: In my view, there are two simple issues on our agenda. The first is to make the Ukrainian Army as strong as possible. In this sense we need, of course, Western assistance. I do hope that the new American administration will be much more effective in this sense than the current administration. Secondly, we should create an international coalition against an aggressive Russia, explaining to our colleagues in the West that this Russia represents an absolutely different way of thinking and a different way of doing business. This is a Russia that rejects Western values and style of life, of being a member of international community. The West should really wake up and remove these rosy glasses and understand that Russia, unfortunately, is not a partner. It is only a challenge and global threat.

Dyczok: And one more question. Where do you see this headed? Is this just rhetoric coming out of the Kremlin? Or is this a real threat?

Ohryzko: In my view this is another form of political blackmail. They use this instrument very often. Now we have, in my view, the same situation. Economically, Russia is very far form being an economic power. I do not know the exact figures, but Russia has a bit more than 1.5 % of world's GDP. If you are looking at Russian military capacity, they are also very far from being at least adequate [as compared] to NATO or to the United States. The only way they can threaten Western societies is by saying, "We will use technical nuclear weapons," or, "We will attack not only Ukraine but also some of the Baltic States and you will never use Article 5 of the Washington Treaty." Unfortunately, many people in the West are really afraid that Putin can do this. In my view, it is only political blackmail to show everyone in the West that he will do whatever he can do. We should stop this policy all together. Otherwise it will be a great threat to all of us.

Next we spoke with Brian Mefford and Michael Getto in Kyiv.

Dyczok: In the studio today we have Brian Mefford, a business and political consultant based in Kyiv for 17 years, author of *Popular Ukraine* political blog and Non-resident Fellow with the Atlantic Council. And Michael Getto who worked on 1984 LA Olympics and is now an international development elections consultant in Kyiv, who reportedly is an encyclopaedia of sports and politics. Thank you very much for joining us.

Mr. Mefford, I would like to start with you. We were planning to talk about politics and sports but with everything that has happened with Russia recently, let's talk about what's happening. Many are focusing on the Olympics, and Russia is making statements, ramping up pressure, causing the UN to have an Emergency Council Meeting. Is the timing of these significant? Ukraine is about to face its 25th anniversary in a few weeks. And the Olympics. And the escalation. Why this timing?

Brian Mefford: There are two historical precedents. First of all, August 8, 2008 when Russia invaded Georgia during Beijing Olympics. And number two, the Sochi games in February 2014, when days afterwards Russia annexed Crimea. The third thing, Ukraine is coming up to the 25th anniversary of its Independence. Something that Russia or Vladimir Putin does not like to talk about. He considers Ukraine to be part of Russia. Perhaps it's an effort to spoil Ukraine's celebrations on the 25th (of August) and remind Ukraine about the Russian army on the borders to the north, east and south…That could explain some recent activities in Crimea.

Michael Getto: I would agree with what Brian said. In addition, there is an on-going diversion by Putin from what's happening in Russia. Economic growth is negative. Russia is an emerging market, which means it needs to grow significantly and the Russian economy did not grow for the last couple of years because of the variety of reasons. Even before the annexation of Crimea and the beginning of the hostilities and the war in Eastern Ukraine and Donbas. Putin is a master at diverting Russian people from what's happening in their own country.

Dyczok: And international attention…

Getto: Absolutely. And sometimes we easily fall for it. There are some other factors that may have played into the bitterness of Russia. The Russian Olympic team has been thinned down. Many people believe they should be left out of the Olympics. That's yet another grievance that Russia has and that could play a role here as well. And just to back up what Brian said earlier. The 25th anniversary is something that really sticks in Russia's craw.

Dyczok: You touched on the Olympics which is I really wanted to talk about today. You were involved in 1984 Olympics and they were very political games. Sports and politics are always related. The Olympic games are about politics as much as they are about sports because it's nations competing against each other. Sometimes nations pull out of the Olympic games as a political statement. What's the political dimension that you see in the Olympic games of 2016? You started talking about the doping scandal. But is there more there?

Getto: I would say the Olympics and global [sports] competitions are always political. As long as they run flags and medal ceremonies there is a certain amount of nationalism that goes with the Olympics and global championships and global sport. There is nothing really wrong with that. Ukrainians should be proud to see their flag and their athletes doing well. As Americans, Canadians and anybody else. That's positive. But in Russia sport has become a part of the political hierarchy and the political system. It's intimately involved. This doping scandal has hit hard at Russians because they like to think of themselves as a sporting superpower. In many respects Russia has been. The Olympic event is a crown jewel. But they basically defrauded it.

Dyczok: And the crown jewel being?

Getto: Sochi. They spent over 50 billion dollars putting on this elaborate show. It turns out that at least half of their medal winners were doped up. First there was a lot of denial and now they are trying to throw themselves at the mercy of the international sports community. They have admitted some problems, but this is a part of the larger narrative that the world and the West in particular are against Russia, excluding Russia from international institutions whether it's trade, security, or in this case sport. There are some athletes participating in Rio but in the big sports, the name sports, Russia is not going to be in the equation.

Dyczok: When politics enter sports, especially when Ukraine and Russia are at the state of war, how does this affect the athletes?

Getto: I think there is some rivalry to be sure. Russians and Ukrainians have competed against each other before in past Olympics. In Rio there have been a couple of dust-ups between Ukrainian athletes and Russian news media.

Dyczok: Can you tell us about this?

Getto: There was a Ukrainian athlete... By the way, I should say that doping is not a Russian problem. They have massively institutionalized it, but it is not a Russian problem. In the US we had some dopers. Specifically, there is one sprinter who will be participating and there are a lot of second guessing if he is going to win the gold medal. But it is not institutionally, as it is in case with Russia. It would be like the Central Intelligence Agency managing the US Olympic effort in Rio. CIA does not do it unless you are a conspiracy theorist.

Dyczok: You were about to tell us about the dust up between the Ukrainian athlete and the Russian media...

Getto: There was a Ukrainian sprinter who had served a doping suspension. She was asked by a Russian journalist, "So what's the difference? You are here and our people aren't." She said that, "I do not think it is quite fair that the Russian athletes are not here because some of them perhaps have not doped." She was missing the point that this is an institutional problem in Russia. And of course, the Russian journalist, or "journalist", went running back to Moscow saying "See, even this drug cheat in Ukraine admits that we are not being treated fairly." After that the Ukrainian Athletic Federation said, "Do not talk to Russian journalists. Stay away from them."

Dyczok: Brian, back to you. We started with the timing of this. Are we likely to see further escalation of tensions between Russian and Ukraine during the Olympics?

Mefford: There is only one person who knows that, and it is Vladimir Putin. That's a "How deep is the ocean?" kind of question. We hope and pray that's not going to be the case. We hope and pray that worst of the hostilities are over. Unfortunately, it is always a question. Everyday Vladimir Putin wakes up, he makes a decision. The elements are there for an increase in hostilities, no doubt about that. If you look at the number of casualties that have taken place this summer they have actually escalated quite dramatically to the highest point since August 2014. That is very worrisome. There's been a steady drumbeat, the tension has been turned up all summer. That could be guns of summer. If you going to make war it is easier to do it in the summer, than try to do it in the cold of January in Kyiv. Without a doubt it is a worrisome sign. We hope that these are simply manoeuvres, that are not going to be escalated to a full-fledged invasion or conflict.

Dyczok: Russian President Vladimir Putin likes to portray himself as an athlete. We know those images of him in a judo outfit or on horseback. Is there a dimension here that president/athlete is waging further escalation during the Olympics?

Getto: It could be. It's hard to get inside Putin's head sometimes. Sport is a part of the Russian narrative because Russians during the

Soviet days were very successful in sports. That could be part of that. The Olympic year is also the US presidential year. I also think this year is particularly profound given the fact that Russia has allegedly been involved in US political process. That could be a factor. I still do not think we know what exactly happened down in Crimea. It seems that the timing does seem rather strange.

Dyczok: Well, the UN's Security Council is meeting over this issue and we will wait to see what if anything comes out this meeting.

And then we reached Jairo O. Nascimento in Brazil.

Dyczok: Jairo O. Nascimento is an active member of the Ukrainian community in Brazil. He has served numerous positions including the Director of Ukrainian Central Representation. He was very involved Brazil's Euromaidan. We have reached Mr. Nascimento via Skype in Curitiba. Thank you very much for joining us. You are in Brazil now where the Olympics are happening. Could you tell us what the mood is like when the games have started?

Jairo O. Nascimento: Of course, we are involved in the atmosphere of the Olympic games. People are very excited about the Olympics. It is also important to say that we are almost finishing the process of impeachment of the President. The day before yesterday the senators voted, and it is almost the last step to kick off President Dilma [Rousseff].

Dyczok: With the Olympics and the political scandal how much attention is Russia receiving in Brazil's mass media? The issue of doping of the athletes and the war in Ukraine broadly?

Nascimento: I can say that for the press here Russia is too far from Brazil. It is almost on another planet. The tension over Russian activities including the invasion of Crimea…We can watch this on television, but it is not very much. It is a little…

Dyczok: Not a lot of attention?

Nascimento: Very little. About the doping scandal, the repercussions were more serious. We can see the athletes who could not come to the Olympics all the time on TV, in the headlines.

Dyczok: How about the latest statements that are coming out of Russia that Ukraine is planning terrorist activities and trying to destabilize Crimea and the peace process is failing. Is this receiving attention given the Olympics and given your own political scandal in Brazil?

Nascimento: No, almost nothing. The Ukrainian community here in Brazil is about 500,000 people among 200 million Brazilians. We are not a very big community. We are very active, especially here in the south of Brazil in the state Parana and Santa Catalina. Even in San Paolo, the biggest city of the country, there are a lot Ukrainians. So we here follow the news on what's happening in Ukraine. But Brazilians in general are not informed and they do not have an idea on what is going on in Ukraine right now.

Dyczok: As you said, Russia and Ukraine are too far from Brazil. Perhaps it is one of the reasons.

Nascimento: Maybe. The government of President Dilma was aligned to the Russian government. So this did not help much. For example, Brazil until now did not take an official position regarding what Russia is doing in Ukraine. We are complaining. We have requested an audience with new Minister of Foreign Relations. We have not received an answer yet.

Dyczok: Well, let's hope that the new Minister will listen to requests and more attention will be drawn to the issues on what's is going on in this part of the world. Thank you very much for joining us and sharing the perspective on what the war in Ukraine looks like from Brazil.

Nascimento: Thank you very much. Slava Ukraini.

"Shadow of the 1991 Moscow Coup Today"

with Oleksander Tkachenko and Serhii Plohkii
18 August 2016

https://hromadske.radio/en/podcasts/ukraine-calling/shadow-of-the-1991-moscow-coup-today

Twenty-five years ago, on August 19th, 1991, the world woke up to news of the Moscow coup. Marta Dyczok decided to take a look back at those events from two different perspectives, that of a journalist and a historian.

Marta Dyczok: Oleksander Tkachenko is today the CEO of one of Ukraine's largest media corporations, 1+1 Media Group. Back in 1991 he was a young journalist working for Ukrainian state television (because all television was state owned back then), and he was one of the first Ukrainians to report for a Western media outlet. He was working for *Reuters*. Mr. Tkachenko, thank you very much for joining us.

Oleksander Tkachenko: I appreciate this, thank you.

Dyczok: Let's go back to 1991. What was it like reporting on the coup, a crackdown, from within the Soviet Union, working for a Western media outlet?

Tkachenko: It was one of the rarest opportunities. Because on state television during the three or four days of the coup, there was no opportunity to report what was really going on in Ukraine. So for me it was an opportunity to remain a journalist. And in fact *Reuters* became the first news outlet that reported on voting in Verkhovna Rada [Ukraine's Parliament] during those days. And I'm proud that I was the person who did it.

Dyczok: So you broke the story!

Tkachenko: Yes.

Dyczok: Amazing! Now at which point? You mentioned that you reported when Ukraine voted for independence when the coup failed, at which point did you realise, did you feel, that the coup was going to fail? It was very tense for a few days. There were tanks on the streets of Moscow.

Tkachenko: One day I was in the yard of Verkhovna Rada, Ukraine's Parliament, and I suddenly saw two helicopters flying overhead and they flew away and did nothing. So I realised with all their opportunities if nothing happened from the military side, nothing else would. So there were no real tensions, apart from nervousness among the democratically-oriented population about what would happen. But when I saw that they [the military] did nothing I realised that it would be a peaceful end to the coup.

Dyczok: That's quite a difference scenario from what we saw in Ukraine in 2014. Can we look at any parallels? Is there anything that we can learn from the events of 1991 that are relevant for Ukraine today, when it's had part of its territory annexed, and is on the receiving end of a war?

Tkachenko: Its two completely different situations. Because in 1991, Ukraine voted first in parliament, and after that in December in a referendum for independence. It was a peaceful breakdown, a legal decision of the majority of the Ukrainian people to become independent. Now we have military intervention by Russia, annexation of Crimea, and it's [Ukraine's] fight for independence in a physical way. Because in 1991 it was an occasion that came as a result of the coup in Moscow. Now it's a real fight for a free, European-oriented Ukraine.

Dyczok: One more question, if I may. You broke the story of Ukraine declaring independence for *Reuters*, and you mentioned earlier that you could not report what was happening in Ukraine on Ukrainian media. What's the role of journalism and journalists in the current crisis in Ukraine?

Tkachenko: Ukrainian media has become really independent and free and a lot depends on Ukrainian journalists. During the Revolution of Dignity we had a successful resolution of the crisis because of the many media outlets who reported what was going on. It was not peaceful, because there were deaths of many people, but I mean a legal resolution of the crisis. And now, during the period of war, the support [informational] of media about what's going on, about reforms, about struggling in a war with Russia, helps Ukrainian people to realise how we can continue to fight for the Revolution of Dignity, how we can continue to fight against corruption. And at least have optimism for what we will be facing in the future.

Dyczok: Mr. Tkachenko, thank you very much for joining us, sharing your unique insight, and once again congratulations on that scoop back in 1991.

Tkachenko: Thank you.

Dyczok: Serhii Plokhii holds the Harvard University Chair of Ukrainian Studies, named after an eminent historian Mykhailo Hrushevsky. He recently wrote an award-winning book *The Last Empire. The final days of the Soviet Union*. And in that book Professor Plokhii reframed the way we see the collapse of the Soviet Union back in 1991. Professor Plokhii, thank you very much for joining us. Can you briefly tell our listeners what your book reveals about how the USSR collapsed that we did not previously know.

Serhii Plokhii: Thanks for your invitation, it's a pleasure to talk to you again, and to a wider audience. My book argues against a number of dominant narratives here, in the US, in North America, and also in Eastern Europe. According to the American narrative, it's President Reagan or maybe President Bush who really ended the Cold War by causing the collapse and disintegration of the Soviet Union. The story starts with President Reagan going to Berlin, standing in front of the Berlin Wall and saying, "Mr. Gorbachev, tear down this wall!" and the rest followed. I looked at all available documents, in particular, the documents now available in the Bush Library, and got a very different story and a very different narrative of what was happening on those last few months of 1991. According to those documents, the American administration of President Bush was doing everything in their power to prolong the life of the Soviet Union. And it was only in late November when the news reached Washington that there will be an overwhelming vote for Ukraine's independence that the decision was made to change the policy, abandon it, and stop the support, cut the lifeline for President Gorbachev and his Union project in Moscow.

Dyczok: We are now approaching the 25th anniversary of the failed coup in Moscow in August 1991. In the wake of that, Ukraine declared independence and the events you have just described followed. How important was Ukraine in the collapse of the Soviet Union?

Plokhii: Ukraine was extremely important. That fact is widely known in Ukraine itself, but largely forgotten in Moscow and Washington and all over the world. It was a few days after the Ukrainian referendum, when more that 90% of voters supported the declaration of independence, leaders of the three Slavic republics gathered in Belarus and decided to dissolve the Soviet Union. A few weeks after that Gorbachev resigned and President Bush declared American victory in the Cold War. All of that was a direct result of that overwhelming vote for independence in Kyiv and the rest of Ukraine.

The question that people normally do not ask, either in Ukraine or outside of it, why did Ukraine become so important and so crucial? And President Yeltsin, the President of Russia at the time, provided an answer to that question more than once in communications with President Bush. Without Ukraine, he said, Russia would be outnumbered and outvoted by Muslim Republics in that new structure that would be called a "renewed union" after Ukraine's exit. So Russia saw no reason to continue with the Soviet Union without Ukraine, the second largest state in terms of economy and population, a Slavic state, to be part of this imperial project. Once Russia was not interested, the rest of Republics, including Central Asian republics that relied on Russia for the economic support, were not interested in the Union either. Gorbachev had to resign, as there was no state for him to rule any more.

Dyczok: Ukraine was already moving towards independence in 1991, but the coup seems to be an important turning point that speeded things up and led to the result that it did. Could you comment how the events of 1991 are relevant today, given what has happened in Ukraine in the last two years—annexation of Crimea, outbreak of war in Donbas. Is there some sort of a relationship there?

Plokhii: There is a relationship. The disintegration of the Soviet Union happened as a result of a number of factors, but first of all in a position that Ukraine took after the referendum. Ukraine' goal was true independence. Russia had a very different view on that. Yeltsin was thinking about a confederation in which there would be a façade of some joint state, and Russia would be running that state from behind the façade.

When President Putin addressed the Russian legislature on March 18, 2014 with his famous, or infamous "Crimean speech," he said that when the Soviet Union was dissolved, he believed and others in Russia believed that the Commonwealth of Independent States (CIS) is just a new form of joint sovereignty, a different form of a Russian state. And that's not what happened.

So from the very beginning, since 1991, there were different visions in Moscow and Kyiv on what should come out of the CIS. The Soviet Union pro-forma stopped to exist in December 1991, but it is only then that the real struggle began over what would become of the Commonwealth of Independent States.

Ukraine wanted it as a form or structure that would help a so-called civilised divorce. Russia looked at it as a new imperial project where Russia would still run other republics, not as part of the

Union but with stronger and enhanced sovereign prerogatives and capabilities. The roots of the current crisis should be sought in 1991.

And as was the case in 1991, the future of the Soviet Union for Russia was not desirable without Ukraine. Now the reintegration project, of economic, political and military reintegration on the post-Soviet space by Russia is incomplete without Ukraine. The reasons are the same: the second largest economy, and second largest by population. Slavic peoples, culturally close to the Russians. Russian thinking in Moscow from that point of view has not changed much since the fall of 1991.

Dyczok: You mentioned that Russia and Ukraine had very different visions of their future in 1991. Ukraine is about to celebrate the 25th anniversary of its Independence. You have just written a new book about Ukraine, *The Gates of Europe*. Can you tell the listeners what that book is?

Plokhii: In many ways it is a story that covers two and a half millennia of East European history. But also, in terms of its last chapters, it is a continuation of *The Last Empire* in the sense that I go into the 1990s and the current crisis—Russian annexation of Crimea and the conflict in Donbas.

Ukrainian independence is an outcome of an alliance of a number of forces. And those forces include national democrats, largely based in western Ukraine, who acted more or less like reformers in Poland and the Baltic States. Then there was the party elite led by Leonid Kravchuk. There were liberals in big industrial cities like Kharkiv, Kyiv and Dnipropetrovsk. And there was a workers' movement, largely based in Donbas. These were four main players who came together to form an independent Ukraine. What that meant in the long run was that sometimes it was very difficult to make decisions, but also that created a political culture of negotiation and compromise. That became the foundation of the Ukrainian democracy that is certainly much stronger, despite all its problems, that the type of democracy which evolved in Russia, or the absolute collapse of democratic institutions in Belarus.

The roots of that different political culture are in the ways in which Ukraine acquired its independence in 1991. Now, unfortunately, many things have changed and came to an end in early 2014. Today Ukraine faces the fact that an independence which was won at the ballot box and the democracy that came peacefully in the last years of the Soviet regime, all of that has to be defended with arms. It's a new situation, Ukraine is in a situation of war, even though it is not that noticeable on the streets of Lviv or the streets of Kyiv. But it's a real war and a real threat to the sovereignty and integrity of Ukraine. And unfortunately, violence became part of the Ukrainian political scene, that's what we have seen in the last two years. Ukraine is now really in the new stage of its struggle for independence.

Dyczok: Professor Plokhii, thank you so much for putting current affairs into a historical perspective, both 25 years and two millennia. I hope our readers and listeners will have a chance to look at your new book, *The Gates of Europe*.

Plokhii: It was a real pleasure, thank you.

"Ukraine: 25 Years of Independence, a Thousand Years of History"

with Serhiy Holovatyj and Bohdan Nahaylo
26 August 2016

https://hromadske.radio/en/podcasts/ukraine-calling/ukraine-25-years-of-independence-a-thousand-years-of-history

Marta Dyczok: 25 years ago Ukraine declared independence. Since then there are a lot of people who say that it was very easy. The process just sort of happened. Lately Ukraine is fighting for its independence. Mr. Nahaylo, Head of Radio Liberty Radio Free Europe Ukrainian section in 1991, I would like to start with you. You were sitting in Munich and carefully watching what was happening in Ukraine. Radio Liberty was the ideological enemy at that time. How did you have information coming from Ukraine? How were were following the story?

Bohdan Nahaylo: In the old days, when it was still very difficult to travel here and when programs would be jammed… It only stopped in November 1988 (as late as that despite so-called glasnost and perestroika)… we were monitoring the Soviet Ukrainian press very closely. Americans were running and financing Radio Liberty. Before 1971 it had been financed by CIA but then after 1971 it was run by a bi-partisan commission. There was a phenomenal apparatus for gathering information and monitoring. The main radio and TV broadcasts would be monitored on a regular basis. When I would come to work in the morning, I would already know what *Radio Kyiv* had been saying or what was on program *Vremia* the night before. [*Vremia* was all-Soviet evening TV news show]. I'll give you an example of how sophisticated it was. The Soviet Union had 11 time zones. But to make sure the first page of *Pravda* in Vladivostok was the same as in Kaliningrad, early editions were sent by satellite to Vladivostok. The Americans would pick this up so we would know what would be on the first page of Pravda that morning and prepare our programs and counterarguments.

Dyczok: However, when it was breaking news like the emergency session of the parliament on the 24th of August 1991 you were telling us. How did you follow that story because that was a very difficult one?

Nahaylo: Marta, you are jumping ahead. A lot changed between 1988 and 1991. You had the occurrence of informal groups, a burgeoning civil society who had their own independent press, and who were courageous enough to spread information, and to try to contact us via telephone. It was very difficult, but by 1989 -1990 we already had stringers in Kyiv, in Lviv reporting by telephone, sending us faxes. So it became a much more sophisticated operation. I always emphasize for those younger people who are now so used to social media that we were the Twitter and Facebook of that time.

But you asked me what happened on that very memorable for me day. It was a Saturday and it was an extraordinary session of the Ukrainian Parliament. This was two days after the collapse of the "putsch" attempt in Moscow. Let's remember those dramatic days. Orest Subtelny, a renowned historian from Toronto, said before his death in an interview, when he came here to oversee the publication of the Ukrainian edition of his History of Ukraine, that week, when he called his editors here they said, "What book are you talking about? There is no such book being prepared." People were very frightened, and for a few days even that theme disappeared from the radar screen. But once that trauma had subsided and once it was clear that the putchistes had failed, here [in Kyiv] expectations were following along the lines of what Yeltsin was doing in Moscow, that perhaps the Communist Party would be banned. That would be already a major achievement. But it was not clear by any means that the issue of Ukraine's status (it was supposedly a sovereign state already by a former declaration) but it would now proceed to declare itself an independent state.

As Director, I brought in the staff on Saturday. Usually we prepared programs in advance. But I said that I felt something important was going to happen. So all day we were sitting at our desks, waiting for news from Kyiv, from our correspondents Serhiy Naboka, Svitlana Riaboshapka and Leonid Miliavsky. At 6 pm Kyiv time, 5 pm Munich time, we were supposed to go live with a broadcast of international news. But at ten to five there were still no news. So I got to the phone to our correspondents in Kyiv and Svitlana Riaboshapka picked up the phone. She said, "Pane Bohdane, Kravchuk, the Speaker of the Parliament, is putting the act declaring Ukraine's independence to a vote." I said, "Come on, this can't be true." She said, "No, listen for yourself," and she took the phone receiver, held it to the TV in Kiev. I am listening over the phone in Munich to Kravchuk reading the text and I hear cheers and applause. I realise something dramatic had happened. My response as a director was "What do I do?" Do I run with that news? Do I believe what my ears and my correspondents have told me? Or do I play it safe and wait an hour until everybody else has broadcast. I ran to the news booth. The red lamp was already on saying "No entry." But I had the prerogative of going in, as the Director. My colleague Vasyl Darchuk was supposed to read the international news in 2-3 minutes and I scribbled a note and passed it to him, "According to preliminary information Ukrainian Rada or Supreme Soviet has just declared…"

Serhiy Holovatyi: Supreme Soviet…

Nahaylo: Thank you, Serhiy. He is a legal specialist and was there. I said, "Read this out." He put his finger to his head to show that I am crazy through the glass. I said, "Read it or you will get into trouble." He pointed to his throat as if somebody is going to slit his throat. "You know what it means if I read this out." I said, "Yes, you lose your head if you don't." So he went ahead, followed my instructions and at 6 pm Kiev time we were the first to broadcast the news. We beat *UkrInform, TASS, AP, Reuters…* Why was that important? Because it was a Saturday and even though there was a relief after the failure of the putsch a lot of people were at their dachas. They had not been glued to their TV sets watching what's happening in the Verkhovna Rada. We were the first to bring that news abroad. Millions of people were listening to us. One footnote: we had to celebrate. Of course the canteen in *Radio Europe* in Munich was run by Germans and the store was closed at 5 pm. I had to bang on the door saying, "Ukraine has declared its independence, please give us some champagne!" They said, "No, it's 5 o'clock". I said, "History is being made in front of your eyes. Do you want to be a part of history or you will be bores?" So they opened the store, gave us champagne and we drank to Ukraine's independence.

Dyczok: Mr. Nahaylo broke the story of Ukraine's independence to the world. Serhiy Holovaty was one of the people that made it happen. Mr. Holovaty, is co-author of Act of Independence of Ukraine, then a Member of Parliament and one of the founding members of RUKH, please tell us how this Act of Independence was prepared? You were one of the authors. We have in studio with us the original draft.

Holovatyi: We have to go back to those days in renewing our memory of the composition of Rada.

Dyczok: Ukrainian Parliament at that time …

Holovatyi: The composition of the Supreme Soviet of the Ukrainian Soviet Socialist Republic. It was not yet Rada. It was the Supreme Soviet. 450 members. Among them not more than 110 those who were anti-Communists.

Dyczok: Democrats.

Holovatyi: The democrats formed an informal alliance which was called Narodna Rada, or the People's Rada, or People's Council. It means that less than a quarter of the MPs were in favour of independence. All the rest were orthodox Communists, members of the Communist Party of the Soviet Union. When the coup occurred in Moscow on the 19th of August, it was not clear what was going on. I was in Russia that day, because it was vacation time for MPs in August. Some of us were on holidays in a resort area near Rostov-on-Don—Mineralnye Vody, a resort for all MPs from all over the Soviet Union. There were also MPs from the republics and Moscow. When we arrived for breakfast, we heard from radio about the coup. Immediately we started to find a way how to get out to Ukraine. It was almost martial law. Everything was blocked.

It took about one day to come to Kyiv by plane, the only plane that was allowed to take off from Rostov-on-Don to Kyiv and Moscow, was that plane registered at Boryspil airport. That is why even MPs from Moscow (members of the Supreme Soviet of USSR) could not get directly to Moscow. It was blocked by military. The captain on board was from Kyiv, from Boryspil. That's why we were lucky to be back in Kyiv around 10pm or even 11 pm on the 19th. Immediately with our luggage we came to the building of the Supreme Soviet and joined the group that demanded to convene an extraordinary session. But the Speaker of the Supreme Soviet Leonid Kravchuk was really hesitating. He did not do that on the 19th, 20th, or 21st. He still was waiting for…

Dyczok: The end?

Holovatyi: What direction events would take place. And only after it was clear that the coup is failing, he convened the extra session. The members of the People's Council met in the House of the Writers Union. There was a special meeting of the democratic bloc to work out the plan. According to the unanimously adopted scenario we drafted the agenda for this extraordinary session. The agenda consisted of 12 points.

Dyczok: That's a big agenda…

Holovatyi: Number one was the resolution on banning the Communist Party. Number two was de-communziation or lustration—banning possibility for the former Communist bureaucrats, apparatchiks, nomenklatura to take any positions in the offices of the government. Possibly proclaim independent

Ukraine. Then number three, denationalization of the property of the Communist Party and making it the property of the people. The last item, as I would say the culmination, the crowning point, is proclaiming independence of new Ukraine as already decommunized, already democratic and so and so on. That what was be the last point. That was the agreement or the decision of Narodna Rada. It was adopted on the 22nd of August and was decided that Narodna Rada will prepare the draft of all these documents. We had only one day—the 23rd—to do it one day and it was done. Then we met on the 23rd in the evening in …

Dyczok: In the Writers Union building?

Holovatyi: No, already in the Parliament. We had already discussed the prepared drafts and the scenario was supposed to be like this. When we came on the 24th, the plenary meeting was opened. The first secretary of the Communist Party, Mr. Hurenko, was admitted, allowed to speak on behalf of the Communists, on what they had done in Moscow and what was their line in Kyiv.

Finally we came to the moment when we had to start to adopt the drafts, the agenda, the documents according to our plan. However, the Speaker of the Parliament Mr. Kravchuk suddenly announced that the floor is given to member of Rada of the Supreme Soviet Mr. Yavorivskyi for announcing the Act of Independence.

Dyczok: Mr. Yavorivskyi was a member of RUKH.

Holovatyi: Exactly. He was a member of the Presidium which was at that time the Presidium of the Supreme Soviet. And it became clear that during the night there was a special agreement between the Presidium and the Speaker that they will not follow our scenario and that they will only vote for one issue—for proclaiming independence. Only this. As they were afraid if they put the scenario like we have planned, we could fail to proclaim independence because the communists were majority. Super majority. 200 people a super majority.

Nahaylo: Mr. Lukianenko said a few days ago that he suspects that Yavorivskyi was being secretly prepared as a possible leader if Kravchuk were to be removed and he would be acceptable to the communists.

Holovatyi: I don't know about that. But I remember Lukianenko, who was authorized by Rada to pronounce that document, was standing in front of me. I was sitting in the first row, so he was standing in front of me with this sheet of paper which was already written with text which had to be voted, but suddenly Kravchuk called for Yavorivskyi and he [Yavorivskyi] just came and pulled out this sheet of paper from Lukianenko and Lukianenko started to cry. Because that was a betrayal, something unexpected. Lukianenko was crying. His tears were coming out of his eyes.

Nahaylo: It was also his birthday.

Holovatyi: Yes. But finally it was done so unexpectedly that nobody could tell what to do. It was put to a vote and there was nothing we could do except vote. By the way, some RUKH members, me and my colleagues, we voted against during the first voting because we also were feeling betrayed. Because it was not our agreement, not our plan. We didn't want to vote for an independent Ukraine of that quality, when the Communists have the power. I voted against the Act which I had co-written. I had to vote against my Act. That was one attempt.

Then when we had voted against the Act, Kravchuk called a vote on the second issue—the resolution, an additional document on the proclamation of independence, along with the announcement of the referendum for people approval on the first of September. Certainly, when that was proposed, we voted. There were 346 who voted.

At that time there was a very active anti-communist minority with just over 100 deputies. They managed to achieve their goal which was for them "their ideal". Our idea was independent Ukraine, independent from Moscow, independent from the Soviet Union. An independent country gaining independence as all other nations in Europe or other nations in the liberal world. At the same time this independence was supported by the communist majority that was aggressively orthodox because it was in their interests. They never pursued an idea of independent Ukraine. But they voted for it because it was their interest to keep power. I voted the first time against, and only then for, because I understood that voting in favour was preserving power.

Nahaylo: They were saving their skins.

Holovatyi: And finally it was a victory for many MPs and RUKH members. They were happy. I had mixed feelings. I was happy and unhappy. For me it was a day of joy and happiness, and of sadness. In the evening they went to a restaurant in a hotel in the Stolichny on Khreshchatyk Street. Communists, RUKH members, they went for *kholodets*. They were drinking champagne. They were singing songs. They were euphoric.

I didn't go there and I didn't join them. With my friend, who was at the time a RUKH member, Valeriy Ivasiuk, we went to the National TV station, to Yevdokia Kolesnik, a journalist who had a live TV program at 11 pm. We went there explaining why we are not singing, dancing and drinking champagne with the others. Our message was that we didn't want Ukraine's independence to be voted in by communists preserving power. We do not believe in that.

Exactly 25 years ago I said on TV I don't believe that Ukraine will be independent in such a way. I said that Ukraine's freedom couldn't be gained without bloodshed. Ukrainian history has proved that only if it is conquered in battle against an external enemy such as the Moscow horde, the Tatar horde, the Mongol horde, invaders form the east. As we see now that is what exactly happened in 2014. There is still a fight for independence. Maybe due to this bloodshed we will preserve our independence as the main goal of Putin's regime is to destroy Ukraine's independence.

Nahaylo: If I may just come in for a second. As Marta suggested at the beginning, a lot of people suggested that independence was handed to us on a plate, that Ukrainians did not do anything. They don't take into account all the centuries of struggle.

Holovatyi: I disagree.

Nahaylo: The major achievement of that movement was that it had a clear concept, thanks to people like Serhiy, of Ukraine for all its citizens, not just Ukrainians, you know, Ukrainians with just one version of history and one version of religion. As you know it embraced all the citizens and it made Jews, Bulgarians, Poles, Catholics feel at home. That was a major achievement.

Holovatyi: It was written down…

Nahaylo: It could have gone wrong. It could have turned into bloodshed.

Holovatyi: I meant bloodshed not inside Ukraine. Bloodshed as the war between Russia and Ukraine, Moscow and Kyiv.

Nahaylo: The point I want to make that even though there was the semblance that it was happening rather smoothly, what has happened since 2014 -15 is that the political nation, and particularly the younger generation, is that freedom comes at a price. The blood and the lives, this has been the price, maybe belatedly, that we are still paying for that independence. That was one of the major messages of the Revolution of Dignity, the Maidan etc. that you don't get things for free and if you want to stand up for democracy, for Europe, for self-identification, for being Ukrainian, at the end of the day you have to be able to and ready to give your lives for it.

I am encouraged by the younger generation who have a different outlook, who already have a sense of Ukrainian history not in any narrow chauvinistic way but in a European sense. They certainly don't want a Eurasian tyrannical model here. If you ask me: after 25 years, is the glass half empty or half full? I would say it is more than half full. 25 years later we are stronger than have ever been despite internal shortcomings.

Dyczok: The feeling of a political nation has spread over 25 years but I'd like to go back to 1991. Mr Holovatyi, you and your colleagues were real revolutionaries and visionaries. You were one of the co-authors of this document that made Ukraine an independent state. Coming out of a Soviet tradition, Soviet education, you had the vision how to draft this document, what to put into it. Can you tell us about the actual Act of Independence?

Nahaylo: Before Serhiy does I want to interject. Serhiy represented that rather limited elite of very sophisticated people legally trained with a broad international outlook, aware of international standards.

Holovatyi: The main factor in this circumstance is that I graduated from Taras Shevchenko University as an international lawyer. I was trained in international law. If I was trained as a simple Soviet lawyer, I could not have known all the things that I knew at that time already. While studying international law we even were trained in human rights law, which was in the Soviet Union almost unknown. Human rights law was a part of international law only. In the Soviet Union, it was not a part of a national law because there were socialist rights. According to the Soviet tradition, Ukrainian lawyers could not be trained in understanding human rights as rights and freedoms, freedom of speech, freedom of assembly, freedom of demonstrations, freedom of expression... No, never... Only in the right to labour, right to housing, right to health, to education, social rights...

I was studying international law. I knew something about the Universal Declaration of Human Rights, about the Charter of the UN and the rights of a nation for self-determination. That's why in our Act there is a reference that Parliament on the 24th of August proclaimed independence based on the Charter of the UN, and other international instruments which contain the right of a nation for self-determination. We were trained as specialists in international law, so we had to know English, French or another language.

That certainly helped very much when I was consulting the RUKH movement and the leadership in the RUKH on how to write documents. I drafted, for example, the whole Charter of the RUKH movement in 1989. I drafted two chapters in the RUKH program on human rights and the rights of individual, rights of the nation, on the state based on the rule of law and so on. That was the knowledge we'd got even during the Soviet Union's legal education system.

Dyczok: This document that Mr. Holovatyi has brought into our studio, which we will photograph and put up to our webpage, was inspired by international documents, by international visions. When you were drafting this what were the key ideas that you put into this document?

Holovatyi: The first key idea was that proclaiming Ukraine's independence means that we reaffirm our long historic tradition of statehood. It is precisely stated that by this we proclaim the continuation of our history of more than one thousand years starting with Prince Volodymyr who baptised this Kyiv land in 988 at the same time when the first king in France was put on the throne in 987. From that year the French dynasty of monarchs was started. At that time we were are almost the same: the French monarchy and Kyivan Rus monarchy or as it was said in Latin, Rossica, which was then stolen by Peter the Great for the name of Tsar of Russia. Ukraine, that is, Kyivan Rus' or Kyiv Rossia. That long history that was put as the first thesis.

Dyczok: So the long history…

Holovatyi: The second was the idea of the right of a nation to self-determination, as this is prescribed by the UN Charter and other instruments of international law.

Dyczok: So immediately referenced to international norms.

Holovatyi: Yes, to the UN Charter and, I would say, International Covenant of 1966.

The third thesis is that we were continuing our action in coordination with the Declaration of Sovereignty, which was passed by the same Soviet republic on the 16th of July 1990, not knowing that we would be voting for independence later. That was our basis for our future statehood, our military forces of Ukraine, which we never had because there was Soviet forces, national currency hryvna and economic independence from Moscow. All these basics were put down in the Declaration of State Sovereignty because the Soviet Republics were not sovereign. On 16th July 1990, we laid the foundation for future state sovereignty. There is a linkage of these three basic things: the long historic tradition, the international basis for independence, and national basis for independence, which was laid down a year before.

Dyczok: So very sophisticated conceptually and legally well-grounded. Quite a historic moment...

Holovatyi: It had to be very short. If it was formulated longer, it could raise debates in the Parliament; and with the super majority of aggressive orthodox communists, we could fail. It could not be a very long text like the American Declaration of Independence.

Nahaylo: You had to be concise. You had to win them over as well, you had to find the right language.

Holovatyi: The priority was independence based on these three things.

Dyczok: Thank you very much.

Nahaylo: I want to mention one point we forget now in the context of the Russian aggression in the East. In 1990 when Ukraine declared its sovereignty an important role was played by the strike of miners in Donbas.

Holovatyi: It was organized, it was an artificially-made strike.

Nahaylo: It was. But it was their involvement and their presence on the streets that helped us get sovereignty because it also helped frighten the Communist elite. That's now forgotten. But that's something we should be aware of because it is not how it was portrayed by Moscow. Donetsk was connected with Kyiv and with the rest of Ukraine, its politics and its aspirations.

Dyczok: Thank you. We have co-author of the Act of Independence and we have the man who broke the story to the world. Thank you very much for sharing your insight and for joining us.

Nahaylo: Thank you Marta for having us. I think that for all three of us it is a very important anniversary.

Holovatyi: And in conclusion I would like to agree with what Bohdan said earlier, that Ukraine is stronger at 25 years than ever before. It has such prospects for the future as never before.

Dyczok: Because it was built on a strong foundation, thank you very much for your contributions, and contributions to come…

"IMF Loans & Economic Challenges: Western Sunrise in Ukraine"

with Olena Bilan, Cameo by Boris Johnson
16 September 2016

https://hromadske.radio/en/podcasts/ukraine-calling/imf-loans-economic-challenges-western-sunrise-in-ukraine

United Kingdom's Foreign Secretary, Boris Johnson visited Hromadske Radio and made a statement about the relationship between the UK and Ukraine. And the new host Marko Suprun interviewed top economist Olena Bilan about the IMF loan.

Boris Johnson: I'm very proud to be here in Ukraine on my first-ever visit. The reason I wanted to come to Ukraine so soon after being made Foreign Secretary of Britain because I want to show my country's passionate support for Ukraine.

And we in the United Kingdom are going to fight to make sure that we keep the pressure up and keep the sanctions on Russia that is responsible for aggression against this country. And we want to see a strong, free, democratic, sovereign Ukraine, with a European vocation. And it's wonderful to be here and to see how much good the United Kingdom is doing. We're training some of the Ukrainian military forces, which is very important. We're also helping with a lot of the humanitarian work and of course we are contributing to the OSCE monitors. And helping also to make sure Ukraine embarks on a sustainable program of political and economic reform and stamps out corruption.

And I wish everybody in the Donbas region particularly, while I know how difficult things are at the moment, and I can tell you that all of us in Britain are hoping and praying the Minsk process will be successful.

And that there is a security solution: a withdrawal of the Russian forces, and of course that we get a democratic solution in that part of the country as well. Nobody could pretend this is going to be easy. But I am sure it can be done. And I want everybody to know that Great Britain, the United Kingdom is here to help. Thank you everybody.

Marko Suprun: Today with me in the studio is Olena Bilan, Chief Economist of Dragon Capital. Dragon Capital, one of the Ukraine's leading groups of companies in the field of investment and financial services. Olena joined Dragon Capital in 2006 as an economist and fixed income analyst and in 2009 was promoted to the position of Chief Economist. She was named one of the top three analysts in the Ukrainian financial markets by Thompson Reuters Extel survey of global institutional investors in 2013 and 2014. She graduated with a Masters in International Economics from the Kyiv Mohyla Academy. Olena, thank you very much for joining us today.

Olena Bilan: Thank you for inviting me.

Suprun: One of the issues this week is the IMF tranche, that we are expecting or not expecting? Could you tell our listeners why Ukraine needs IMF support?

Bilan: We are expecting that tranche very much because the previous tranche was disbursed more than a year ago in August last year. There was a huge delay. Usually IMF tranches come according to a quarterly schedule. The next tranche would come in three months after the previous one. But that tranche was delayed for various reasons. We had a political crisis in Ukraine. We had discussions about the budget. Time passed, the economic situation changed, and then a new round of negotiations started. So the country needs this tranche very much. It is not about the money. Ukraine's economic situation is much better than it was before. The economy has stabilized. The financial markets are stable and there are some initial signs of recovery. But the overall situation remains fragile because we still have military conflict with the Russian separatists in the east. There is no political resolution found to the conflict. It is calm now. It is absolutely safe in Kyiv and on more than 90% of the Ukraine's territory but there is always a risk of some escalation that would definitely hit confidence and the economic situation.

Suprun: You mentioned the war in the East. I know many friends of mine worked with Dragon Capital and your fund was helping out with the war effort.

Bilan: That's true. Many people are volunteering in different ways. My colleagues and myself we give money and medicine whatever we can.

Suprun: Could you tell us why it is important for IMF loans to continue?

Bilan: The participation of Ukraine in the IMF program is a strong signal to the international investor community in indicating that Ukrainian authorities are doing good work in putting the economy on the right track of sustainable growth, to overcome the crisis, restructure the economy, and implement reforms. Reforms are very important to be able to escape the legacy of the Soviet Union and the previous oligarchic structure of the economy. We are definitely happy to receive the funding, but what's really important is to remain in the program and continue with the reforms according to commitments made by the government.

Suprun: You said that that this memorandum between Ukraine and IMF has been subsequently changed?

Bilan: Overall, the main direction of the reforms will remain the same in the energy sector, fiscal sector, banking sector, state-owned enterprises, and big anticorruption component.

Suprun: Indeed the last Memorandum had a notion of increased tariffs. Regarding gas and central heating retail prices, the increase was 285% and 67% respectively. That brings me to this interesting issue that raising tariffs and pension age is part of the Memorandum.

Bilan: Tariffs are clearly part of the Memorandum. I am not sure about the pension age, but some element of the pension reform will be also included in the Memorandum. Whether it will be related to pension age or other measures is not clear yet. Regarding the gas tariffs, I would like to stress that Ukraine has increased gas tariffs dramatically. The 285% increase is only the first step. If you look at the tariffs from two years ago, they were at $17 for 1000 cubic meters of gas. Now it is 11 times higher. You can imagine that in almost three years the increase was 11 fold.

Suprun: Doesn't this put a lot of stress on the country and the people who live in the country?

Bilan: That is true. Definitely there is a short-term negative impact on the population and households, but this is mitigated by quite generous subsidies to the poor. This is very important because low prices meant that everyone was subsidized including very rich people. We have many rich people in Ukraine. They do not reveal their real incomes. In reality some people were heating their outdoor pools with gas and paid this very low price. Definitely it is not the role of the state to subsidize these rich people. Now there is more targeted subsidization directed to those who are really in need.

Suprun: So the subsidies will not be "blanket" subsidies in Ukraine.

Bilan: Not anymore. They will be targeted and based on income and on the share of utilities bill in the income. If it is very high, the part of the utility bill will be compensated and is currently compensated by the state.

Suprun: This is interesting. I spoke with some insiders in the Verkhovna Rada [Parliament] last week and they said that Ukrainian budget requires 120 billion hryvnas to cover the subsidies, which is about 20 billion hryvnas more than the budget for the Ministry of Defence. There is a fear that there will be *taryfnyi Maidan* [protests] in the fall. Do you see this happening?

Bilan: I would like to see the estimates and calculations behind the numbers. You can cite any numbers to generate headlines. So far what was budgeted for this year is 40 billion hryvnas, which seems enough to cover this year's subsidies. Maybe there will be some small increase when we will see who will apply. I do not think it is really 100 billion.

Suprun: So these numbers are often used as a political football to start fears that the crisis is coming may be in fact artificial?

Bilan: I do not know. I would like to see the estimates. That is what our community is missing. Someone presents a number/figure but it is not supported by proper calculations.

Suprun: Do you expect any political risks to these reforms that are coming?

Bilan: The increase in tariffs has been already done. This was a very unpopular but very important step to improve public finances. Ukraine really did a very good job in consolidating the budget, in reducing the deficit. You cannot imagine: in 2014 the budget deficit was 10% of GDP. Last year it was already 2% of GDP. Partially it is thanks to the gas tariff increase. It was very important for the future of the economy and its growth, and for overall economic stability.

Suprun: So it is a part of an energy independence program…

Bilan: Yes, it is. It would definitely help to reduce gas consumption. Because people will think very carefully whether they really want to use gas and to keep the temperature very high in their houses.

Suprun: Interesting. Often you can see in wintertime in Kyiv people who always have their windows open.

Bilan: Kyiv and large cities are really a problem. Because in large cities we have central heating which is very difficult to adjust in your individual apartment. Many people who use gas have individual heating systems. Those that live in the suburbs and some small towns live in individual houses, they have individual heating systems, they can really use only as much gas as they need.

Suprun: So the Memorandum with the IMF is on the road of modernization and would bring Ukraine closer to the 21st century.

Bilan: The important part of the Memorandum is a macroeconomic stabilization. Another part is called the Extended Fund Facility and it is on much longer term. One of its structural components is an anti-corruption initiative. That is what would make Ukrainian economy stronger and would help to recover quicker.

Suprun: Part of me wonders. This is clearly a loan. This means it had to be paid back. What are some of the conditions of the term of the loan?

Bilan: It is not a typical IMF Program. It is a long-term program. The first payment, if I am not mistaken, will be paid in five years after the first disbursement came. It is quite extended over time. The interest rate is below 3%. For Ukraine which has its sovereign Eurobond traded at 8% at the moment it is a source of very cheap financing.

Suprun: I did not know that.

Bilan: The yield compressed quite substantially over the last months. Ukraine has quite high yield. This is a reflection of the absence of an IMF tranche for a long time. There is still some uncertainty about the economy and the conflict in the east…

Suprun: How closely is the exchange rate linked to the IMF program? I remember in the former document the exchange rate was something like 22 to 1 [hryvnia to US dollar]. Today it is 26 to 1. Would receiving the loan stabilize the currency?

Bilan: The currency has already stabilized. It was 25 several weeks ago. Now it is close to 27. This was kind of expected. Usually we have some pressure on the devaluation of currency in the end of summer-beginning of fall. IMF recommends and advocates for Ukraine to have flexible exchange regime. Do not fix the currency. Ukraine had a pegged exchange regime for many years. For the structure of the economy it did not work very well. We always had a period of stability and then an economic crisis because the pegged exchange rate created an illusion of stability. It distorted how people behaved. Many people underestimate the risk of exchange rate fluctuation. They prefer all operations in foreign currency. They do not take into account the exchange rate risk. Now the Central Bank is moving from a pegged exchange rate system to inflation targeting which is a very popular monitor policy regime adopted in many countries. It means that an exchange rate will not be stable, it will be moving, but the Central Bank would step in to confront extreme movements in the currency.

Suprun: With the exchange rate falling to 26-27 now, how do you think Ukrainians will be able to pay some of the subsidies? What is your projection of the currency in five years?

Bilan: The current level is close to a fundamentally justified level. Ukraine now runs very small trade deficit, close to zero. There is no major under or overvaluation of the currency.

Suprun: Essentially economically things are looking good…

Bilan: Yes, but it depends whether we will have an external shock or not.

Suprun: Such as a war with Russia.

Bilan: The escalation of the conflict… I do not see us on the brink of war. I do not see this. For Russia it is quite expensive. Plus the potential geopolitical cost and cost to domestic politics But an escalation of the conflict is still not off the charts. This might be an external shock. Ukraine is also a commodity-based economy. About 60% of all the goods we export are commodities such as steel or grain. An adverse move in prices may trigger turbulence and affect the markets.

Suprun: Minister Danyliuk says that even without the tranche Ukraine has resources and tools to stabilize the economy. Do you think it is possible?

Bilan: Ukraine does not need money as much as it needs a signal. Working without extra funding for some period of time, not forever, would be possible for Ukraine to survive for another several months, maybe for a year. But it is much better for the country to get this financing, to get IMF on board, and to send a signal to the rest of the world that we are moving forward in terms the reforms.

"Ukraine Commemorated the 75th Anniversary of the Babyn Yar tragedy"

with Timothy Snyder
30 September 2016

https://hromadske.radio/en/podcasts/ukraine-calling/ukraine-commemorated-the-75th-anniversary-of-the-babyn-yar-tragedy

New host Bohdan Nahaylo.

Bohdan Nahaylo: What a sombre week... A week of remembrance... I am honoured to have in the studio with me Timothy Snyder, Professor at Yale University, a leading intellectual figure of our time. Let us begin by focusing on Babyn Yar itself. You gave a brilliant presentation yesterday in which you so lucidly talked about such complex and tragic events. I will be very happy if you could share with us your main thoughts, your main theses that you presented. From today's point of view, what do we know about what actually happened at Babyn Yar?

Timothy Snyder: We know a great deal. Although we continue to learn more, and it's very important as we remember Babyn Yar, as we commemorate Babyn Yar, as Ukrainians think what kind of museum to establish, how do they want to institutionalize the memory of Babyn Yar, to remember that Ukrainian and Western historians are still at work to figure out some basic facts. We know the following. We know that on the 29th and 30th of September 1941, 33,771 Jewish children, women and men were marched from Kyiv to a meeting point from which on one day or the next they were shot, kneeling over the ravine at Babyn Yar, or lying on top of people who had already been killed. We know that the killing, the shooting was carried out by the so-called Sonderkommando of the Einsatzgruppe, a special group led by the SS, assisted by two battalions of German police, and also assisted by some local inhabitants of Kyiv and perhaps some other Ukrainians as well.

This we know. This event, horrible and significant to us as it was, is in a way only a beginning of a larger event which is the mass killing, the Holocaust of Jews on the occupied Soviet Union.

Nahaylo: What is the significance, what is the broader meaning of Babyn Yar for our understanding of the Holocaust?

Snyder: It is very appropriate that the Jews who come from Eastern Europe would remember Babyn Yar as a symbol. It is very appropriate that scholars of the Holocaust turn their attention to Babyn Yar as well because Babyn Yar demonstrated how the Holocaust could be carried out. It was at this moment, the summer of 1941, that the Germans realised that the thing Hitler and others called "the final solution" could become the horrible reality that we remember as the Holocaust. This method that was carried out by in Babyn Yar—the cooperation of German institutions, the mass shooting in the open air, the increasing collaboration of local people—this was the method that was applied all over the occupied Soviet Union, not just in Ukraine, but in Belarus, the Baltic Sates, western Russia, everywhere the Germans went killing. Not on this scale—this was the largest. Killing of this kind was carried out as the German army moved to the east, and even as they came back to the west as in Kerch, for example, there were further mass killings. In this way Germans learned that the Holocaust was possible. In this way more than two million human beings lost their lives and in this way we also learn what human beings are capable of. When we think of Auschwitz, of later methods of killing, we often separate ourselves from the horrible reality of our own capabilities by metaphors like "death factories" or "machines." Whereas Babyn Yar and the way the Holocaust begins teaches that getting large numbers of people to kill even larger numbers of people is unfortunately not as difficult as we might think.

Nahaylo: At the end of the day, how could it have happened? That only a few days after the Germans marched in [to Kyiv] they were able to round up tens of thousands of people and just shoot them?

Snyder: Part of the answer, unfortunately, I have already given. Namely, it does not actually take much to turn a human being into a killer. Unfortunately, the question is the opposite. How do we preserve the institutions, the ways of life, the laws, the habits that prevent us from doing things like this? But back to your question. I think most historians would emphasize three factors. The first one is an idea, a big idea, an ideology in which Jews have a specific and central place. In Hitler's world view Jews are responsible for all evil because it is Jews who prevent Germans from being always victorious, from taking what they want, which is the second idea. The second idea is Lebensraum: empire, colonies, and the notion that Germans as a superior race deserve to conquer Eastern Europe and, in particular, need to control the fertile soil of Ukraine. Without the idea of racial war in Ukraine, without the quest for Lebensraum, German forces would not have come to Kyiv in the first place. That is another very important component of what happened. The third idea is lawlessness, statelessness, the separation of Jews and everyone else from the normal pattern of daily life by the alteration, mutilation or even the destruction of the Rule of Law, and the states themselves. The Germans, wherever they went, created legal or political chaos. We stereotype Germans as being orderly. In fact, the German march into the Eastern Europe through Austria, Czechoslovakia, Poland and finally the Soviet Union was a constant generation of chaos, of lawlessness, of statelessness, which allowed people to do things they would not have done in other situations. Those are three big factors.

Nahaylo: We recall that for many decades Babyn Yar as the place where so many Jews and others—including Ukrainians, gypsies, and invalids—were killed. This fact was hushed up. It was presented by the Soviet authorities as simply a place where many Soviet citizens had been killed. I was also struck by the fact yesterday that a renowned German historian said, "You know, we did really not know that much until recently about Babyn Yar itself. We knew about the Holocaust." How would you explain this, and how this affected remembrance of what happened?

Snyder: The history of the Holocaust shows that history is hard work. Even the events that seem to screamingly demand our attention can be forgotten or altered in such a way that they seem less significant. In the case of Babyn Yar and the Holocaust in the East there are several kinds of forgetfulness. There is forgetfulness of Nazi perpetrators who, in order to hide their tracks, forced the Soviet prisoners of war in 1943 to cover the site. There is the forgetfulness of the Soviets themselves who, wanting to define German aggression as fascism against communism, ignored the specific hostility of the Nazis against Jews. There is forgetfulness of some nationalists in Ukraine and elsewhere who in a time said, "Jews deserve this, therefore there is no reason for us to remember it because no harm had been really done." And finally, there is forgetfulness of the West.

According to the model of the Holocaust we generated during the Cold War in the West, the Holocaust was mainly about West European Jews or German Jews. Something that mainly happened after deportation in trains to some distant gas chamber, which meant metaphors of the Holocaust like confusion: people were sent to places they did not know, and in the end it was a kind of mechanised form of death. Whereas, in fact, half of the Holocaust happened in a very different way in places the Jews lived as well as died: Poland, the Baltics, the Soviet Union. Face to face. This never reached Western consciousness for a couple of reasons. The first is that in order to have Holocaust memory you need the survivors. You need survivors in places like France and Italy where they can write and where Western Europeans can read them. The second is that even German memory of the Holocaust impressive as it is contains a minimization.

Germans associate the Holocaust with Auschwitz, but in doing that, they protect themselves from the basic reality that long before the Auschwitz tens of thousands of Germans were killing millions of people as hundreds of thousands of other Germans looked on. In other words, German society knew all about the Holocaust even before there was Auschwitz. When Germans accept Auschwitz, which of course they should, they have been displacing the other part of the Holocaust. Our German colleague was right. It was really only after 1991 that this half of the Holocaust began to impose itself on the German memory. Of course it forces Germans to ask other questions. The main question during the Cold War was, "How could had this happened without our knowing?" which is a false question. The real question is, "How could people like us do things like this?"

Nahaylo: How should we remember Babyn Yar today? The way that the Ukrainian–Jewish Encounter and the state of Ukraine today are trying to commemorate it 75 years on? Is this a good start? Is enough being done at this stage to remember it in a dignified way, in a way that has lessons for all of us?

Snyder: I should say as an outsider, and as a historian, that I am always impressed if the politicians giving all the demands on their time and all the pressing concerns especially in places like Ukraine can find the time and place, a moment of dignity to recall an event like this. It seems to me it is a good thing that the state of Ukraine is taking this week and devoting so much attention to these events. How should this be done? Now I offer what I think, but very modestly and as a proposition. Because the business of memory is a business of national societies and they have to work things out.

As I see it, there are three levels. There is the Holocaust as a general problem, a problem how humans behave. This is a universal. It is relevant for you and me as well as for Ukrainians in Kyiv. Then there is a problem of the Holocaust in the Soviet Union, which we have been discussing today. The history of the Holocaust in Belarus, Ukraine, Russia is very much the same. Trying to explain why local people took part in shootings, for example, is just as relevant for Russians, Belarusians, Lithuanians, Latvians, Estonians, as it is for Ukrainians. Because that is how the Holocaust happened here.

That said, and this is the third level, we cannot expect that Russians, Ukrainians, and Lithuanians will carry out remembrance together. Remembrance should be done nationally. It seems to me that the history you share might be universal or might be broader than your own nation but how you choose to remember is characteristic of your nation. Or better yet, how you choose to remember is how you choose to build your nation. It's very much my sense that if Ukrainians wish to build a political nation with a future they have to be able to look reflectively upon the past. Not to take responsibility for everything because that would be too much, but to find a way to take responsibility for something. If there is zero responsibility, there is also zero nation.

Nahaylo: At this stage of historic development, at least in Europe, we do not try to build nation states anymore.

Snyder: That is an excellent point. A political nation means an ability to converse within the political society where not everyone has the same cultural origins, maybe not even the same language. Political nation means the ability to converse. And it could arise only through the ability to converse about the past. If we have no ability to get over our own position with the past events, then we have no ability get beyond our political narcissism in the present. For me the process of creating a political nation is always a historical process as well. It always involves the ability to be reflective on the people you identify with in the past and to see other points of view in the past. If you cannot do that, if you cannot create a conversation about the past, it is going to be very hard to do it in the present.

Nahaylo: It is obviously a very interesting set of questions that you raised. On one hand Ukrainians need to have an inclusive view of their past and the past of their neighbours who shared the territory, who suffered or may have suffered on this territory. On the other hand, in a parallel process, as your books indicate, there is a need for western audiences to understand more globally the interdependence or interconnectedness of these tragedies and atrocities in terms of what they mean for the human psyche and the human development. Where do you see Ukraine in the scheme of things? You are a historian of not just the 1930s and 1940s and these tragic times. But you are also someone who is looking at the positive developments and movements. You are interested in Poland, for example. You show your interest in Europe more broadly. Where would you place Ukraine in the scheme of things now, before and after the Maidan?

Snyder: This goes back to your previous comment what Westerners need to understand. I think the fate of Ukraine was central in the entire history of the 20th century and is also central in the history of 21st, at least in the West. Ukraine was at the centre of the rivalry between two different kinds of empires. The National-socialist attempt to conquer Ukraine for their own purposes. But also the Soviet Union's attempt to exploit Ukrainian territory to build what Stalin understood as socialism. Ukraine was right in the middle. That is why so many people died in Ukraine.

That is why Ukraine was the most dangerous place in the world between 1933 and 1945. Happily, the nature of political composition today is different from what it was in 1930s-1940s. But nevertheless Ukraine is still in the centre. After the end of the empires we have a new Europe. It is an age of integration where European nation-states rather than seeking to dominate people around the world have built a construction. That construction is called the European Union. It is awkward. It is imperfect. It is sometimes funny. But it is the largest zone of peace and prosperity in the world. It has a bigger economy than China. It has a bigger economy than the United States. It has a better-developed set of social welfare regimes than anywhere else. It is on the list of the least corrupt countries (most of them are members of the EU) and so and so forth. In other words, it is a success. It's a non-imperial success.

Ukraine is once again at the edge. If the European model is going to continue, it is because it continues to be attractive. If the Ukrainian state is going to succeed, it is going to succeed because it joins the European Union at some point. In the meantime, the crucial question is, "Can the West help Ukrainians to build a rule of law state that functions?" If so, that state will eventually move closer to Europe. Likewise, as we look even further down the line, Ukraine is basically the only hope for Russia. I mean if one thinks the current Russian model of development is not ideal, there has to be a success in the post-soviet sphere, which shows people from here can also follow the Rule of Law. It is terrifically unfair for Ukrainians that they are in the centre of things. But they are. It is just the way it is.

Nahaylo: As Poland was for many decades and centuries…

Snyder: And some people in Poland now seem to be longing now to return to that state. Yes, exactly…

"Ukraine, Canada & a Satellite Phone: How History Happened in 1991"

with Nestor Gayowsky
2 December 2016

https://hromadske.radio/en/podcasts/ukraine-calling/ukraine-canada-a-satellite-phone-how-history-happened-in-1991

Marta Dyczok: On December 1st, 1991 Ukrainians were given an opportunity to vote for their future for the first time in modern history. There was a referendum on independence and over 90% of the population voted "yes." A day later, Canada recognised these referendum results, in fact, confirming Ukraine's independence internationally. The Hon. Nestor Gayowsky was the Canadian diplomat in Kyiv who navigated this process. He kindly agreed to speak with *Hromadske Radio* and give us a peek behind the scenes of what was going on, what led to this decision. Mr. Gayowsky, thank you very much for joining us.

Nestor Gayowsky: Thank you. It's a pleasure to be here.

Dyczok: Can you pull back the curtain and tell us what led to the decision that Canada made to recognise Ukraine's independence back in 1991? We remember that the US opposed the Soviet Union falling apart. They wanted the USSR to stay together. They were not interested in Ukraine's independence. They did not recognise it until Gorbachev resigned. Yet Canada took this step right after the referendum results. They were the ones who came in and said "yes, we recognise this." What was happening behind the scenes? You were at the negotiations and were a key player in this.

Gayowsky: We have to go back in time a little bit remembering how we opened our office, our consulate in Kyiv. Prime-Minister Brian Mulroney was working hard on the East-West relationship, particularly with German Chancellor Schroeder. In fact, Schroeder mentions Mulroney by name in one of his books, saying how Mulroney made a tremendous contribution to East-West relations, particularly with respect to the Soviet Union, Europe and the west situation. Mulroney was eminently political. He understood the aspirations of Canadians of Ukrainian origin wishing to see some sort of activity on behalf of the Republic of Ukraine. He responded to that over time. When he was visiting Moscow in 1989, he announced there that Canada was going to open a consulate (in Ukraine) and that was against the current, as you said, because the Americans were trying very hard to support Gorbachev for various reasons. One, they were able to obtain many concessions favourable to themselves with respect to the Soviet Union, such as the armament race and human rights. Secondly, I think a very warm relationship had developed between the American politicians and Gorbachev. One politician trying to help another. So, they weren't very focused on Ukraine and there was Mr. Mulroney…

Dyczok: The Canadian Prime-Minister…

Gayowsky: The Americans once upon a time had intended to go into Ukraine back in the 1980s, but Afghanistan intervened, so they withdrew an option to open a consulate in Ukraine. And here was Canada butting into the business. There was some resistance within the Canadian political establishment to the idea of the consulate. It worked out in 1991. After I got there…

Dyczok: Can you remind us when you arrived?

Gayowsky: I arrived in January 1991 to open an office. In that period from January to roughly March the Canadian budget was being developed. At one point very serious attention was given to the question whether we should open the consulate in Kyiv.

Dyczok: May I ask, what were the reasons for and against it?

Gayowsky: I think within the Department of External Affairs at that time we were pretty much accepting the American line that we should support Gorbachev. He is doing a terrific job in the country.

At least they thought he was doing a terrific job. Whereas various Soviet republics, as well as the population, were thinking otherwise. I think it was a big misreading of the situation. The External Affairs people sympathized with the American point of view. It was a budgetary crisis. The Department of External Affairs was hammered by some budget cuts. We were looking through ways of cutting expenses, and Kyiv came up on the chopping block. That was a situation then, but people in External Affairs also forgot that 1991 was also the 100th anniversary of Ukrainian settlement in Canada, and to open an office and then try to close an office was politically unacceptable. After a short tussle, I learned that indeed we were going to maintain the office.

Dyczok: Good thing that they did not close it, because important things happened. You were there during the coup and during Ukraine's declaration of independence.

Gayowsky: Canada was very lucky with the timing, because other countries were not there, particularly from Europe. The French were already trying to establish themselves in Kyiv. The Germans had already been there for a couple of years. There were not many Western countries represented there [in Ukraine] and only when the business of the coup and the independence of Ukraine began to come forward, other countries suddenly started to send their diplomats to establish representation in Kyiv.

Dyczok: So, you were one of the few Western diplomats to be posted in Ukraine at that historical moment. In between the declaration of independence in August 1991 and the referendum in December 1991 you must had been a key source of information for Ottawa, and other countries, since you were on the ground and you were watching things. Could you give our listeners a sense what were the discussions were during those months leading up to the referendum?

Gayowsky: It's a little bit of an exaggeration to say how much influence or role I or any Western diplomat played at that time.

Because you have to remember that it is the Embassies that provide political judgements that are sent back to the home countries. Certainly, consulates and the officers there can provide information to the Embassies. This was particularly the situation for Americans. The American Consul-General arrived there in February 1991, about a month after I did.

Dyczok: Was that John Stepanchuk?

Gayowsky: No, it was John Gunderson. The situation there was interesting because I learned over time that if he was reporting on the Ukrainian situation, he had to go up to Moscow and write his reports in Moscow. In Moscow they were very much against the view that Ukraine was really pushing that hard, and that independence was looming on the horizon. There was a difference between opinion of the American Consulate in Ukraine and the American Embassy in Moscow, which was presenting Bush's line, "We have to keep Gorbachev in power." That idea also led to the famous August 1991 "Chicken Kyiv" speech by President Bush during which he said, "You've got to be careful about breaking up a big monolith like this. Think carefully about this." The Americans were very hurt by what happened in Yugoslavia. They did not want to see the break-up of the Soviet Union leading to the same consequences. So there was some tension between the reports that probably John [Gunderson, US Consul-General in Kyiv] was sending and information that I was sending.

Sending information from Kyiv to Canada for me was extremely difficult. We had the time difference of 8-9 hours depending on the time of year. My day would be ending and Ottawa would just be coming online. I had no means of communication other than the telephone line, which, as you will remember very well, telephones didn't work very well in Ukraine. If I had to make a long-distance call, I had to reserve a time and ask that a call be made at such and such a time, and the call had to proceed through Moscow. There were often large delays and the times that I had set were often ignored, so that sometimes I would be staying up in my apartment office, waiting for a phone call as long as 10 and 11 o'clock at night. Written communication was difficult because most consulates and embassies of Canada at the time had some direct communication with Ottawa through a particularly secure system. I had no such arrangement from Kyiv. I had to rely on the telephone system. Faxing was almost impossible. The reason was that there were very few fax machines at Ukraine at the time. The hotel had one. But to access it, we had to get permission. Permission had to be granted by a security staff member. I don't know if that staff member was in the hotel or if they had to go to the local secret service office to get permission. Fax machines, you will remember, were printing presses and therefore controlled.

Dyczok: Fax machines were communication devices controlled by the state. Thank you for all that rich detail. You've touched on two questions that I wanted to follow up. I remember that on the 2nd of December, right after the referendum results had come in, and the 90% yes vote was in, there was a celebration organized by the RUKH, the democratic opposition at the time. I remember you rushing in late, and the band was asked to stop playing. You were given the microphone and made the announcement that Canada had recognised Ukraine's referendum results for its independence. Now how did you manage to do that so quickly, given the communication challenges that you faced and that you liaised with Moscow and Ottawa? Could you describe that day between the referendum results and announcing them?

Gayowsky: Certainly. I think it was September, soon after the August [1991] coup, Barbara McDougal, our Minister of External Affairs, visited Ukraine, to set the record straight as to what Canada was hoping and expecting from the new Ukrainian leadership. While she was there, she brought with her a satellite phone setup. That satellite phone setup was sort of brought in illegally, because we never sought permission from either the Soviet or Ukrainian establishment to operate a private telephone line out of Kyiv.

Anyway, Barbara McDougal left that telephone system with me and it was put into the third room of my hotel apartment, which was also serving as my administrative office area. We had this telephone ready to go on the 1st of December.

December 1st came, we had an observer group from Canada. You may remember that parliamentarians and some people from the Prime Minister's office came to take a look at the vote and to see how the election was conducted. They reported back to Ottawa at the same time using the satellite phone explaining that everything had gone very nicely and properly in the best kind of voting standards available.

By that time, we had a pretty good idea that if the vote was large enough, Canada would be prepared to recognise Ukraine as an independent nation. So I received a phone call on that illegal satellite phone in the evening and it worked like this. The message came over the phone to me. I repeated the words to Anne Collins who was down from the Moscow Embassy. She took the words down, and once I had received the entire message, she went down to our other office and typed out the statement on velum paper, so that we could then present it to the new president of Ukraine. I was ordered to take that document to the new President of Ukraine.

So I picked up the phone and called the Ukrainian Foreign Minister, Anatoliy Zlenko, with whom I had very good relations. I had his private office number and I got him and I said, "Look, I received this document, which I think you'll be very interested in, and I've got to present it to President Kravchuk." He understood what was involved, so we got together a party. Patrick Boyer, who was a Member of Parliament at that time, helping the Minister of Foreign Affairs Joe Clark, was part of the party as well as a representative from the Office of the Prime Minister.

We drove out to President Kravchuk's dacha, passing through several checkpoints, and we delivered the message there and then. And that is how we worked on this phone. Another story about the phone that I think is amusing. Barbara McDougal had left the phone in September, sometime in late November Foreign Minister Zlenko called me up and said, "I've got to get an urgent message to Czechoslovakia. Can I use your phone?"

I had never told anyone that the phone was there, but I'm sure that hotel staff had reported it, so I said, "Sure, come on ahead." So, he came in, made his phone call, thanked me very much, and that was it. Things were very loosey-goosey at the time as you remember, and it was a charming time indeed. And that's how that event transpired. And that stopping the band, I think it was at the Lybid hotel at the time…

Dyczok: Yes, you actually anticipated my next question. I was wondering about the sequence of events, because you came in and made the announcement to the then opposition RUKH. I was wondering who was the first to hear the news, and you've already answered that. How much contact did you have with Kravchuk, who was Speaker of Parliament and who then became president on December 1st How much contact did you have with both sides? Because there was the majority and the opposition and you as the diplomat watching and reporting, presumably, you had to have discussions….

Gayowsky: If I did any reporting, it came later, I think, after the independence. Up to that period it was very difficult. I was a one-man show. I hired some staff. I had actually been looking forward to a very easy summer. By August the office was working very comfortably, and I was thinking, "This is a breeze. I've got nothing to do." I can hardly communicate. I knew what was going on. I was talking to the opposition. We rarely talked to the communist side there. For some reason, they didn't want to contact us, the foreign, Western diplomats, and we didn't go after them very much.

Dyczok: But you did have contact with Leonid Kravchuk, who was a Speaker in Parliament?

Gayowsky: Yes, I did. I had a fair amount of contact with him and his staff. Particularly his staff because after all he was extremely busy. He had just been promoted very quickly from Propaganda Chief of the Communist Party. He became the Chairman of the Ukrainian Parliament, which was a very powerful position in Soviet times. And then, when the head of the Communist Party went to work for Mr. Gorbachev, effectively Kravchuk became the leader, the undeclared leader of the Communist Party, and of the country. Then, in a short period after the coup and the election in December the 1st, he became President. So, this happened very quickly, in about a year, to a man who had been hidden in obscurity for a long time.

I'll tell you another story, which will be in the memoir. This was at the time Kravchuk was going to Canada [in September 1991]. Well, while I was there, I developed very, very good relations with particularly people in the Ministry of Foreign Affairs. [Borys] Tarasiuk, for example, became a very good friend and a few others, and Zlenko as well. I was always kidding them about the flag on their car because they had the Soviet Ukrainian flag on their official cars. I said, "Listen, if you go to Canada and you have that flag, you're going to cause a riot." And I talked to them about that and to Mr. Kravchuk and I kept reminding his two assistants, who really handled the details of his trip. So, they came up with that Act of the... not an Act... postanova...

Dyczok: Decree.

Gayowsky: A kind of Declaration. Yes, kind of Decree, saying that for the purposes of travel abroad etc. etc., they would use the traditional blue and yellow flag. So I persuaded them, I said, "Listen, if you're going to Canada, you better do that, because it's very, very important." So a few days later, after having discussed this again, my friends from President Kravchuk's staff came to me with three pieces of paper, and it was the document that had been approved in Parliament to have the blue and yellow flag as representative of Ukraine. The ink was still even wet on one of the documents Mr. Kravchuk had signed. So, they said to me, "Is this satisfactory?" And I said, "Absolutely!" And that's one of the things. I feel that I really reminded them that they had to go to Canada with a blue and yellow flag.

Dyczok: In 1991 you were the right man in the right place at the right time to navigate this very complicated process and Canada's recognition of Ukraine's statehood. You are now enjoying retirement on Canada's West coast, and you've had time to look back. What is it that strikes you now, looking back at those events, as being something that was surprising, significant, that you only realised in retrospect?

Gayowsky: I think the degree to which, what I would call, Sovietism and communism, the 75 years of sort of Soviet power, how deeply it had penetrated Ukrainian society. It's a way of thinking, a way of… it's a very kind of corrupt approach to civic life. It's a very deadly cunning one in many ways. I regard some of the politicians who emerged out of the Soviet system as being top-notch politicians, in the sense of being able to achieve their objectives. No-one has been able to control a former Soviet bureaucracy. It hasn't happened in Russia and it certainly hasn't happened in Ukraine.

And one looks back at this and wonders why it was so difficult for Ukraine in 25 years to make changes, such as changes occurred in the next-door neighbour Poland. When in 1991 they were roughly economically equal and now Poland has pulled far ahead of Ukraine in terms of economics and GDP and average salaries and so on. That's really what has struck me is, what has prevented Ukraine from becoming a modern, democratic state.

The aspirations are there. There's much hope with the young, but the problems of extricating themselves from communism, from Sovietism, that kind of thinking, is very, very difficult. You see it everyday in the newspaper reports. People are being arrested for this or that corruption. But I read very rarely of anyone going to jail. What is it that is preventing the legal system from responding? It appears the judicial system has been totally corrupted. And it wasn't just Mr. Yanukovych, the deposed President, that corrupted it. It had already been well established by the Soviet system. So, I think, looking back, that is the thing that troubles me most. Why is it proving so difficult to move that society to the democratic tradition, when there are some wonderful people there, the young people are coming up, pushing forward, but my goodness, how slow the progress is.

Dyczok: Well, you have a perspective of 25 years, you've seen various presidents leading Ukraine, let's look forward. What do you see happening in Ukraine in the next 25 years? What would you like to see happening, and what do you think needs to happen?

Gayowsky: Well I think you do need a reform of the legal system, you need a reform of the judiciary, the business with the Procuracy, and now the Corruption Bureau. All these mechanisms either have to be improved or changed. There has to be a will and it has to be decisive because you just cannot afford to stand still. I think that Russia is sliding backwards and I think that Ukraine has the opportunity to move forward. In fact if Ukraine wants to regain Crimea, or even have some appeal for people living in Eastern Ukraine, in the Donbas, I think it has to show how much more beneficial a democratic way of life is to what is now being offered to those areas and to Russia.

Dyczok: You mentioned Crimea that's been annexed by Russia. Eastern Ukraine that has entities calling themselves the Donetsk People's Republic, Luhansk People's Republic. They've had events that they've called referenda there, but they have not received international recognition. And that underlines the importance of international recognition of events that are referenda, that have to be democratic, properly observed, in order to be recognised.

"Read This Book with a Martini. Shaken, Not Stirred"

with Serhii Plohkii
9 December 2016

https://hromadske.radio/en/podcasts/ukraine-calling/read-this-book-with-a-martini-shaken-not-stirred

Marta Dyczok: 2016 is drawing to a close. This week we are going to take a look what has been published in English about Ukraine over the past year or so. Joining this conversation is Harvard Professor Serhii Plohkii the Mykhailo S. Hrushevs'kyi Professor of Ukrainian History and Director of the Harvard Ukrainian Research Institute. He is an award-winning author of ten books including *The Gates of Europe: A History of Ukraine* and *The Last Empire: The Final Days of the Soviet Union*. His latest book, *The Man with a Poison Gun: A Cold War Spy Story*, has been just published this week and has been already named 'Book of the Week' by the *London Times*. Professor Plohkii, thank you very much for joining us for this conversation and congratulation on a publication of your latest book. Let's start with that. The title of the book *The Man with a Poison Gun*. Sounds like a spy thriller, but it's actually based on real life events. Could you tell our listeners what the book is about, and why you chose to write about events from back then in 2016.

Serhii Plohkii: First of all, thanks for having me. The book is a spy thriller. But it's an unusual spy thriller in a sense that it's a non-fiction book that is based on significant research, including research in archives in the Unites States and also in Ukraine, in the KGB archives. I'm the author of the book, but when it comes to its title, I have a predecessor or co-author and this is Ian Fleming. The title is modelled on the "Man with the Golden Gun," Fleming's last James Bond novel. That novel starts with a very interesting episode, where James Bond tries to assassinate his boss using a spring pistol loaded with cyanide, which later became the Stashynsky gun. He fails, he is arrested, and poisons himself in the process. But it's also interesting that before that happens, Bond and his boss discuss two killings in Munich of people with strange names. This is certainly a reference to the Stashynsky gun and the killings Stepan Bandera and Lev Rebet, which were committed by Stashynsky in 1957 and 1959. So, with Bandera back in the news, and Stashynsky being there as well, I wanted to take another look at what happened in Munich in 1957 and 1959. With the partial opening of CIA archives we now have access to the CIA investigation into the causes of Stepan Bandera's death. And the opening of archives in Ukraine, including KGB archives, allowed me to gain access to the personal file of the KGB officer who was Stashynsky's handler at the time of the assassinations.

Dyczok: You mentioned Stashynsky. For our listeners who might not be familiar with the name, could you please tell us who was Stashynsky? This is the man with a poison gun, right?

Plohkii: It is the man with the poison gun. He is the main character of the book. He was a native of Ukraine who was recruited by the predecessor of KGB in summer 1950. When the recruitment was taking place, he was faced with the choice to either start working for KGB or he and his family would be arrested. Because he had a close connection to the Ukrainian nationalist underground, which at that time, in 1950, five years after the end of the WWII, was still fighting behind the Iron Curtain in Western Ukraine against the Soviet regime. Once recruited, he was sent to Kyiv for training and then sent to Germany. His base of operations was East Berlin, but most of his activities were in Munich at that time. Post-war Munich was centre of the American Zone of Occupation, and that was also the place where the headquarters of a number of anti-Soviet organisations (Ukrainian, Baltic, and others) were located. So that was the primary target of KGB operations, which included assassination, kidnapping, and other so-called 'active measures,' including disinformation campaigns.

Dyczok: Would it be fair to say that we now know what happened because archives have been opened and history is becoming familiar to us? Is that why you chose to write about this now?

Plohkii: Well, not all the archives have opened yet, but certainly those that are opened allow us to better understand what was happening during the Cold War. In this book there is a personal story of a youngster who was recruited against his will to spy on his family, to spy on his people, and who eventually rebels and escapes. That's how we know the bulk of the story. Now, with opening of archives we know what the person was telling interrogators, and that is extremely important. Because when he first told his story of a lone gunman going to Munich with a strange spray pistol that no one knew existed, the CIA didn't believe him. After three weeks of investigation they dumped him on the West Germans because they didn't believe him. In the CIA files we have a report that was prepared as late as April of 1976, where they were still trying to figure out whether he was a defector and the person he was saying he was, or if he was a KGB plant. With the documents coming from CIA archives, from some German archives, Polish archives, and finally KGB archives in Ukraine, we can not only collaborate parts of the story, but we can also understand the broader context in which these assassinations were taking place. And what impact they had on the conduct of the two main parties in the Cold War, The Soviet Union and the United States.

Dyczok: History has been a major battleground in the current conflict in Ukraine now. People are writing based on archives, and not just that. What sort of trends do you see in books published in English about Ukraine over the past year or so?

Plohkii: Normally it takes a while to research and write a book. The exception would be people who write on current history, and political scientists. In that sense the most amazing authors are in Britain. We know Andrew Wilson's book on the so-called *Ukrainian Crisis,* and Richard Sakwa's book *Frontline Ukraine,* books with different takes on what is happening in Ukraine. They appeared almost immediately. When it comes to history, there is work in archives libraries and not just following the news, so it takes longer to write and publish them. There are some interesting books appearing now. One of them was published this year in Toronto, a book by Paul Robert Magocsi and Yohanan Petrovsky-Shtern, *Jews and Ukrainians: A Millennium of Co-Existence,* which doesn't necessarily deal with the current crisis, but is very interesting in the sense of the formation of the political nation in Ukraine. There are two parallel stories of Ukrainians and Jews and how they interconnect over millennium as the title of the book suggests.

Another book that made strong impression and interestingly enough was published in Toronto is George Liber's *Total Wars and the Making of Modern Ukraine, 1914-1954*. It looks at the Ukrainian history in the context of global history from WWI to the end of WWII, and the immediate years after the war. Putting Ukrainian history in the context of global history is something that we've been talking in the field for a while for long period of time. This is one of the first books. Not just a collection of articles that, but a book with this goal. I think both books indicate new interest in trends that emerge in writing on Ukraine here in the west in the last two-three years.

Dyczok: You've mentioned books that are written by scholars and experts on Ukraine. A trend that I have noticed is that since Euromaidan erupted there has been an increase in attention to Ukraine, and people who are not experts on Ukraine have been writing on Ukraine with more or less success. Would you like to comment on that?

Plohkii: Overall, this is a very welcome occurrence, that people who write on Ukraine are not necessarily Ukrainians or are not necessarily focused exclusively or primarily on Ukraine. This trend brings new perspectives. It creates new framework and formulates new questions. Of course, it's a very difficult task to write on the country that you really in many cases don't know much about, and that's why we have here really a very mixed blessing. It would be better for some people not to write or not to agree to give interviews. But there are some very important editions, and really very strong informed voices. One of them belongs to an author who didn't write on Ukraine before, and this is Marci Shore. Those who are interested in Ukraine noticed her recent publication in *The New Yorker* on Serhiy Zhadan. She also publishes in Britain, and in the US on Ukraine, Maidan and the Revolution of Dignity. She is now working on the book that deals with that subject. Overall, it is difficult to characterize the situation positively or negatively, because we have a lot of people who really don't know much about Ukraine. But the fact that there is an interest in Ukraine, that there are people who were not doing research on Ukraine before are now trying do it, and that is very positive.

Dyczok: The increased interest in Ukraine you have just mentioned. Do you see an increased contact between scholars in Ukraine and outside of Ukraine that is improving the quality of scholarship on Ukraine?

Plohkii: Absolutely, that is indeed what is happening. It doesn't matter who you are. If you are a journalist researching current crises, you go there. You meet locals, you have a fixer normally, you have a person who helps you to do that and that provides a perspective on the events that is inside perspective, something that people normally don't have. The same is true when you are a political scientist. You go and work with people in the field, either in the field of political science, or for example sociologists, gathering data. This is also true for historians who go to the archives and work together with colleagues in Ukraine. When it comes to history, like everywhere else, it increases the field for cooperation. My concern is that sometimes you have a situation which reminiscent of a colonial type of relationship, where the data, for example, is harvested in Ukraine, but then the final academic product is really produced somewhere else outside of Ukraine. I guess the trick here would be that with this increased traffic to Ukraine, and increased interested in Ukraine, the Ukrainian voices would be heard here as well and that those would be the voices that would talk and be on par with the commentators here in the west.

One obvious thing is that there is a lot of expertise, a lot of talking, a lot of publications on Ukraine but mostly what we hear more or less well-informed voices coming from the West. We rarely have Ukrainian academics and journalists publishing their materials here in the West and making their voices heard. I hope that will change in the future. Things don't change overnight, but I think this increased context eventually will lead to reformatting, reimagining the field of Ukrainian Studies and commentary on Ukraine here in the West.

Dyczok: You actually anticipated my next question. I was wondering have you seen any books published by Ukrainians in English that have made it to an international audience? The book that I remember from the Maidan period was Andrey Kurkov's The *Ukraine Diaries*, which became quite well known in the West. But I haven't come across really anything this past year by Ukrainian authors in English. So, the voices from Ukraine, I don't see them making it into the western audience. I don't know if you've seen anything.

Plohkii: Exactly. Kurkov, Andrukhovych, Zabuzhko. These are names that are recognizable in the West, but again not by the general public. It's very good that those people are there, that there is name recognition, that those voices exist. You have also people from Ukraine, like Volodymyr Kulyk, for example, publishing in Western scholarly journals. So that is happening. The question is whether there are people who would have name recognition and would be able to talk if, let's say, if CNN is interested in the commentary. Normally they are not interested. They have a bunch of journalists who can talk on almost anything. But there are not really people who can contribute to the debate, not just on the academic level, but can speak to a broader audience.

Dyczok: So, contacts between experts in Ukraine and Western audiences is still an area that needs to be developed. Book distribution is something I also wanted to ask you about. Is that something that you see could be improved, the distribution of work produced in Ukraine to international audiences?

Plohkii: Yes absolutely. As far as I know the Canadian Institute of Ukrainian Studies in Edmonton and Toronto is now involved in the project of translation of Stanislav Kulchytsky's work on the Famine of 1932-1933, making the work of one of the leading Ukrainian experts on this subject known to the academic world. But these are projects that unfortunately take years, a lot of effort, a lot of resources. So we can't expect an immediate return on those kind of investments. But on the other hand, there is no other way, so the trick is that either people from Ukraine have to write in English and German, or those works have to be translated. And that's how this situation can be changed. On the other hand, Ukraine is not exactly unique in this case. Look at any other East European country. Look at Romania, even at Poland. The situation there is not much better. This is a common challenge that intellectuals, writers, from the region face when they try to enter the debate that is happening in places like London, or New York, or Toronto, or Boston.

Dyczok: Books. How many people are reading books these days? As professors we assign books to our students and the foundation of our knowledge and our understanding about Ukraine really continues to rest in books. What are the formats that you can think of to transmit, to get people reading more books, whether they are students or the general audience?

Plohkii: The book publishing industry is of course out there. It is healthy. It of course changes the way how it tries to reach readers. Kindle is one of the examples, that people read relatively less in the traditional format and more and more from the screen of their laptop, their i-phone, and so on. So that is changing. But at the end of the day, you still have to have the text. You have to have a message. You have to have an argument. That didn't change. And the challenge is how to make whatever you say not just topical but interesting for other people to read. That's a challenge for the entire field of all of us working on Ukrainian topics, not only Ukrainian topics. How to make what you do interesting, not only for yourself. And how to make the argument that you are making important enough for other people to care about. That is an ongoing challenge. In my opinion, the British are doing much in this sense. It's almost a job description of British intellectuals to go out there and write for a broader audience as well. But it's a different situation in Canada or the United States and Ukraine, or Eastern Europe as a whole for that matter, where the tradition is rooted in the value of the academic knowledge per se and it is, "I wrote something interesting, I wrote something important, but it is not my task to go out there and to inform people about these things, or present them in a way that would generate interest if not excitement. It is the task of people out there to discover what a wonderful thing I have written." That has to change.

Dyczok: Well Professor Plohkii, your writing is an example of that. You not only have great ideas and extremely solid research, but you write so well that your books read like novels. And I really look forward to reading *The Man with the Poison Gun*, and I hope others will be able to enjoy it over the holidays as well.

Plohkii: Oh, that would be wonderful. There was a short review here in the *New York Post*, and it ends with the suggestion, "Read this book with a martini, shaken, not stirred." So that's the advice for the Christmas season.

"How Ukraine Was the Testing Lab for Russia's Information War against the United States"

with Yevhen Fedchenko
13 January 2017

https://hromadske.radio/en/podcasts/ukraine-calling/how-ukraine-was-the-testing-lab-for-russia-s-information-war-against-the-united-states

Marta Dyczok: Yevhen Fedchenko is Head of the Journalism School at one of Ukraine's best universities, the National University of the Kyiv Mohyla Academy. He has also set up and runs the project called StopFake, which is in response to the information war that Ukraine has been experiencing for a number of years. Mr. Fedchenko, thank you very much for joining us. Fake news, information wars, state sponsored cyber attacks, foreign interference in elections. None of this is new. But it is new for Americans. They are just learning how it is to be on a receiving end of that kind of activity. Over the last few weeks, the US has been just buzzing about Russian interference in their recent elections. Ukraine has been experiencing this for a number of years. Usually Americans go to Ukraine and offer advice on how to build democracy, economy, a free press. What can United States now learn from Ukraine, given that Ukraine has been on a receiving end of this type of activity, information war?

Yevhen Fedchenko: Ukraine has been living with this for the last two and a half years. There was a reactive stage, but also, we experienced a lot of propaganda through television, which was around for years since Ukraine's independence. And before that, we had the experience of Soviet propaganda. We really are pretty much immersed in this environment and we are learning how to cope with this. Trying to make sure that we differentiate journalism, and something which is definitely not journalism, or just a pretension or masquerading as being a journalism. And make sure that our audiences will also understand this difference.

We are working with the StopFake project to increase people's awareness of the dangers of propaganda. But we are also talking to audiences beyond Ukraine, to explain how fake news is ruining journalism, how they influence public policy, decision-making and elections in different countries. We now have a big dataset of all the fakes we debunked over the past two and a half years, we have more than 1000 of them. This is a systematic approach to create the atmosphere of untruth, lies. This is evidence of not just bad journalism or low-quality journalism. This is evidence of a very well created system, created by the Russian government and run top down, very well resourced, with money and people. It has a huge impact, and now we see how it works from one country to another. Ukraine was just a testing laboratory for all these. Now we see how all those tools out of this toolbox are used in many other countries, including the United States.

Dyczok: In this type of warfare, this type of information warfare, one of the aims is to create confusion, to create doubts, to get people to not really believe anything, because so many different narratives are put out there. Can you give us some of the examples how you actually tried cut through this cloud of confusion and mixed information, and sort out fakes from the truth? How you really know what the truth is? How it can help others to learn?

Fedchenko: This is great question because as we talk about era of post-truth, the atmosphere around is that the truth is almost non-existent anymore. But this is not true, because still we can find a lot of high-quality journalism. But we also see a lot of fakes. We do a lot of monitoring in order to find them. We have a list of Russian media outlets, or so-called "media outlets", which we monitor on a daily basis. Also, we have a set of markers, which allow us to differentiate real news from fake news.

Dyczok: Could you tell us what those markers are?

Fedchenko: It's pretty simple, and any journalist can give you those examples. The problem is that many journalists are not using them much anymore. So first of all, we are looking at the headlines of stories, because often the headline of the story, and the story itself, tell the different stories. Because people are mostly reading stories from social media and the title, 140 characters, is the only thing most of the people now consume and share with others. It is very important to see what is inside the story. Unfortunately, that is what most people are not doing.

At the second stage we are checking the sources, because as we speak about Russian propaganda, we can see that they often quote each other. They often quote many anonymous sources. They quote unnamed foreign media. Or just generalizing American or European media. When we start to look for where the story originated, we just find a lone-standing blog, which may have been created two days before the publication, or just some information from social media from pretty much an anonymous account. Very often they just cross–quote each other, and you cannot find where the story has originated. Also, we check the quotes they are using, because if they do a translation, they change the wording and the meaning of the quote. With a purpose of course.

We had many stories like this. For example, the story on the West lifting sanctions. They tried to find this information, and every piece of news they are trying to fake. When we start to fact check this information, we find those sources or speakers, which Russian media had quoted, say completely different things. For example, we had a great story coming from one of Russian media outlets saying that the US Ambassador in Moscow said that they are considering lifting sanctions. When I contacted the US Embassy they said, "No. He said just the opposite. We are looking into continuing sanctions." So, the meaning of what had been said was completely different.

So, we're looking for these very small scenes, but they're really important, because they completely change the whole meaning, not only the alone-standing news, but the whole narrative. Because they produce it on a mass scale and then they translate it into many, many different languages. For example, *Sputnik* [a Russian government owned news agency] now publishes in more than 40 languages, so by the end of the day they take one fake which was produced in Russian or English, and then it's translated into all those many languages. And then it's everywhere on Google searches. And many media outlets just republish it because they still consider *RT* and *Sputnik* to be traditional media, and don't realise its an arm of the government conducting information warfare.

So, we just want to set the record straight, and we collect all those stories and put them in an archive, which is available on our website to show the scale and the system behind it. Also, the data collected by us allows us to make an analysis of all those fake stories. We've identified 18 main frames of Russian propaganda, for example, on Ukraine, and all of them are very, very famous already. For example, the narrative of Ukraine as a fascist state, or Ukraine as a failed state, of the junta, who came to power as a part of the coup d'état here in Ukraine. And every week or sometimes every day they try to find some supportive facts for all those frames, to make sure that they're repeated all the time and keep them alive.

Dyczok: It sounds like it's a lot of work to fight this sort of an information war and expose all the fakes. A question I wanted to get your thoughts on is journalists in the United States, in established liberal democracies, they're now facing this sort of information war coming at them. What sorts of challenges does this new kind of warfare pose to established journalism? Where the norms require that all sides of the story are reported? You need to report even news that apparently is fake. So, how's that changing the whole face of journalism?

Fedchenko: I think that we are now witnessing huge changes in journalism, and all previously existing rules and norms seems to move very fast. And it escalates very quickly, which makes the work of journalists sometimes very difficult and sometimes even pointless. Because now, to distribute fakes, or manufacture fakes, you don't even need journalists. You can just go to social media and you could get an even bigger audience than any traditional media outlet. So, for journalists now the biggest challenge is how to re-create the system, how to introduce the new rules for our work. It's really very difficult, because we exist in an environment where there are no rules. If journalists stick to the rules, and all other audiences or other newsmakers just do whatever they wish, our rules and our norms wouldn't do any good, because then journalists would look very marginal and pointless, because we would be steps behind all the time. We would be just explaining what went wrong, instead of being more proactive, which is really, really a big challenge right now.

Journalists looking at all sides, seems to me, a very outdated approach. Because now you very often even cannot define who the sides are in any particular situation. Because you have so many actors, and each of them is playing kind of their own game, by their own rules, that it's impossible to define whose sides they are. Or very often we see the competition between facts on one side and opinion on the other. That's what *RussiaToday* and *Sputnik* are pretending to do. They're saying, "We're giving you the other side of the story," but they're not using any facts, they're just giving their own opinion. And it's very difficult to compete with them, because they use it in a very irrational way, emotional way, without providing any facts, and just being loud and that's finding a huge audience for them. Like for conspiracy theorists, those people actually do not need any facts. Because again, all those years of propaganda created the atmosphere where people are not interested in facts. Because they've been told many, many times that facts are irrelevant, the truth does not exist anyway. Everybody is lying, so what's the point in looking for reliable sources or what's the point of reading reliable media? You can just listen to the loudest voices around, and it's very misleading and very confusing, and I'm sure it would have a very long-lasting effect on audiences.

Dyczok: We see a lot of these trends now moving to the United States. You have been working on this issue for a number of years. What implications do you see of this type of behaviour in, arguably, the most powerful country in the world? What advice would you give to your fellow journalists in the United States?

Fedchenko: Well, I think journalists should basically bring their profession back and start to do what journalists were always expected to do. Just checking facts. And presenting those facts to audiences, even when audiences are reluctant at some points to hear that. To regain their profession back. But, on the other side, we really need to reinvent journalism. Because the old rules, as I mentioned, are dying. And it's not a problem of journalism only, because we do not exist in a vacuum. So, for example, the Ukrainian lessons with the war in Crimea and the war in Donbas were very painful because journalists were not quick enough to adjust to arising issues and arising challenges, and we've been losing this. For example, when the occupation of Crimea started, journalists spent quite a lot of time trying to find out who are those polite green men who are occupying Crimea and they were really sincerely looking for the other side of the story and waiting for sound bites. But it took a lot of time, and the momentum was lost, and that basically created a good atmosphere to move and start the war in Donbas.

That really was a situation when slow journalism or old-style journalism played a very wrong role. Because journalists were expected to get the second opinion of what's going on, the facts from the other side. And the other side was just creating *fait accompli* on the ground and did not care much about what journalists would be doing in this situation. And then they said OK, we will produce facts on the ground, and then we will explain everything to you, and you will see by yourselves. So, this definitely means that old-style journalism is kind of outlived, and we need to reinvent it. And probably to become more cynical, because policymakers and politicians are really using these weaknesses of journalism sometimes, and those are moments where journalism is losing, it seems to me.

"What Can Ukraine Expect from Trump: Temporary Insanity or a Permanent Shift?"

with Daniel Drezner
20 January 2017

https://hromadske.radio/en/podcasts/ukraine-calling/what-can-ukraine-expect-from-trump-temporary-insanity-or-a-permanent-shift

Marta Dyczok: Joining us is Daniel Drezner, Professor of International Relations at the Fletcher School of Law and Diplomacy at Tuffs University. Professor Drezner is not only an award-winning author and lecturer. He a media commentator and regular contributor to *Washington Post*. He has a unique perspective on Ukraine because he lived in Donetsk in early 1990s where he lectured at Donetsk State University. Last fall he spoke at the conference in Russia where Russian President Putin also spoke. Professor Drezner, thank you very much for joining us.

Daniel Drezner: Thank you very much. Happy to be here.

Dyczok: Every time the Americans elect their president it has consequences for the whole world. On my way to the studio, a song came on the radio, which, I think, was a nice preview to our conversation. It was REM's, *The End of The World as We Know It*. There has been a lot of talk about changing the international order, Trump's relations with Putin, cyberattacks, information war. In summer Trump was already talking about changing US policy towards Russia and Crimea. Let's start with this: what can Ukraine expect from the Trump presidency?

Drezner: To be blunt—not much that is good. At least to start off with this. It's been very clear that one of the consistent elements of Donald Trump's foreign policy world view has been to argue that some certain bargain or deal should be struck with Vladimir Putin. He has been extremely reluctant to say anything critical of Vladimir

Putin ever since he came into the race in the middle of 2015. Over the weekend in the interview he talked about an idea that he would be willing to lift US sanctions on Russia, which were originally imposed because of their interference in Ukraine, in return for nuclear arms reduction. The very fact that he is willing to talk about this, in this kind of way, suggests that he cares a great deal more about Russia that he does about Ukraine. That said, it is entirely possible Russia and Putin will rebuff him, and if that is a case, we still do not know how Trump would react to that. That is one of the "no-one-knows" for US the "no-one-knows" for US foreign policy going forward, which is that Trump has a lot of out-of-the-box ideas in terms of what he wants to do with American foreign policy. But we do not know what happens if they do not work terrible well. At least in the short-term Trump, I believe, re-wrote the Republican National Convention's platform with respect to Ukraine ruling out arms transfers. He's been much more dovish on Russia than any Republican or Democrat in the race. From Ukraine's perspective, nothing good will happen in the first few months.

Dyczok: There has been a lot focus on Trump, and what he's been saying he is going to do. The US is an established democracy, with well-entrenched rules and procedures, checks and balances. How much can Trump actually change the way how foreign policy is exercised? To what degree his chosen advisors will have the power to do what he says he is planning to do?

Drezner: There are some things that Trump can do with great deal of ease. Trump will find other things more difficult to do, because of Constitution and statutory laws. One of the hidden trends within America foreign policy, since 9/11 has been the slow shift in power from the legislative branch to executive branch. You can argue that if you take a look at Barak Obama's signature foreign policy achievements, such as the Iranian nuclear deal, the opening of Cuba, the pivot to East Asia, and indeed the Paris Climate Change Accords. All of them were executive branch arrangements. There was little to no buy-in from Congress on any of them. There are ways in which Donald Trump, if he wants to, has a capacity to reverse a fair amount of existing foreign policy, because a lot of existing foreign policy has been done without any real legislative buy-in. So, in that sense he can change a fair amount. Other issues like trade, for example, the presidency has been endowed with a considerable amount of authority. There are other things that he will run into in terms of Congressional reaction to it. In other words, if Trump exceeds his authority and starts pursuing policies that maybe Congress does not like so much, Congress would react by trying to pass legislation designed to reign Trump in. For example, in case of Russia it would not shock me, if, after Trump tries to launch some sort of new détente with Vladimir Putin, you'd see a push in Congress that is bi-partisan towards more Magnitsky–style sanctions.

Dyczok: So that's the political elite's level of things. Let's look at society. As I have already said, the US is an established democracy. Ukraine is often descried as a politically divided nation. It seems now that the US now has become a politically divided nation. What happens in Ukraine when people exhaust all democratic avenues of protest, they take to the streets. We have seen two major revolutions in the past ten years where Ukrainians protested and changed the course of events at the presidential level. Since Trump's election campaign, we have seen a rise in activism in the United States. Do you see any potential for American society taking an active role in possible mass protests against major changes in policies?

Drezner: You have already seen this take place. We are expecting to see this will take place. A day after Trump's inauguration, major protests are planned for most major cities in the US. Let me stress, these are peaceful protests obviously.

Dyczok: They were peaceful in Ukraine as well.

Drezner: That's true. The question will be to what extent these protests will continue. There are a couple things to think about. First, to be fair, there is actually some geographic concentration of opposition to Trump in the US much like cleavages in Ukraine, which are also geography based. California is implacably opposed to Donald Trump. A lot of New England and East Coast as well. One of the questions is whether because of geographical concentration you do see this kind of schism you are talking about. To tell the truth though, I would expect more, is to see activism through Congress. You are already going to see that. For example, as Republicans wanted to reinvent their ethics rules as a way to weaken the ethics watchdog when Congress was first brought into session in early January. There was an immediate outcry. It was truly by-partisan in a sense. Even Trump tweeted he disapproved of it. Apparently, a lot of Members of Congress started hearing phone calls and so on. There is nothing Congress responds to more than constituent complaints, the phone call, an email, and showing up at Congressional meetings or Congressional Town Halls. I think that will be the first sign you are going to see of enhanced levels of social protest against Trump. And it's worth remembering that, part of what happened in terms of Republican opposition to, let's say Obamacare, was in fact, that you had Tea Party members showing up at these Congressional Town Halls, and putting pressure on Republican Members of Congress to resist.

Dyczok: There are splits within the Republican Party over many issues and one of those issues is Ukraine. Someone like Senator McCain has been very supportive of President Poroshenko in Ukraine, very tough on Russia, and this is diametrically opposed to what Trump is saying. Do you see that the divisions within the Republican Party might play a role in how policy towards Ukraine is formulated?

Drezner: Yes, absolutely. You can even see that in the state of the Confirmation Hearings. Both Rex Tillerson, who's essentially supposed to be the Secretary of State, and James Mattis, who's supposed to be the Secretary of Defence, and Mike Pompeo, who's supposed to be the CIA Director, all three of them in their Confirmation Hearings were making statements about Russia, that were far, far more hawkish and dissented pretty strongly from what Donald Trump said. So, the real question going forward is:

where will the centre of gravity for American foreign policy towards Russia be? If it's the White House, then you are likely to see Congress, the Defence Department, and maybe the State Department trying to push back on it. If on the other hand, Trump winds up giving up on this, after an initial overture's rebuffed, then indeed you should expect US foreign policy to revert very quickly back to a more hawkish perspective.

Dyczok: Would you care to speculate where you think it's going to be?

Drezner: Oh, that falls under what I call the "yacht question", which is to say, that if I had the answer, I wouldn't be talking to you. I would be on my yacht. I will say this. There does seem to be a surprising amount of evidence that Trump in particular has been very consistent on this. He's been all over the map on a whole bunch of things, but I think at a minimum you are at least going to see an initial overture towards Russia as a way to substantiate all of the rhetoric during the campaign. That said, my expectation is that within six months you will see a worsening of relations between Russia and the Trump Administration to the point where it wouldn't surprise me if we're back where we were during the campaign. And I think, to some extent, Trump himself might have underestimated the degree to which all the reports of Russian interference in the 2016 election has truly altered public opinion in the United States. You know, Democrats, for partisan reasons, are obviously shifting towards a more negative perception of Russia. But truthfully, a lot of Republicans and Independents also have negative perceptions of Russia. And I think there's actually limits to the degree to which Trump can shift public opinion on this issue.

Dyczok: Professor Drezner, you have a lot of expertise in international affairs. If Ukraine's President Poroshenko was to invite you to be his strategist under the new regime of Donald Trump, what advice would you give him? What would you advise Poroshenko to do with Ukraine's policy?

Drezner: I would advise Poroshenko to do things that might not necessarily be in Ukraine's long-term interest. In the sense of, if I wanted to make sure that Donald Trump paid attention to me, I would probably try to offer some sort of joint investment project with a member of the Trump Organization, or some sort of concrete deliverable, whereby there is Ukrainian foreign investment in the United States that generated jobs. Because this is clearly the thing that Donald Trump reacts to. He reacts to concrete tangible deals. So, if there is something that Ukraine can put on offer that Trump would see as a concrete win, he might pay more attention to Ukraine.

Dyczok: And in the long run?

Drezner: Well in the long run, this is obviously problematic because it basically suggests the way to curry favour within the United States is to ignore things like the Rule of Law and essentially try to bribe, formally or informally, members of the Trump Administration. And of course this also raises the obvious question of what happens after Trump either leaves power or becomes disinterested in Eastern Europe. So, I'm not sure that would necessarily be the long-term best kind of advice, but if nothing else, making the offer might be interesting, because it might actually get his attention.

Dyczok: And on the question of Crimea and sanctions? Is there anything that Ukraine can be doing?

Drezner: The only thing I can think, is somehow to change the calculus so that Trump realises that lifting the sanctions would be problematic. But that entails much greater risks, such as cutting off access to Crimea from Ukraine in terms of energy, in terms of what have you, and/ or pursuing a brinksmanship strategy towards Ukraine. None of this is really in Ukraine's short-time interest, because it would risk a much wider conflict. But on the other hand, if there's one thing that Donald Trump responds to, it's anything that generates headlines on *CNN*. So, the more that you can get

Crimea mentioned on *CNN*, the more that Donald Trump will pay attention to it.

Dyczok: Well perhaps President Poroshenko will be listening to our show and take some of your advice. Professor Drezner, is there anything that you'd like to add that I didn't ask you about? Looking into the future, is this the end of the world as we know it?

Drezner: The word 'disruption' has been used way too much in this century, but unfortunately, I think it actually applies relatively aptly to what we're about to experience over the next year. The interesting question is going to be whether this is a temporary disruption or genuinely permanent shift from the sort of post-war US-created international order that we've all understood that has existed since 1945. I'm enough of an optimist to still think this is a temporary disruption, but I'm enough of an international relations scholar to fear that it actually will be permanent.

Dyczok: So, a cautious optimist! I share your cautious optimism. But I can't believe Trump's going to be able to get away with as much as he wants to. Call me an optimist but I believe the American political system is strong enough to resist this person.

Drezner: I would have said that too, I would have said that as well, but the fact that he got elected has sort of shaken my confidence in a lot of things. But yes, I'm hopeful that this will actually be a temporary moment of insanity and hopefully we'll return to normal soon.

Dyczok: Professor Drezner, thank you very much for joining us and look forward to having you on the show again.

Drezner: Diakuyu!

"I Participated in a Pro-ukrainian Protest against Russian Occupation"

with Hennadiy Afanasiev
3 March 2017

https://hromadske.radio/en/podcasts/ukraine-calling/i-participated-in-a-pro-ukrainian-protest-against-russian-occupation-afanasiev-tells-his-story-of-what-happened-to-him-after-that-in-2014

New host Oksana Smerechuk.

Warning: interview contains an account of being tortured, some readers may find parts of what follows disturbing.

Oksana Smerechuk: This week the attention has been on Crimea and Crimean issues as people remember the events three years ago in 2014 when Russian Special Forces seized control of the Crimean Parliament and other administrative buildings in Crimea. Today in this studio is someone whose life took an unexpected turn due to the annexation of Crimea. Hennadiy Afanasiev was a law school graduate working as a photographer when he was detained by police in what by then was Russian-ruled Crimea, and imprisoned. He managed to survive two years of being tortured in Russian prisons. Since his release in a prisoner exchange he has been involved as a community activist, and working as an advisor at the Ministry of Foreign Affairs [of Ukraine] to help other Ukrainian political prisoners. Welcome to the studio, Hennadiy!

Hennadiy Afanasiev: Thank you.

Smerechuk: How did it happen that you were detained by the police on 9th May 2014, a few months after the annexation of Crimea? Had you been working as an activist before?

Afanasiev: I was born in Simferopol in 1990, just before Ukraine gained its independence. I have a university degree in Law. I was also working as a professional photographer. During Russia's occupation of Crimea I was helping Ukrainian soldiers who were in Crimea. I took part in protest actions against the occupation of the peninsula. At first, I had not accepted the Maidan [the Euromaidan protests of 2013-2014] because of Russian propaganda in the peninsula. Later I understood what was happening and became a supporter of the Maidan. On May 9th, 2014 I took a part in Victory Day commemoration in Simferopol. I was walking in the group, holding a photograph of my great-grandfather. He is the pride of our family. He participated in WWII. Suddenly, men in civilian clothes with automatic guns kept stuck me in the back. Later it turned out they were FSB officers. [FSB is Russian Secret Service] They pushed me into a car, where they threw me onto the floor, and put a bag on my head. While driving, they were punching me in the stomach, and inquired about the names of participants of a pro-Ukrainian protest. They threatened me, saying that they would take me to the forest, and I would dig my own grave there. Finally, they dropped me at my house. They already knew where I lived. They took out the keys to my apartment and guided me inside with a bag on my head. Then they threw me on the floor. They did a search but did not find anything. Then they took me to FSB office and put me in a cold basement where I spent ten days. All this time they did not let me sleep, eat, or drink water.

Smerechuk: So that was when you were first detained?

Afanasiev: Yes.

Smerechuk: Then what happened?

Afanaisiev: On the first day they only beat me. I was chained to an iron chair. I did not have a lawyer. I was surrounded by investigators from Moscow and FSB officers. They tried to threaten me. When they understood that I did not have any interesting information, they demanded that I self-incriminate myself. I must have admitted that on May 9th I tried to explode the war memorial. The absurdity of these demands was that they detained me in front of people, as I was walking with other people in the procession, without any explosives or guns. During the first five days FSB officers tried to get me to talk. They beat me about the head, wearing gloves to avoid bruises. They put a plastic bag on my head, suffocating me, and beat me again and again. But I kept silent. But it turned out to be a good attitude. Then the real tortures began.

Smerechuk: This is still in Crimea.

Afanasiev: Yes. I have to tell you what I had to overcome again and again, because people have to know what happens to someone who is under unlawful imprisonment in Russia. I am not the only one. They put a gas mask on my head with a lot of holes. Then they unscrewed the mask and sprayed some gas inside. I started to throw up and choke with my own vomit. When I was losing consciousness they took the mask off and gave me some ammonia to smell, and then repeated the whole process. Because of the cruel tortures, I pleaded guilty. Then they became interested in Oleksandr Kolchenko and Oleg Sentsov, other political prisoners. I refused. Then they put electric wires to my genitals. That was the way how they prepared documents. In the end they demanded from a plea agreement. They took off my clothes, pressed me down, and started passing an iron nail over my body telling me what would happen with my body when the iron tools will be under me [touch me]. They said the same would be done to my mother, and that got the desired effect. [HA agreed to give testimony against two other activists detained and charged in Crimea.] During the trial of Oleksandr Kolchenko and Oleg Sentsov [the other Crimean activists] I refuted my previous testimony in front of many witnesses. And told everyone about the torture, and the ways they made me testify against innocent people.

Smerechuk: So what were you charged with? What were you doing wrong when you were arrested? What was the grounds of this arrest?

Afanasiev: I participated in a pro-Ukrainian protest against Russian occupation.

Smerechuk: How long did you spend in prison in total?

Afanasiev: In total I spent 767 days there. It is more than two years.

Smerechuk: Were you held in Crimea? Were you imprisoned in Crimea?

Afanasiev: Only for the first 10-20 days I was held in Crimea. Then they took me to Moscow, to the FSB prison, which is called Lefortovo. The worst thing was that all people who tortured me work at that place. And I saw them every day, during the one year and six months I spent there. When I rescinded my public testimony, they transferred me to the Republic of Komi [in Russia]. It is a modern GULAG, it is near Vorkuta. The transfer was really hard, the temperature reached minus 40-45 degrees.

Smerechuk: Was it a special prison train?

Afanasiev: Yes, it is a special prison train. The railroad cars were so hot that they should have been cooled down by firefighter vehicles. There was neither water, nor toilet inside those railroad cars. Then in the Republic of Komi I caught several illnesses. My body was covered with wounds. But when they finally gave me some pills, those pills caused inflammation of my digestive organs.

Smerechuk: So you are saying there were wounds on your body that did not heal?

Afanasiev: Yes, they did not heal, so I had to take a knife and cut myself, cut those wounds. That was horrible. And after that they took me to women's colony. It is closer to Vorkuta and I was there for 3 months in solitary confinement. I have not eaten at all, because they said that I am a Russian citizen and I am fighting for my nationality, for my Ukrainian citizenship, so I have not eaten. [HA went on a hunger strike] And my health became very bad. There was inflammation of digestive organs, wounds etc. Putin was scared that I was probably going to die over there and they released me just before the moment when sanctions had to be prolonged.

Smerechuk: So that was a strategic move. Were you allowed to receive letters, as a prisoner? Did you receive those letters?

Afanasiev: For the first year and six months I did not get any letters. I did not know that somebody knows about me and that I have support from people and my country. And everybody around me said that I was alone and nobody would help me.

Smerechuk: That is intimidation. So, when did you realise that people were advocating on your behalf, that Ukrainian government was working to get you released?

Afanasiev: First I got real advocacy when I rescinded of my previous witness statement and normal work started with me. And my defender [lawyer] started fighting for me. But it was really hard to the end to realise that somebody in Ukraine, politicians and people, supported me. It was really hard for a simple man. Until the end I did not realise how great was the support that I got.

Smerechuk: You were released on 14th June 2016 together with Yuriy Soloshenko in exchange to two Ukrainian citizens who have been charged with separatism. From that day you said you wanted to work to help free Ukrainian political prisoners. What have you been working on since you were released to Ukraine?

Afanasiev: For the first nine months after my release I worked as a volunteer in different NGOs. I tried to create my own human rights defenders' group, but I decided that it is not necessary nowadays, because we have enough human rights defenders' groups, which are stronger and more experienced. I became an advisor in the Ministry for Foreign Affairs of Ukraine. And I am working there on the platform where NGOs and deputies from parliament can consolidate and fight together for our goals.

Smerechuk: Can you say how many Ukrainian political prisoners there are in Russia and how many have been released?

Afanasiev: For now there are 48 political prisoners and this number grows up every month. There are a lot of people who were arrested for 10 or 15 days in Crimea. It is a horrible situation, it is a change in strategy of the Russian Federation, because they try to threaten people and they just arrest them for couple days, and people are very threatened after that. And that is why we should become stronger. Only three people were released—Nadia Savchenko, me and Yuri Soloshenko. The problem is that if Russia releases Ukrainian political prisoners, they have to admit that Russian soldiers are on Ukrainian territory. And all our documents will be proven.

Smerechuk: Just in the past week, five Crimean Tatars were detained by Crimean police for five days when they came to support a fellow Crimean Tatar, Marlen Mustafaiev, who had been arrested. And also this week, the pre-trial hearings have begun in the case of Mykola Semena, who's a Ukrainian journalist. Who's been writing for 15 years through the Soviet times but is not allowed to publish anymore. What are the conditions currently in Crimea? What's the situation with human rights and free speech for people who regard themselves as Ukrainian citizens or Crimean Tatars?

Afanasiev: Crimea SOS [an NGO] created a webpage with human rights violations. There are more than 300 violations of human rights in the peninsula, and all these cases are already proven [documented]. It means that in Crimea, any institutes of human rights, they're almost not working at real advocacy because everybody is working for the FSB. That's why all our citizens and other people they couldn't get any defence.

Smerechuk: Particularly for Crimean Tatars, it seems that if one is a Crimean Tatar, then your rights are curtailed.

Afanasiev: That's why I'm talking about sanctions, like Jackson-Vanik, which was in Russia/USSR in 1970s. It's the sanction by the United States against the Soviet Union, when Russia would not let Jews to go out from Soviet Union territory. It was discrimination against a whole nation. This is the same situation you have in peninsula with Crimean Tatar people, and maybe we should push on the Russian Federation with different kind of sanctions.

Smerechuk: Hennadiy, you have lived through a horrific experience through the past three years and returning home to Crimea is pretty impossible for you at the moment. What are your plans for the future?

Afanasiev: Well, it's impossible for me to go to Crimea because I am a on their terrorist list, but I am studying to become a software test engineer and I really like this job.

Smerechuk: So you're looking forward and moving on to more positive things?

Afanasiev: I should earn some money, and to do some things which are very good for my soul, not just all the time fighting and fighting. But I can do it together, (both). Make it my mission to help people, people who have problems, and are in trouble. And at this time I can do something for myself after almost two and a half years in prison.

"Celebrating Ukrainian Easter: Not Rabbits and Chocolate but Paska and Pysanky"

with Ihor Poshyvailo
14 April 2017

https://hromadske.radio/en/podcasts/ukraine-calling/celebrating-ukrainian-easter-not-rabbits-and-chocolate-but-paska-and-pysanky

Oksana Smerechuk: Hello, this is Ukraine Calling with Oksana Smerechuk. This is the final week before Easter. My thoughts are about how Ukrainians celebrate Easter. With me in studio I have a very interesting ethnologist Ihor Poshyvailo. He was a Fulbright scholar at the Smithsonian Institute, and also former Deputy Director of the Ivan Honchar Museum, a Ukrainian national centre of folk culture. At the moment he is Director General of the National Memorial Museum of Maidan. Welcome!

Ihor Poshyvailo: Thank you so much for inviting me.

Smerechuk: As I walk around the streets in Kyiv. I do not see really many chocolate Easter eggs, which is something you would expect, let's say, in Canada, US or Western Europe. How are Ukrainians preparing to celebrate Easter?

Poshyvailo: Easter is a special holiday for Ukrainians. It has some special features and you can easily distinguish it from traditions in the east like in Russia and from the west like Western Europe and US. Maybe the most typical feature is that it is a family holiday and the most explicit, vivid attributes of this celebration are Easter eggs, special, unique...

Smerechuk: But not chocolate ones...

Poshyvailo: And no rabbits at all. And of course, handmade Paska [a traditional Ukrainian Easter Bread]. Many families even in big cities bake Paska. It is not only an attribute. It is a special symbol. Usually, according to our tradition people have to bake Paska at home with the family. Even in a rural tradition we still have so many connections to the past. For many centuries baking Paska and bringing it to the church for blessing was a special event. I know from many fieldtrips and expeditions to villages when we tried to find out how the process was in our recent past, many people tried to bake a Paska as big as possible. Sometimes in these home stoves people had to take down some upper parts of the stove because with a Paska you can easily put it inside, but can hardly take it outside, because when baking process goes correctly can be twice big the original size. Usually people were in a hurry to bring this Paska to the church to be the first. It was like a competition.

Smerechuk: So, you would say that baking this Easter bread, or Paska, is the central symbol of the holiday?

Poshyvailo: Paska and Easter eggs. Today we have transformations, because painting Easter eggs—pysankas—is becoming much more of a decorative process. On the one hand people mostly accept them as an attribute of Easter. On the other hand, it is kind of decorative art. It is losing its symbolic tradition. Even in the past two types of eggs were used. One was empty and the other was full.

Smerechuk: You mean the ones that you blow out?

Poshyvailo: Yes.

Smerechuk: And raw eggs.

Poshyvailo: Yes. People mostly brought empty pysankas to cemeteries, to the dead, because…

Smerechuk: So they would bring a painted egg as a gift.

Poshyvailo: Yes. It was a part of the Easter celebration.

Smerechuk: Was it before or after Easter?

Poshyvailo: After. In some regions immediately after Easter. It is called the 'dead people remembrance week.One week after, mostly on Saturday or Sunday. In some villages and regions you have Monday a special day. Today this tradition is getting much wider. You can see decorated cemeteries with people bringing to cemeteries flowers, eggs, and Paskas. Usually people bring empty pysankas to the dead.

Smerechuk: Why is this attention is paid to cemeteries right after Easter? Is it tied to Resurrection?

Poshyvailo: Easter has quite deep traditions. In Ukraine it is still a combination of pagan pre-Christian traditions and Christian traditions. Usually we speak about three connotations of this holiday celebration. It can be celebration of fertility. As a symbol of fertility people would put a pysanka in the land when ploughing.

Smerechuk: I guess as symbol of planting life.

Poshyvayo: Trying to guarantee a great harvest. On the other hand, it is a pre-Christian symbol, with ornamentations of the universe, archetypal symbols like the tree of life, solar and lunar symbols. And the third connotation is of course Christian—Resurrection.

Smerechuk: For someone has never been to Ukraine before, what could they expect? How do the events develop? Does it start with Lent? Are there special rituals for lent? You are supposed to fast, right?

Poshyvailo: When a foreigner comes to the streets of Kyiv, s/he cannot see how people fast.

Smerechuk: But you can see it in restaurants. You have special vegetarian, non-meat menus, possible non- diary, for Lent.

Poshyvailo: In supermarkets you have a lot of products for fasting. You can see for fasting even so-called mayonnaise. That's quite funny.

Smerechuk: Do you think a lot of people fast?

Poshyvailo: A lot of people fast. And I know a lot of young people here in the urban environment in Kyiv. Young, modern people are fasting. Fasting is great is not only due to Christian tradition. A lot of people believe it is good for health.

Smerechuk: It's a cleansing...

Poshyvailo: Right. It is becoming fashionable, because young people want to be special in different ways. Fasting is also testing your mental, psychological strength. It makes you kind of a special person. Because on the one hand you celebrate old traditions, you care about your mental and physical state, on the other hand, it is great to have the final point. When you fast, you can feel the celebration much better.

Smerechuk: So during the Lent period there is no meat, no diary, no parties, no music. So this is like a blueprint of a classical traditional model of celebration of Easter. 40 days of Lent and then...

Poshyvailo: No parties usually, no dancing...

Smerechuk: You have these 40 days of lent and then you have the Easter service (which is Easter Saturday, through the night) and the Easter service ends with the celebration of the Resurrection on Easter Sunday. And that's when you break the fast, right?

Poshyvailo: Many people stay at churches during the night ceremonies, and the churches in Kyiv are overcrowded in this period. You can hardly enter inside, so even before midnight many people stay around the church. There are special baskets with not only pysankas, painted eggs and Paskas, but also with wine and sausage...

Smerechuk: I am surprised – wine?

Poshyvailo: Yes, it is a modern transformation. Because people still believe that the food which is blessed on this special day will bring some good health. And they try even to bless the main attributes of the celebration during breakfast and dinner for the next day. So they try to bring products for the feast table.

Smerechuk: This sounds to me like it is a modern tradition to have wine in the basket, because as I understand, the classic traditional food should be the Easter bread, boiled eggs and also butter, which is one of the foods that were forbidden during the fast, some meat...

Poshyvailo: Salt...

Smerechuk: Yes, salt, and horse radish. So, these are the classic foods, and cheese, of course. But this is, I guess, something new that you can have wine?

Poshyvailo: Wine and horilka [vodka] and different kinds of sausages, meat. Because for people who really kept the fast, it is a special day. It is not 40 days, it is, in fact, seven weeks. And so for people who kept the fast, it is a special day to celebrate on different levels. People are so joyful and especially in villages, where tradition is still alive. They exchange food – Paskas and pysankas – and they fight with pysankas...

Smerechuk: Oh, they try to compete, whose egg is the stronger.

Poshyvailo: The person whose egg is stronger will dominate in the family for the coming year. Whose final decision will be accepted in the family. On the other hand, fighting with eggs is also an old tradition. A hundred years ago, or so, it became mainly for children. But earlier than that, according to some beliefs, people believed that with painted eggs it was possible to manipulate demons, evil forces. By rotating these painted eggs it was possible to control the behavior of these evil forces. So, it was kind of a game and an attempt to persuade people that they could be over, stronger than evil forces.

Smerechuk: You are talking a lot about these beliefs that I think go back a long way, this is more than a hundred years probably. What's interesting, I find is that for about 70 years, or 40-50 years in one part of the country, officially there was no Easter. During the Soviet times it was banned. Do you have any memories of this time, of Easter celebrations?

Poshyvailo: Maybe this is one reason why this tradition is enjoying such a revival, importance, and scale. Because in Eastern Ukraine it was forbidden and even the Soviet authorities tried to fight against these old traditions. And I remember while studying in Soviet school, the so called *subotnyky,* special working days, which were organized on the Saturday before Easter. According to tradition it was a big sin to work on Easter and before Easter, because you have special days to make Paskas. And it was really a big harm to Ukrainian traditional culture, for consciousness, for world outlook. And before Easter so many churches were ruined. My grandmother told me a story that those, so- called Komsomol activists, who were in front rows to destroy churches, to take down crosses from domes, were punished later on by some problems in family, health of their children. So, it was a double standard situation, because people were forbidden in general—in schools, especially teachers, my grandmother was a teacher. It was very hard for her when a director of school…

Smerechuk: So, she could not go to the church and bless a basket with Easter foods?

Poshyvailo: Not even her, but she was obliged to control her class, school children. She had to check that people do not go to church. Officially churches in Soviet period were open, but everything what was going on inside was controlled—in Eastern Ukraine, in Central

Ukraine. In Western Ukraine this tradition was much stronger and the tradition was still kept alive there. And I remember that my grandparents were very connected to Ukrainian culture, to folk traditions. And one of my grandmothers was famous Ukrainian poetess from Opishne, a capital of Ukrainian ceramics. I remember when I visited her 35 years ago, I was 14 years old, I never remember a celebration of Easter in that period. So, it was forbidden. Maybe among themselves people tried to keep it sometimes, they painted eggs, but it was in a secret way.

Smerechuk: Something done privately. So what happened then in the 1990s? How did the Easter revival begin? And what do you remember that what was different about the celebrations in the 1990s and celebrations today?

Poshyvailo: When Ukraine renewed its independence in 1991, it was a big wave of national revival movement in different ways and in different fields, especially in religion. A lot of churches were reconstructed. A process started, some people thought it was crazy to build so many churches in villages. But really in the situation, say my native village which my parents are from, had ten thousand people living there at that moment. And there were eight churches, big churches, gold-domed cathedrals. It was quite normal that people, when they got freedom, they started to revive their traditions and religion. The Ukrainian Autocephalous Church was renewed after being repressed during the Stalin times. And of course this revival movement created glorifications, celebrations. People tried to use every moment, every holiday, especially religious holiday, to celebrate their identity, their national and cultural traditions. In Kyiv, as I mentioned, churches are overcrowded.

Smerechuk: Would you say it is becoming more commercial? Do you think business in general is taking the opportunity to make some money somehow of Easter? Are products for Easter more available?

Poshyvailo: Well yes, of course. Easter celebrations are becoming much more commercialized. On the one hand, it's not good. From the other side, it's OK.

Smerechuk: Well, it's because it's all available. You don't have to make it yourself at home, I guess.

Poshyvailo: If we speak about the possibility to buy Paskas everywhere: the market, supermarkets, everywhere, I think it's good. On the other hand, we have seen so many [Easter egg] stickers, which are not connected to Ukrainian tradition. We see rabbits, they ruin our tradition because we have a definite, special, unique, limitations or symbols with painting pysanka. You can paint it in the special liquid prepared from onion, they become golden and brown, and very simple.

Smerechuk: Yes, its the traditional way to use natural dyes.

Poshyvailo: Natural dyes, not refined decoration, but all the stickers which are plastic, which in fact, is not very ecological. I don't like this innovation, but having the possibility to buy Paskas everywhere, and most are very high quality, is great.

Smerechuk: If I was visiting Ukraine for the first time, and I wanted to experience Easter—the best parts of it—what would you recommend particularly in Kyiv, where to go, what to see?

Poshyvailo: I would recommend before Easter day, trying to participate in master classes, in painting Easter eggs or baking Paska. During Easter, I would suggest going to church before midnight. It's a special event. You can see a lot of people, a lot of candles around the churches, especially near St. Volodymyr Cathedral, Kyiv Pecherska Lavra. Overcrowded, a lot of people with their baskets nicely decorated, nicely dressed. It's a great performance for outsiders. On the other hand, I would recommend, as I mentioned, the master classes. For example, our museum organized baking Paskas and painting Easter eggs for the Heavenly

Hundred heroes [protesters killed by snipers in the final days of the Euromaidan protests] and for the soldiers fighting in Donbas.

Smerechuk: Of course, and then you can go to the Andriyivskyi Uzviz, and many other places to buy souvenir eggs, painted eggs, Ukrainian style. I think the nicest ones I've seen were at the Ivan Honchar Cultural Centre, you had a little Easter market.

Poshyvailo: Yes. I would also recommend visiting exhibitions which are devoted to this special event, mostly museums, art galleries, open thematic exhibitions and on the St. Sophia square where you can see modern pysanka installation—huge pysankas, lots of them.

Smerechuk: So, they are not actually real eggs?

Poshyvailo: No, they are huge, they may be one metre high. Lots of them are quite different, traditional, non-traditional, contemporary art. So, it's a big installation in a very special place in Kyiv, I would recommend this event.

Smerechuk: I guess that's an example for how the Ukrainians are adapting these traditions and developing into something bigger, something new.

Poshyvailo: Yes, and it's also amazing to see the making of a pysanka, and the pysanka itself is a model symbol of the universe. Most of the designs are pre-Christian, and the church supports these pre-Christian traditions. In Ukraine, it's amazing, you can see art installations in the Kyiv Pecherska Lavra [Monastery of the Caves] and many others, in St. Michael's Cathedral as well. You can witness this unique combination of pre-Christian traditions here in modern Ukraine.

"Laughter and Strength Featured at Kyiv's Book Arsenal"

with Olesia Ostrovska-Liuta
20 May 2017

https://hromadske.radio/en/podcasts/ukraine-calling/laughter-and-strength-featured-at-kyiv-s-book-arsenal

Oksana Smerechuk: If you are a person who likes to visit bookshops and travel to other cities or whose idea of a lovely Sunday afternoon is just browsing through bookshops, this event is for you. If you started to learn about Ukrainian literature but got only as far as Taras Shevchenko and are wondering what on Earth there is to read, this event is for you. To explain this event, we have Olesia Ostrovska-Liuta in our studio, the General Director of Mystetsky Arsenal or "Art Arsenal" cultural complex. The Art Arsenal is a home of Kyiv Book Arsenal. Welcome Olesia!

Olesia Ostrovska-Liuta: Thank you very much.

Smerechuk: First, I want to bring you to the experience I had yesterday when I visited the Kyiv Book Arsenal. I just want you to imagine how it looks. You have this fabulous centuries old arsenal building build in a shape of quadrangle with high vaulted ceilings, long galleries, long hallways that seem to go on forever. Then you enter inside and you see this huge hall with stands full of books. There are about 150 different book publishers presenting their new publications. Thousands of people are coming through the doors each day. There are also strategically placed coffee corners where you can have coffee, tea and something to go with that to refresh yourself and keep looking at books. Apart from that, dozens of presentations, discussions, workshops, and even art exhibitions are going on. For five days. This something that I saw yesterday but I think Olesia can fill us in on what else is going on. Could you tell me how many people you are expecting in general?

Ostrovska-Liuta: Yesterday we had 6,000 people, which is a lot, even for such a big building like Arsenal. As you saw yourself, it was full of people. There were lots of all sorts of sounds, movements, activities. It was very busy and lively.

Smerechuk: How many are expecting? How many came last year?

Ostrovska-Liuta: We do not have a very precise data at this moment. We will check this year how many people we actually have. Then we will take this year data for a benchmark. For example, in March we had a tremendously popular exhibition about the nature of TV-news. It was attended by 100, 000 people in one month.

Smerechuk: So, you are expecting on the same level…

Ostrovska-Liuta: Maybe less because it is only five days and then it was a month and a very busy one.

Smerechuk: I actually saw the first floor covered with bookstands, but I was told there are many other things are going on, and not just book selling.

Ostrovska-Liuta: The Book Arsenal is integrating the book scene, literature, other art, and cultural practices. That is why we also have a musical program on the first floor. You saw only the ground floor, which is huge enough already but there is also the upper level. For example, we have an exhibition of the old Soviet Ukrainian satirical magazine *Perets* (Pepper). It used to be a very funny magazine, people laughed for 50 years but when you look at it today, it's not funny anymore. The context that brought that laughter has changed. It was a huge propaganda machine. We also have an exhibition of the illustrations to Ivan Kotliarevsky's *Eneida* by Anatoliy Bazylevych.

Smerechuk: This take you to a Ukrainian literature lesson because Kotliarevsky's *Eneida* was the first book written and published in vernacular Ukrainian.

Ostrovska-Liuta: This is its anniversary year. That is why we chose it to talk about laughter.

Smerechuk: When you look at Kotliarevsky's *Eneida*, you suddenly realise Ukrainian printed language originates from a funny text and that is something to talk about.

Ostrovska-Liuta: These are our roots, and our first text. The Ukrainian language that we are using today is a satirical text, a parody. We also decided to focus our discussions on the subject of laughter and humour in times of crisis. We are living in a crisis-driven world. A world that is very different from what we saw five years ago. It is changing from Syria, to Poland, to Ukraine, everywhere. Things are very vulnerable. Borders are changing. It is a very strange crisis, tragic in many senses in Ukraine.

Smerechuk: You were saying "laughter … and strength." So how do you laugh in such a situation? Because Kotliarevsky also published his book at a time of crisis, when Ukraine was vanishing as an entity. Kozaks were declining…

Ostrovska-Liuta: Yes, it was in the 18th century. The Russian Empire was getting stronger. A lot was changing. And now this is a question: is it moral to laugh today? Can you go on, or carry on, without laughing at all? How do we laugh today? Is it irony? Because in the 1990s in post-Soviet countries, at least in Ukraine, the main laughter was irony. People were detached, very ironic. Is it still irony now? Is it a different type of laughter? This is what we want to talk about during the Book Arsenal. That's the main theme, but it's only one of the themes. We have about 150 events, discussions, lectures, workshops, theatre, and other types performances, music, poetry readings, all sorts of things. As my colleague Oksana Khmeliovska said, the Book Arsenal actually serves as a showcase for the Ukrainian intellectual landscape.

Smerechuk: I am getting a sense what is the main attraction for so many people. It's not just book shopping, you can do that in Kyiv anywhere. What other aspects you find attractive that bring the crowd in?

Ostrovska-Liuta: I think two things. One is that you do not often see so many publishers in one place. It's like super-mega-bookstore. It's huge. Also, most publishers prepare their publications to appear either for our book fair, or the publisher's book fair in Lviv in September. So this is a period when you have many new publications. For example, for this Book Arsenal we have about 1,000 new publications. So you will find new books here. You have authors who will talk about their books. You can meet friends to share your opinions and observations. You will have lectures and discussions related to those books. So you are getting not just a book, you get all the context around this book. It's a richer experience than just going to a book store...

Smerechuk: You mentioned the Lviv Publishers Forum. Is that the competition for your event, for the Kyiv Book Arsenal? Because they've been going now for twenty years. I think they started in 1993. Ukraine hasn't had a tradition of having book festivals or book fairs for Ukrainian books, compared to Leipzig where it goes back to the 17th century. So how does Kyiv Book Arsenal compare to Publishers Forum in Lviv?

Ostrovska-Liuta: That's always a question. No, we are not competing with Publishers' Forum; we consider them a very important partner. We are trying to collaborate and cooperate more than compete. I'm full of respect towards the Forum of Publishers president, Oleksandr Koval, who is the pioneer of this field, and who's been carrying on with Publishers' Forum for more than 20 years. Even at a time when we didn't have many books, it was much harder to do it than today for the Book Arsenal. And we're a bit different because the Book Arsenal, as I said at the beginning, also integrates other cultural practices. It originates from the story of Mystetskyi Arsenal itself, which is combining and integrating different cultural practices and arts. It's contemporary visual art, it's academic art as well, historical art. It's problem-based exhibitions as well, it's literature, as we are talking now, it's theatre and music occasionally, not as much as we'd like, but we're working on it. So, as Mystetskyi Arsena functions as a multi-dimensional centre. That's why also the Book Arsenal has this multi-faceted approach. The Forum of Publishers, is not just a formal event in one place, it's the city that becomes a reading city. The Forum of Publishers it somehow inhabits Lviv as a whole city-everyone everywhere reads. It's different with Kyiv Book Arsenal, we're more localized.

Smerechuk: In one location only?

Ostrovska-Liuta: Yes. The Forum of Publishers and the Kyiv Book Arsenal are going in slightly different directions.

Smerechuk: There are readings in cafes all over the city (in Lviv).

Ostrovska-Liuta: They go out to the city and reading is everywhere. Our strategy is a bit different. We're trying to get as many cultural practices in one place.

Smerechuk: I see. This is the 7th year that Book Arsenal is being held. Have you and your team noticed how it has changed, say, from the previous year? Has the idea been more refined, has there been growth in some areas, in terms of books?

Ostrovska-Liuta: This is what we are trained to do, we're trying to focus on the intellectual dimension. That's why we are introducing a focus for discussion on laughter. Also, the number of new publications has grown. Just a year or two ago, we were all complaining that there are not enough, for example, books for teenagers. And now we have a lot of books for teenagers. Then we were complaining that we have very little non-fiction, and look, today we have a lot of non-fiction by Ukrainian authors and translated from different languages. And they are not the old best sellers, but the current ones. We also have non-fiction for children, which we didn't have a while ago.

Again, I would like to stress the important thing is that we are starting to have Ukrainian authors, both writing non-fiction, this intellectual type, and writing also for children. And this is very important because that's how the writers scene is developing as well. There is one more thing we are trying to do very slowly: we are trying to connect the literary process and scene with teachers. There is a huge debate in Ukraine about schooling. We are all very unhappy about it. One of the opinions is that schoolteachers are often very detached from the literary process, and it's very hard for them to make children like reading. You have to understand the literary scene, you have to love it to pass this love to children. That's why we initiated a few workshops for teachers of Ukrainian and foreign literature, so that they can talk to professors—all those professors are also writers of fiction—to immerse, to understand better the literature process. This is just a small thing we started this year. But we are really motivated to develop it further.

Smerechuk: I certainly noticed that the presence of very eager children looking at books and the section with children's literature has certainly grown and seems to be thriving. Also, I noticed that you mentioned there's a lot of non-fiction in Ukraine being produced now. A lot of it is recent translations from English, for example, items from the *New York Times* bestseller list. Growth and translation, does this mean it makes it tougher for authors of Ukrainian fiction? Then they've got more competition, and if the publisher can do something that's a translation and much cheaper, then the Ukrainian authors then have to produce better.

Ostrovska-Liuta: Yes, then they have to shape their writing, they have to become better. But they are very interesting for Ukrainian authors. It is a benefit of living in an open society when you have open access to the international literary scene, either in the original or in translation, and you just become a better reader and a better writer.

Smerechuk: One thing I noticed that wasn't there. I didn't notice any state publishing houses, or publishing houses, which, I guess, started as state owned then developed further. It seemed to me that all these stands are new publishers that probably a lot of them had been founded in the past 10 years or perhaps 20.

Ostrovska-Liuta: Yes, perhaps 20. In Soviet times, all the publishing was state owned. Since then, the industry has developed tremendously, which is a very, very good sign. And if state publishing houses cannot compete… Well, it's not the focus of our attention to help some publishing houses through the state. We need to have good books. We need to have jobs. We need to have books developing. Those are important things. If the private sector is doing that, then it's great.

Smerechuk: What is the feedback from the book publishers on discussions etc.? What are the particular challenges Ukrainian book publishers face?

Ostrovska-Liuta: Well, one thing is the level of reading is not as high as one would like…

Smerechuk: But wait a minute, I think in Soviet times people, Ukrainians, felt very proud that they were such a reading-oriented people. There was great culture of reading. What happened? Is it the electronic age? Everyone is just writing things on the internet, social media, instead of reading?

Ostrovska-Liuta: I couldn't tell you. It might be that this idea of Soviet reading people was a myth. Also you didn't have many things to choose from. Right? So, people read something, maybe. I don't know any serious book or any publication on that, so, couldn't give you better arguments. But when you take the latest research that we have about reading levels, it is as not high as we would like it to be. If you look at the number of publications, or number of bookstores outside of Kyiv, and I am not talking about Kyiv and Lviv because these cities have readers and they have bookstores, but Ukraine is not just two cities. And there you will find not enough bookstores, and not enough readers. One of the reasons for that might be our system of education. How we teach our children to read. Our post-Soviet system of education, which was inherited from the Soviet Union, is a very common base and the process of learning to read for little children is not a very pleasant process in our schools. So, this is how we develop people who do not read later. This needs to be changed and this needs to be addressed. But what is very positive is that the last few years we started to talk about it loudly and openly. The Ministry of Education is very open for such debate. They have started changing things and programs, they have started working with teachers as well, to change that. So, I am quite optimistic, but there is a lot of work to do.

Smerechuk: Possibly, it would help, I think, if a general business environment was more open, because, after all, publishing is also a business just as much as selling shoes is. Everybody has to deal with all these other restrictions and try to figure out the bureaucracy and try to, I guess, figure out marketing. Someone mentioned to me that there was a need of prurient market analysis to figure out how to sell, but these things still need to be developed. I was also very positively impressed that attention is being brought to new areas such as tolerance towards other people, to handicapped people and, for example, an interest in Braille. I noticed they was a hall room devoted to Ukrainian books in Braille. Perhaps something that is a bit exotic for people who are not visually impaired and don't read Braille. But that's another area where this focus on the needs of handicapped children or specially in children's literature. Do you see that has been developing in The Arsenal?

Ostrovska-Liuta: Oh, yes. On the publishing scene in general year or two ago was a lamenting that we don't have Ukrainian books in Braille. And see what happens! That has changed. What is very positive at the moment, we start talking about sort of niche that is an empty, or about certain needs that we have in the publishing field. Some time passes, and something happens to this niche and new books arrive. New authors appear. And we have been observing that for a number of years, which is very good, positive tendency.

Smerechuk: Growth in general.

Ostrovska-Liuta: And more diversity also.

Smerechuk: Another discussion is that there is now a ban on, particularly, Russian books that are anti-Ukrainian in nature, and that there have been steadily fewer books imported, which means books from Russia in essence. And imports are down in general. So, has that has an impact on the growth and demand for Ukrainian books?

Ostrovska-Liuta: I hope so. What do Ukrainian publishers do now? They have started developing the intellectual sector of the book market with intellectual books. Those were the books that were imported from Russia for many, many years.

Smerechuk: Are those technical things?

Ostrovska-Liuta: Well, philosophy, for example, sociology, also business training books. And that is changing now, because Ukrainian publishers are paying special attention to this part of the publishing market. There is also a huge part of the book market, which is devoted to mass literature and that was imported from Russia. I am not a specialist, so I cannot tell you in detail what is happening there, but we have seen a number of Ukrainian mass market books, detective stories, written by local authors or translated from other languages, which is good again, I think.

Smerechuk: Well, that was certainly convincing. I went there yesterday and just saw the crowds and the faces of people and the enjoyment and simply the atmosphere was so positive. So, to sum up, I can say, I think it is fair to draw a conclusion that Ukrainian book is alive and thriving, despite electronic media, despite the iPads and right now there is a great book event happening in Kyiv. So, come and join in, if you can.

"Who Judges the Judges? Peter Solomon on Successes & Challenges of Legal Reform in Ukraine"

27 May 2017

https://hromadske.radio/en/podcasts/ukraine-calling/who-judges-the-judges-peter-solomon-on-successes-challenges-of-legal-reform-in-ukraine

Marta Dyczok: Peter Solomon is Professor Emeritus of Political Science, Law and Criminology, at the University of Toronto. He is one of the co-founders and long-time director of the Petro Jacyk Program for the Study of Contemporary Ukraine at the University of Toronto's Munk School of Global Affairs. He specializes in post-Soviet politics, and in the politics of law and courts. And is one of the world's leading experts on judicial reform in Russia and Ukraine. He has been involved in the Support for Judicial Reform in Ukraine Program sponsored by the Canadian government for a number of years. This week he was in Kyiv to speak at a major international conference on, "Independent Judges and Free Media: Synergy for the Future." Professor Solomon, thank you very much or finding the time to speak to us.

Peter Solomon: It's a pleasure, Marta.

Dyczok: Legal and judicial reforms are arguably the foundation for all other reforms, since if courts don't function properly then it's impossible for individuals to protect their rights. Ukraine has been reaching out to international experts for advice in this area for the past two decades, with, I would suggest, mixed results. Let's start with the conference you were attending this week. Could you please describe the conference to our listeners, what was its purpose? Who were the organizers? The participants? What were the main findings, outcomes from the event?

Solomon: The conference brings together the courts, judiciary on the one hand, and media on the other. It's part of an effort to give some serious national attention a nagging problem, which is how the courts are presented in the media. I do not think it's news to your listeners that public trust in and evaluation of courts in Ukraine is very low. It is actually got worse after Euromaidan. In part because branches of power encouraged criticism of judges. But in any case, we went from the situation when 15% to 20% of the public trusted the courts, which is kind of the norm in Southern and Eastern Europe, to single digits when 5% or 6% had some respect for courts, even though more than that would actually go to courts.

In our project we decided it was particularly timely to increase attention that we gave, or our Ukrainian partners gave, to court-media relations. We are working in two regions: Odesa and Ivano-Frankivsk, with judges, journalists, civil society organizations, advocates, on all measures that people can do to improve court-media relations.

In this case [the Forum in Kyiv] we are trying to give the issue national attention. This is much desired by leaders of judiciary and journalistic world. In fact, at the opening session, we had a line-up of very prominent figures who, I would say, came to 'bless' the conference. There were over 100 judges and media people. Many judges came not only from Kyiv, but from many other parts of the country. People who thought a lot about what could be done in this area.

Now what I was presenting, was a talk on comparative experience, on what is done in the USA and Western Europe. There are two really different traditions. One of them is in USA and Canada, whereby staff of courts take the role of helping journalists, explaining things, defining rules, working with them—in other words—the role of a press secretary. Whereas in the European tradition it is judges who do this. What's emerged in the last 20-30 years is the role of the press judge. One or two judges in a particular court who actually take on responsibility of talking to journalists. Interestingly enough, what has been happening in the last two-three years, both of these roles have emerged.

In fact, if you look at legislation or regulations a year and a half after Euromaidan, orders were sent out in the country that they should have both of these roles. The problem is that most of people fulfilling them, staff positions, have backgrounds in law and not in communication. They do not really know what they should be doing. So training is something we are working on.

I was particularly impressed at this conference by some of the presentations by press-judges and court secretaries from different parts of Ukraine. They were talking about their experiences and their challenges. It was very full program and a lot of speakers. I think the most valuable thing is that judges of different schools and journalists were talking about these issues to each other, and shared perspectives.

One of things that was done by the conference organizers was that they took quick instant polls at the beginning and at the end of the conference. At the beginning people were asked, "What is the state of relations between judges and journalists?" Over 60% said "bad" or "very bad." Then they were asked at the end of the conference, "On having had these meetings, what do you think the prospects are for the future?" Substantial share of those people who had been so negative at the beginning showed some hope and came up with much positive answers. We had a sense that conference had accomplished something for individual members, for people who attended. It is also clear that the subject got tremendous media attention. As an event involving media, naturally, there was lots of journalistic coverage and quick TV interviews. Even I did a couple interviews in Russian, with people from the different parts of the country. In short, that is what this event is about.

Dyczok: That is very interesting. You mentioned that judges are meant to fulfill the role of informing the public. Could you explain how it is supposed to work? I do not know if I even heard about this before. Are they supposed to hold press-conferences regularly?

Solomon: It's that sort of thing. In fact, I was talking about what is done in the Netherlands, in Spain, and so on. Not just any judge but the press-judge, particularly. Say, there is a high-profile case that people are very interested in. Periodically the press-judge (not the judge who is actually handling the case in the court room) would either do a press conference or meet with journalists, explain thing. And if you are lucky enough to have a courtroom where there is also a press-secretary, then the two can work together. In Spain, they discovered that a lot of judges do not know how to talk to journalists.

Dyczok: It's an absolutely different skill set…

Solomon: Exactly. And they need help. I suppose in this part of the world the idea of a judge being responsible to connecting to a society is not that strange as in the Anglo-American world. If you think about, it in Soviet times, judges were indeed expected in the 1920s and 1930s to go out to factories, talk about what they were doing. When you move particularly into the post-Stalin period, when judges were elected (to be sure in a non-competitive elections) one of their duties was to periodically go out and talk in public settings explaining what was going on. The judges even had an obligation to hold office hours and let the members of public come and ask them questions. In various international projects we have been trying to discourage that sort of thing, because it may give one side an advantage, or at least the appearance of that. I have a sense that it may become in the next three-four years, to have the judges doing these sort of things, rather than to have a staff person who can devote a lot of time to it.

Dyczok: That's a very interesting historical context that it might be easier to introduce these sorts of positions in post-Soviet context. Something you said earlier about level of trust towards courts and towards judges that has decreased since the Euromaidan protests, do you have any insight about what is causing this? Is this, perhaps, the matter that there is more freedom of speech, so people are expressing themselves more openly, or is it your sense that the courts and judges have started performing more poorly than before? What is causing this?

Solomon: I don't think they are performing more poorly. It is much more a matter of what appears in the media. I mean, it is more free, of course the media is extremely open. And I think that the overwhelming majority of coverage of what goes on in the courts is negative. But then, contributing to that, what judges have told me in many parts of the country, is the tendency of legislators and people in the executive branch to scapegoat judges. They say that is where the biggest problems of corruption are, or sometimes lawyers, who lose a case that people are following, will go to the press and say, 'Eh, the only reason we lost is because the other side paid more, or something like that. So, you get a lot of that stuff. But you know, hopefully your listeners know that there is a major new wave of judicial reform underway…

Dyczok: That's what I wanted to touch on next, because they've been introducing these reforms. So, in your opinion, how successful have they been if they are still getting all this negative media coverage?

Solomon: Well, this is early. Remember, reform is not something that happens overnight. A key piece of legislation, there was some kind of agreement as to what sorts of changes to personnel and structure they would really go with about a year ago. But let's put it this way, they are doing two things. They are trying to renew the judicial core, review credentials of current judges. Trying to find ways of weeding out people who either are incompetent, or there are signs that they must be corrupt, because of their living style, the cars they drive that they could not possibly afford in any other way. So, there is this big process of re-attestation that's been going on. In fact, that started even before a year ago. And some judges, frankly, don't want to put up with it, they don't want to do it. Either because they find it offensive, or, frankly, because they think they will be shown off. So, a lot of judges have left, retired early or moved out.

There are a lot of vacancies. And actually, this includes judges who had had five-year terms, but it came up for life appointment, but then Rada decided that they had to go through the whole new attestation and appointment process. So, there are actually people who are attached to courts and are being paid salaries but are not allowed to hear cases.

It is very early to know what will come of this. But there will be a lot of new judges eventually. And hopefully, there will be new social expectations that will translate into new norms. It is not clear if that will happen, because if the old structures are there, the old system of evaluation, new judges may behave the way old ones did.

But the other thing that is going on is a big-time institutional change. And we'll see what comes of that. They have changed the functions of the High Council of Judges, of High Qualifications Commission, changed the composition of these bodies, and I must say from what I see of them, they are performing their functions (selection, promotion, discipline) much better than they used to. And certainly, in a more transparent way.

But the other big institutional change relates to the top courts. They reached a point under Yanukovych, when the Supreme Court was cut down and made quite small. And there were three high courts, cassation courts, one for administrative cases, one for commercial and one for civil and criminal, which did most of the work. And if you took three courts plus the Supreme Court, you had nearly, I guess, four hundred judges at the peak of the system. A decision was made that those three high cassation courts are all going to be eliminated. And a new Supreme Court is being formed, which could have two hundred judges, but start with a hundred and twenty. An extraordinary thing of this winter and spring that everybody is watching, is a process of selecting judges for this new Supreme Court.

Dyczok: This what I wanted to get you to focus on: who judges the judges? How do you set up a system where you have a tradition of corruption in the courts and a political will to clean that up? Who is in a position to make these evaluations? What is the process?

Solmon: Well, you are absolutely right, it is a very complex process. First of all, the body that decides on which people will make it through the competition is a High Qualifications Commission. It has a new composition that includes some judges, but also lawyers, scholars, it is a mixture of people.

Dyczok: Who did the vetting of that commission?

Solomon: Well, the different people who are handling the selections.

Dyczok: So, is this a political body?

Solomon: No. The advocates were selected by the advocate organization, the judges by the, I guess, the council or the congress of judges, I do not remember which level. But what I wanted to say, to answer your question it is important to add that there is another body involved—the so-called Public Integrity Council, which is about fifteen people, who work voluntarily. Two thirds of them are from the so-called Reanimation Group, which is a sort of radical reform group, they emerged after Euromaidan.

Dyczok: Coming out of civil society…

Solomon: Coming out of civil society and what they get to review—the dossiers and materials on every candidate, who at least passes the introductory stage and issue an assessment. And they have three of four different grades. And if they issue a negative assessment, say this person should not be a judge because we see signs of corruption or some other ethical problems, it's an ethical review. Then this information goes back to the commission and the person is allowed to proceed the competition only if eleven out of fifteen members of the commission decide to overrule the Integrity Council. We don't know what the total picture will be. But I had a long conversation, actually this weekend, with one of the members of the Council, so I am sort of up to date on what they are up to. They are trying very hard. And one of the other things to say is this whole process is extraordinarily transparent. The reports of this Council are public. The sessions of the Qualifications Commission include not just a group as a whole, but interviews that they do with candidates for the positions on different stages. These are all available. You can watch them online on the website of the Qualifications Commission. It is really quite extraordinary. And the same thing, if you want to get some of it, there is a newspaper *Sudebnaya Yuridicheskaya Gazeta* which also carries a lot of this material.

Dyczok: This sounds like the process is very well organized, you've got political actors, professional actors, civil society actors, transparency. Something that occurred to me as I was listening to you speak, what happens if they can't find enough honest judges?

Solomon: Good question (laughs). I think they are OK. I mean, given the standards. This is a big competition, and what I should mention, it was open not only to people who are working as judges, including all of those people in high courts that are being abolished, but also, for the first time, to academics and practicing lawyers. And in fact, 30% of the applications were from those categories. Some of them are not going to do well, because they could not get the dossiers together or other things. But my guess is that the new Supreme Court in the end will be at least 10% from people who came from the side and represent completely new blood. One of the things that happens through a judicial career is that you become somewhat of a conformist. Remember that Ukraine has the same system as most West European countries, where you become a judge a few years after law school. It's not like Canada or the US where it's something normally for mid-career, where you've worked for 20 years in a legal capacity. So, if you work your way up the judicial bureaucracy, you tend not to be independent minded in the way you approach issues. Some of these other people, I think, may well introduce a new degree of energy and creativity.

Dyczok: I don't know if this is within your realm of expertise but, to attract talented new people with good qualifications, there's an economic dimension.

Solomon: Oh yes.

Dyczok: In your view, from what you know, is there enough economic incentive for these well trained, legally trained people with integrity to enter state service, as it were?

Solomon: Well, I hope so. They've raised the salaries quite drastically. I don't have the figures in front of me, but the position of judge on the Supreme Court will be extremely well paid. And even judges on lower courts are going to get a lot more than they did. And even so, they were doing better than comparable civil servants, better than procurators [prosecutors], for example. There's a recognition that paying judges properly is a necessary condition for a new quality of justice, although probably not a sufficient one.

Dyczok: So, from everything you've said, it sounds like the reforms are moving forward. And yet public opinion about judges continues to be low. How do you fix that problem?

Solomon: Well, you have to develop a communications strategy, for the country, for particular courts. That's the whole idea. You have to remember the tradition, if you go back 10 or 15 years, was for the courts to do almost nothing for journalists. Not only not have nice guidelines to say when you could use cameras, when you can do this, when you can do that. Not explaining what's going on with big cases. Even making it hard for journalists to get into the courtroom. A lot of judges didn't want journalists around. In fact, to this day some of them are quite suspicious of journalists. They say, "Oh, they're all on somebody's payroll. They're corrupt. You think we're corrupt. What about those journalists?" There are all kinds of traditional misperceptions, or exaggerated perceptions, that need to be overcome. And I think that when most courts start dealing with journalists and society around them in an effective way, I think public trust in the courts will change. It's not something you expect overnight. You don't measure this in months, you measure it in years, as a minimum. And if in that same period you have new judges, you have courts that work better, that help people better, and all that gets reported, that's the whole idea.

People in the courts have to give journalists something newsworthy, that's positive.

Dyczok: Maybe Ukraine needs a *Law and Order* type of TV show, to explain how things work?

Solomon: I think it has some, but that's a whole other subject. But those have to be done very carefully too. I remember from the Spanish story. When the press judges started working, one of their goals was to overcome, to correct misperceptions that a lot of the journalists had about what courts did, which were based on American television shows that were shown in Spain. It's like everything else, it's a question of how good they are.

Dyczok: Well, it sounds like there's room for hope in this area, that reforms are on track, and it's just a matter of keeping them that way. Is there anything you'd like to add that I didn't ask you?

Solomon: Well, there's the Constitutional Court, which is having all sorts of trials and tribulations. I think that the judges there are afraid, they've got some very big, controversial cases that they're ducking. It's kind of a weak spot that I worry about. The biggest problem, of course, is the context. This is a country that everybody knows, is at war, has a declining economy. It's not easy to change institutions in that context. And when you talk about corruption, corruption is not something that was ever unique just to judges and courts. It's a general government problem.

So, I stop and think. Suppose we have a regional court. What about their staff? Staff in courts in Ukraine are paid miserably. There's a huge gap. As judges salaries kept going up and up and up, much of the staff salaries did not. There's no question that in some courts, money is paid by litigants that basically goes to support staff. Often, it's both sides that pay money, and it's more of a service fee than an inducement. But again, if that kind of practice continues, the public will remain cynical. So, these are complicated matters.

Dyczok: They are indeed. But you've given our listeners a very insightful picture into what is happening and what still remains to happen. Thank you very much.

Solomon: Everybody should remember that the work of this Forum, Conference was above all part of a wonderful Canadian Support for Judicial Reform Project, as you said at the beginning.

"Putting an End to the 'Wild West Pharmo-Mafia' in Ukraine"

with Ulana Suprun
7 July 2017

https://hromadske.radio/en/podcasts/ukraine-calling/putting-an-end-to-the-wild-west-pharmo-mafia-in-ukraine

Marta Dyczok: Our guest today is Dr. Ulana Suprun, Ukraine's Acting Health Minister. She is spearheading a package of reforms that, I believe, will be voted on in Parliament this week. Something our listeners may know about are the health care reforms we've been reporting on our program. But something they may not know is, this Minister is actually US born. She's a medical doctor from the United States, born in Detroit, was practicing medicine there. She is also a Professor of Pathology. And now she's in Ukraine. So what brought you to Ukraine? What made you stay? And how did you become Acting Health Minister?

Ulana Suprun: Thank you for the invitation to come and speak to you and your audience. I practiced medicine in the United States for about 15 years before I moved to Ukraine. I was born in Detroit, as you said, from Ukrainian parents. They were forced to leave Ukraine after World War II, with their parents. They spent half of their lives in the United States and I was born in Detroit. However, as I was growing up I went to Ukrainian schools, Ukraine church, I belonged to Ukrainian youth associations. And I really felt very close to my Ukrainian background. Back in 2013, my husband and I decided to move to Ukraine on a permanent basis. We had been always planning on moving to Ukraine, but something would always get in the way. We would have school to finish, jobs, parents were ill.

And finally in 2013, we decided to put all our stuff in storage and to move to Ukraine. We happened to be in London when the Revolution of Dignity began here in Kyiv. And after about three or four days in London we chose to come to Ukraine earlier than we had anticipated, so we could take part in what was going on with the Revolution of Dignity. The two of us arrived in Ukraine on November 29th [2013] which was the day the students were beaten up on the Maidan. And after that we took part in the Revolution of Dignity.

Then, when the war started, we started helping the military with humanitarian aid and with teaching tactical medicine. That's battlefield First Aid. Teaching combat medics, providing them with first aid kits and medical equipment. And then eventually we started to teach physicians, doctors, how to perform surgery and how to help those who had been involved in battlefield and non-battlefield trauma.

After about a year and a half of being in Ukraine, the President awarded myself and my husband Ukrainian citizenship. And a year later, I was asked by the Prime Minister to become the first Deputy Minister, and then Acting Minister of Health of Ukraine.

So we've had a long road getting us to where we are. But one of the things that's very important about being here at this time, is that really Ukrainian independence didn't begin in 1991, when there was a referendum, when there was a Declaration of Independence of Ukraine. Ukraine really became most independent and chose its path in the direction of the West and of civilization and of Europe, after the Revolution of Dignity. And in the last three years, there have been quite a few changes that have occurred in Ukraine. We've chosen that we want to go into the civilized Western world, and I believe that part of this is also changing medicine, changing the health care system in Ukraine, which is a left-over of the Soviet system. Ukraine is one of the few countries that still has the Semashko system of medicine, which is a way of financing the actual infrastructure of medicine, the existence of hospitals, and the number of hospital beds. But it doesn't pay for the services provided in those hospitals or in the medical facilities. So one of the big changes that is happening in Ukrainian medicine now with the reform package, is that we're changing the way that we're financing medicine. We're going to a national health insurance, where we'll be paying for services rather than the existence of a hospital. We'll be paying for operations rather than walls.

Dyczok: That is quite revolutionary reform. You've been Acting Minister for less than a year but have already introduced a number of really radical changes to the way the health care system is delivered in this country. If I understand correctly, there are two key pieces of legislation that you and your team have prepared. Could you outline the key points for non-experts?

Suprun: There are two bills in front of the Parliament. One of them is creating financial guarantees for payment of medical services and for payment of pharmaceuticals or medicines.

Dyczok: So who's going to be paying?

Suprun: We're creating a national health insurance. It's similar to the NHS system that exists in the UK, where the tax hryvnias that are paid now into the budget will be administered differently. Right now, taxes are distributed equally across Ukraine to pay for the infrastructure. And the idea is that patients come to this infrastructure and they should be receiving services. However, at this time, there is not enough funding to pay for services. So we pay for the walls of the hospital, for the existence of the beds, and very low salaries for the medical personnel who are in those hospitals or medical facilities.

But the patients don't receive any services. They have to pay for everything themselves. They pay the doctors, they buy the medicines, they buy all the disposable materials. They pay for everything.

Dyczok: This is something that theoretically should be provided for by the state budget but, in reality, patients are asked to pay for these. Am I correct?

Suprun: Yes, it's a very inefficient system. Because again, you're paying for the existence of the hospital itself without looking at how many procedures they do, how many doctors you really need. Are they fulfilling the needs of the population or not? It's all based on the existence of a system rather than the services provided. Since the beginning of the century, and very discretely after World War II, many countries in Europe, as well as in other parts of the world, changed from paying for the existence of hospitals to paying for hospital services, to an insurance system, whether it's a national insurance system or private insurance system, where payment goes as a fee-for-services provided.

And in Ukraine we haven't had that system at all for the last twenty-five years. So what we've done is we've put forward a change in the way we're distributing the budgetary funds already in place. We're not asking for additional funds. We're saying the funds that we have can be effectively distributed by paying for services, and that we can provide better services, higher quality services and more of them for our patients, if we're not just supporting an infrastructure.

Dyczok: So it's a conceptual shift. Or redistribution.

Suprun: Right, that the financing follows the patient. So where the patient chooses to go, that's where the money goes. If I choose to go to my primary care doctor in my neighbourhood, that's where the payment will go for the services. If I choose to go to the primary care doctor across town, in a different region, because that's where I heard the doctors are better, I make that choice, and the money will follow me.

On a primary care level, that will be a capitation, or fee-per-patient, given to each of the doctors that are chosen by the patients. When it comes to the higher level of care, specialized care or hospitalization, it will be by DRGs or Diagnostic Related Groups, and these are more fee-for-service payments through a national health insurer.

Now we're rolling this out over two and a half years. We begin with primary health care on January 1st, 2018, and then January 1st, 2019, we start on specialized care and on hospitalization. So that by 2020, the entire system is financed differently. We already have promises from the Ministry of Finance, that every year they will help us to increase the amount of funding available, because of the kind of change that we're producing with the financing of the healthcare system, where we're able to prove where the money's going, and also because there actually are results. It's a results-oriented manner of distributing the financing. They're more willing to provide us more funds.

Right now, we have a very large amount of money, over 62 million hryvnia, that are spent just on the *medychna subventsiya* or the financing of the hospitals and the medical facilities. And we can't really say that that money is being used effectively, because we don't see positive effects. At this time Ukrainians live 10 to 11 years less than our European neighbours.

There are several things. We have a problem with the HIV epidemic, with antibiotic-resistant tuberculosis. We have a very high incidence of hepatitis C, we have a very high incidence, 67% of Ukrainians dying, from cardio-vascular disease every year. These are the kinds of diseases that are preventable, if we had a strong primary care service, if we could do preventative medicine, if we can have early detection of disease and do the intervention early, so that it does not get to the point where you have a heart attack or where you have a stroke...

Dyczok: Because you have already been monitored...

Suprun: Right, because we have discovered high blood pressure early and we are able to treat it by lifestyle changes and dietary changes and also by medicines, so that we never get to the point where strokes and heart attacks are occurring in 30 and 40-year-old men the way that it is now.

We have already started several programs which have been quite successful when it comes to the reforms. One of the things we have done is we started a program called "Accessible Medicines." It is a reimbursement program for medicine taken on an ambulatory basis for cardio-vascular disease, bronchitis, asthma and for type 2 diabetes. These account probably for about 70% of ambulatory care that is given to Ukrainians at this time. And what patients do is they go to their primary care doctor. They receive a prescription for the medicine. They go to the pharmacy and receive the lowest price generic at no cost. They have to pay a small co-payment if the medicine they choose is not the lowest price generic but it is one of the other brand names. They pay the difference in the prices and they get the medicines and they are able to take them.

Dyczok: Is this already in place?

Suprun: This is already in place. And in the first month, April 2017, there was a 62% increase in the use of these medicines over April of 2016, a year ago. And also because we spoke to the manufacturers and the distributors and we had them lower their prices to get into a range of reference pricing that we did with our neighbouring countries. We have actually lowered the prices on these medicines by 23%. Just this one program has been extremely successful and now we would like to do more of these programs, so that we can pay for the medical care for patients. 640, 000 families go bankrupt every year in Ukraine because of the payment for medical treatment for their own family members or their loved ones. They have to sell their cars, they have to sell their houses, they have to borrow money from people, because there really isn't any guarantee from the government. So what we are providing is a financial guarantee that will be able to pay for these services 100%. There are some services where there will be co-pay, but everyone will know what that co-pay is. It is a single tariff across the whole country for each of the services. The amount paid will be known, it will be all transparent, the information will be given to the patients. And there will be programs in place for those who cannot financially afford that co-pay.

Dyczok: Subsidies…

Suprun: There will be subsidies as there is for energy now in Ukraine. It has been very specifically even put into law, that the soldiers who have become permanently disabled because of injuries that they received in the Russian-Ukrainian war in Eastern Ukraine, that they will have 100% free medical care for the rest of their lives. And there will be additional programs that will be provided by local authorities as well as by businesses such as Ukrzaliznytsia [the National Railroad Company]. We are now in a discussion with them about their providing additional insurance for all of their employees to pay whatever co-pay there needs to be. So there is a lot of different areas that we can work with to help patients who cannot afford to pay the co-pay. But very many Ukrainians right now can afford to pay the co-pay.

And we need to stop lying to ourselves here in Ukraine—medicine and healthcare is not free. It is not. Everybody pays for almost everything. We need to provide financial guarantees by the government to use the money that is already paid into the tax system, not only through the regular taxation of income tax, but also through VAT and sales taxes. It is already there, in our budget. Let's use it more efficiently. Once we start using it more efficiently, we can talk about having additional private health insurance, perhaps other types of programs through the national insurance, and we will be able to provide more services to our patients.

There are also several programs that continue, that we are not cutting out. We do national procuring of medicines. We buy very expensive medicines on a national level. So for patients who have cancer, for patients who have hepatitis B and C, for patients who need treatment for tuberculosis, for orphan illnesses or very rare illnesses that children have. We actually buy these medicines on a national level. And this year, in 2017, 5.9 billion hryvnia are going to buy these medicines. That was also one of the very successful programs that happened with reforms and as an anti-corruption program. In 2015 Parliament voted for a law where we gave the national procurement to international organizations, rather than doing that within the Ministry.

Dyczok: So basically changing the way…

Suprun: Changing the way it is procured. Because through the ministry there were a lot of problems with tenders, there was a lot of corruption that was involved. So now the Ministry just forms the order, which medicines we need, and we give it to international organizations like UNICEF, UNDP and crown agents to actually do the purchasing. In 2015, we were able to buy 5% more medicines than we had bought in 2014 with the same amount of money, and this year the savings are even greater. We already have over 17 million dollars—dollars!—in savings for just the vaccine program. That allows us to buy additional vaccines and additional medicines for our patients.

Dyczok: This all sounds wonderful. You touched on the issue of corruption, when you were speaking about procurement. From what I have been reading there has been some opposition to these reforms that you are introducing, plan to introduce, have successfully introduced. Listening to you talk, this sounds amazing, that there are savings, that there are more people getting access to services they need more efficiently. Why is there opposition to what you are doing, where is it coming from?

Suprun: Especially when it comes to procurement of medicines and procurement of medical devices, there has been a very strong lobby against the changes that we put in force, because a lot of people are making money on corrupt practices in these particular fields. A lot of … what is called the pharmo-mafia. Here in Ukraine there are several pharmaceutical companies and conglomerates that have pretty much been monopolizing the system for many years. And they made billions and billions of hryvnia off of the illnesses of Ukrainians.

Surprisingly, medicines and pharmaceuticals here in Ukraine are more expensive than for our neighbours like Poland, Estonia, Latvia and Slovakia and so on. Even though our economy is much worse off and our hryvnia is much lower in value compared to their currencies or their Euro. However, medicines are less expensive there, because there is some regulation of prices. In Ukraine until now the pharmaceutical industry has basically been the Wild West. They could put any prices they want and they would be agreed upon.

Now we are creating competition. Just in the first year of change in the purchasing and procurement of medicines through international organizations, 40% more Ukrainian companies and manufacturers were able to get involved in the tender process. Because until then they have always been pushed aside and they were squeezed out by the big conglomerates. So now there is a much better chance for those honest Ukrainian pharmaceutical companies, distributers and importers to get in on what is happening and purchasing and producing Ukrainian needs for pharmaceuticals.

The other thing that is a big problem, is about 7% of Ukraine's GDP is spent on healthcare. Only about 2.6% of that is through government funding. The rest is grey economy. It is all paid under the table, not taxed, not controlled, pricing is absolutely not regulated and more than 50% of what is spent on healthcare is paid in cash under the table with no control and no regulation, and we have a very difficult time even knowing exactly how much it is. It could be up to 10%, we are not really sure, that is an estimate that the World Healthcare Organization gives us with the 7%. And with that what we want to do with the new reforms with the laws and the change in the legislature, we are trying to bring this out into the open.

Dyczok: One example, please, because we're about to run out of time.

Suprun: Sure, one example of this is that Ukrainian doctors have traditionally written out prescriptions for a lot of different medications, most of which don't even have any medicinal effect. They're vitamins or some kind of supplements. And about 70 per cent of the medicines that are written out by prescription in Ukraine really don't have any pharmaceutical effect. But because the pharmaceutical companies come and sell this to the doctors and tell them it works, the doctors are writing it out and sometimes even getting a cut from the sale of these pharmaceuticals. We have to re-educate our physicians so that they're only giving those medicines that are really necessary for patients. We need to re-educate patients so that they're not taking medicines that are what we would call over the counter, but being sold as prescription medicines that they need to take, rather than just something to treat their symptoms. And one of the ways we're doing that is by way of another reform. We've created a new formulary of what medicines can be bought by government agencies and that formulary of medicines has decreased from 1200 registered pharmaceuticals in Ukraine to only about 360.

Dyczok: That's quite the cut.

Suprun: That's quite the cut because the things we cut out are either unnecessary or unaffordable by Ukrainian government, and so that smaller list is now the only medicines that are allowed to be bought by the government agencies, whether it's local government or national government. It will also decrease quite a bit what physicians will be writing out in prescriptions, because patients won't be willing to pay for all these medicines, unless they really have some medicinal effect.

Dyczok: Thank you. This week the second law is going to be in front of Parliament. Last time the vote happened, one of the laws squeezed by one vote and the other one didn't. What do you see happening with this in the next round of voting?

Suprun: What happened, was that Law 6327, that's the Bill that is financial guarantees for medical services and pharmaceuticals, that law was passed through in the first reading. Barely passed. It got 227 votes [226 are required for a bill to pass in Ukrainian Parliament]. But now we got the pass, and now a working group is taking all of the changes that the deputies from the Parliament have submitted. And this week they're supposed to work on all of those changes, and see which ones will be suggested when the voting is in the second reading. We anticipate that the working group will be able to finish, although there are a number of changes. Over 800 were submitted by deputies, many of them are repeat changes (the same thing repeated over and over again). The working group should be working every day this week to narrow that down to a smaller number. Then we anticipate that the week of July 10, Bill

6327 will be put up for a vote in Parliament. And that no significant changes will be made to it that will change the actual philosophy of the law.

The other law didn't pass and that was changes to the budgetary code. Now those are necessary so that we can pay for the new type of financial guarantees. However, what we did was, we resubmitted the second law about the changes to the budget code.

We need to pass these healthcare reforms to show that we as a government, as a country, care for the health and wellbeing of our people in a way that will be providing guarantees, and providing security. 97% of Ukrainians are afraid of going to the doctor, of getting a diagnosis where they won't be able to pay for their care, and this is something we really need to address. The only way we can do that is by fundamentally changing the way that we provide care for our patients, and that first step is changing the financing.

Dyczok: Well, let's hope the Parliamentarians hear this interview. Dr. Suprun, you and your colleagues are going to England, what is the reason?

Suprun: The Prime Minister and the Cabinet Ministers were invited by Foreign Secretary Boris Johnson to come to Great Britain and to talk about the transformation that's happening in Ukraine. We're going to be presenting several different changes, but healthcare is being highlighted as one of the successful reforms that have happened in Ukraine. The reason that we've been able to be successful is because we've gone through the entire policy cycle of how you make reforms or make transformations in a country. We didn't start healthcare reforms 10 months ago when I came into the Ministry. Healthcare reforms started many years ago with a discussion on how Ukraine needs to transform its health care system, but in 2014 a special advisory group was formed at the Ministry of Health. They were inviting experts from all over the world, including the World Health Organization. There were members of USAID, members of the Renaissance Foundation, of the Canadian government, Ukrainian experts, and also international experts that got together. They wrote a road plan, a strategy of how Ukraine needs to change its healthcare system to improve it.

This was then presented at Parliamentary hearings and a collegium of the Ministry of Health. It was presented to the government and discussed over about a six month period. When we came into the Ministry, we took this document and we divided it into two concepts: one, the reform of financing and the other, the creation of a public health sector, which doesn't exist in Ukraine. We took the portion about financing first to the Prime Minister and presented it to him, talked it through three-four times, long meetings, lots of discussions. It was put into a document. We then made the audience wider and invited Parliamentarians, representatives from the regions. We had discussions with them, we presented the concept of the reform, we included their suggestions, and then we went wider. We actually have traveled to all 24 oblasts [regions] and we have presented these reforms together with the Organizations Centre UA, which does a policy dialogue. We come with them, we talk about healthcare, the changes that are happening, we present it to the stakeholders, which is the administrative staff of the departments of health, we present it to the medical community, we present it to civil society, and to patient organizations.

Once we discuss it with them, then the Centre UA, what they do is, they further that by sitting and talking with the organizations, with civil society, with government structures and tell them how they should implement this healthcare into their own systems. What we're doing is using healthcare as an example to build civil society in Ukraine and to create that new contract between government and society, to tell them that they're involved with what's happening. Because really healthcare touches each and every one of us every day, every year. We either have been a patient, or will be a patient, or we know someone who has been a patient, or someone in our family who has been a patient. So all of us have a stake in what's happening, and what we've done is instead of doing reform from the top, which is the way it's always been done in Ukraine, where laws are written in Kyiv and forced onto the local governments, what we've done is written a concept, we've gone to the regions and taken their suggestions. We've incorporated their suggestions and their points of view into what we're doing. And we're coming back with both, from the top where we have experts that are giving us advice, as well as the practical portion of it which will be implemented into the regions. So this policy, this entire procedure that we've gone through, has created a difference in the way society looks at how these reforms are happening.

Dyczok: You're a success story. Why is it not possible for other ministries to be successful? Your Ministry is showing that your reform is possible, so why is it not happening in other ministries?

Suprun: It is possible. I think that there is a traditional block in many government structures here in Ukraine that they don't include society. They're not open to having discussions and having a national dialogue about the issues at hand. All of it is done behind closed doors and much of it is done in a paternalistic way. What we've done from the very first day that we came into the Ministry is we opened the doors to civil society and we include them in what we're doing. And I think that that really brings that connection between what the people want, and what the people need, and what the experts tell us. And we put it all together into a reform that will not only be the right thing to do theoretically, but practically will work from the very top down to the level of the patient.

Dyczok: So that's a formula that maybe could be suggested to each and every ministry. Thank you very much.

"Assisting Ukraine's Uprooted – UNHCR and Partners in Action"

with Pablo Mateu
11 August 2017

https://hromadske.radio/en/podcasts/ukraine-calling/assisting-ukraine-s-uprooted-unhcr-and-partners-in-action

Bohdan Nahaylo: I have the great pleasure today in welcoming Pablo Mateu, who is the Representative of the United Nations High Commissioner for Refugees in Ukraine. I am particularly pleased because I am a former UNHCR employee. I spent 20 years with the organization and had the privilege of working alongside Pablo. He has served in many countries. It's fortunate for Ukraine in time of misfortune to have such an experienced and seasoned UNHCR manager, campaigner, and humanitarian. So welcome to the program, Pablo!

Pablo Mateu: Thank you so much for having me here, Bohdan.

Nahaylo: I am not going to assume that all of our listeners know all the legal aspects of defending refugees and IDPs (Internally Displaced People), or the scale of humanitarian challenges in this country. In these 20 minutes or so let's put things in perspective. Let's begin by asking how many internally displaced persons does UNHCR have on its books at this moment in Ukraine?

Mateu: The Ukrainian Ministry of Social Policy registers Internally Displaced People. According to their latest statistics there are 1.6 million Internally Displaced Persons (IDPs) registered.

Nahaylo: Which is a large figure. It's certainly up to the scale of the former Yugoslavia conflicts in the 1980s.

Mateu: Indeed. For a country of 43 million, I think it is quite a large percentage of the population. We have to keep in mind that some of displaced people have decided not to register.

Nahaylo: Are these displaced just in Ukraine? Russia claims a large number of displaced people there. Belarus also claims it has refugees.

Mateu: That figure, 1.6 million, reflects only the Ukrainians that have decided to remain within the territory of Ukraine. We have a significant number of Ukrainians who have gone abroad. They have not all asked for asylum. Many of them have also looked for alternative forms of residency. If we take, for example, Belarus, they have about 2,000 Ukrainians who are recognised as refugees. But they have about 250,000 Ukrainians who have a different form of residency, which has been granted by the Belarusian government. Poland has taken a similar approach. In other words, those who have been recognised as refugees are very few, but they (neighbouring countries) have decided to grant different type of migratory status to quite a few thousands of Ukrainians.

Nahaylo: Is this a kind of humanitarian status?

Mateu: No. Some of them have received student visas or temporary work permits. We have to keep in mind that Ukrainians traditionally migrated. I think the crisis has accelerated that process. Some neighboring countries have been generous enough to grant different forms of residency permits.

Nahaylo: We had a huge outflow at the beginning of the 20th century to Canada, USA, South America and a lot of economic migrants in more recent times to Italy, Portugal, etc. If we take the Russian and Belarusian figures, the numbers would suggest that there about 2 million displaced people from Eastern Ukraine now?

Mateu: It is difficult to say that all of these people are from Eastern Ukraine. There are people from different parts of Ukraine who have decided to go outside of the country and look for better economic opportunities, and some of them have decided to apply for refuges status. But they are not necessarily all from Eastern Ukraine.

Nahaylo: If you could also explain for our listeners clearly: they (the IDPs) have material and social needs, but they are also in need of legal protection.

Mateu: Correct. When we discuss with IDPs and when we look at some of the surveys conducted, for example by the World Bank or by the International Organization for Migration, there are two concerns that come to the top of the list of displaced people problems. One is housing, as many of them are struggling to find affordable housing. Second is employment. There are also legal issues on the list of problems. For example, being able to legalize small business when sometimes there is an internal document that says they are residents of a different province. Some of the children who are born in those areas which are not currently controlled by the government of Ukraine and registering them as Ukrainian citizens can be problematic. There is a process established by law, but that process has quite a few requirements that some families are not always able to meet.

Nahaylo: I am just reminding our listeners that I am talking to Pablo Mateu, Representative of the United Nations High Commissioner for Refugees in Ukraine. Tell me, Pablo, about what the government has actually done. How well has it coped in dealing with this unexpected and large challenge in recent years?

Mateu: A lot of people highlight the initial response of the civil society to the displacement crisis. We have to recognise that civil society in Ukraine were the first responders. But we also have to admit that the regional and municipal authorities also reacted quite quickly. We also have to recognise that the central government in Ukraine has taken very positive steps from the very beginning. Let me just give you three examples. First, they refused to establish IDP camps.

Nahaylo: What is the significance of that? It is not apparent…

Mateu: When you establish camps either for refugees or IDPs, you are basically isolating them. There are quite a lot of social problems that come with it. Sometimes you are going to create ghettos. Instead, the government refused the pressure from some organizations to establish camps and they decided that displaced people should integrate into communities. That was a very positive move. Second, they passed legislation on internal displacement, which is not perfect, but it incorporates some of the international standards and principles. That is also a very positive measure taken by the central government. Third, they created a dedicated Ministry in 2016 to look after not just Internally Displaced but also over the temporary occupied territories. This happened much faster than in Georgia, for example, where there is also a dedicated ministry. Does this mean that everything is perfect? Obviously not.

Nahaylo: Are there new pieces of legislation in the pipeline, that have been there for a long time?

Mateu: There are quite a lot of amendments to Internally Displaced legislation, and there is quite a lot of legislation in the pipeline that would affect those who are living in areas not controlled by the government. As the UN Refugee Agency, we are trying to advise the government and the Parliament on this legislation. We are trying to point out some potential negative impacts of some of the articles that are currently being discussed. Sometimes they follow our advice. Sometimes we have to advocate more.

Nahaylo: In real practical terms, how is the government is assisting the IDPs apart from allowing them to settle in other areas? Are these unfortunate people, victims of the conflict, receiving social assistance? How are they receiving assistance with finding employment? Is it difficult to find, as you said?

Mateu: I think they are. A lot of times we give recognition to the international organizations, or to NGOs that are supporting the displaced. But the government has actually also established certain measures and certain programs to support them. There is a decree that stipulates a monthly payment to the Internally Displaced. Let's say that in real terms that's not a lot, but if you add it up, it's 1.6 million people who are receiving that particular kind of stipend. That's like a cash grant and they can use it for any type of need that they have.

Nahaylo: In terms of the geography of the displacement, is the bulk of IDPs still in Eastern Ukraine or are they scattered fairly evenly over the country?

Mateu: I think most of them decided to stay close to their places of original places. It means they stay in Eastern Ukraine's five provinces. Many also came to the capital where obviously there are employment opportunities. Some of them also went to Western Ukraine. Provinces like Odesa and Kherson also have significant numbers of the displaced. But the bulk is still in Eastern Ukraine.

Nahaylo: Tell me a little bit about UNHCR's activities and work. First, let's clarify one thing. You represent the UN High Commission for Refugees, yet you are dealing with IDPs.

Mateu: Correct.

Nahaylo: Does this mean that in practice UNHCR now is recognised as a lead agency by default?

Mateu: As you rightly pointed out, UNHCR is the UN Refugee Agency. We deal with persons who come to Ukraine and look for refuge or asylum here. That's our main mandate. That is what we have been working on when we established our office more than 23 years ago here in Ukraine. We are still working on that issue and still supporting the government of Ukraine.

Nahaylo: Could you tell us how many refugees recognised by the government there are at this moment in Ukraine?

Mateu: There are about 3,000 recognised refugees in Ukraine at this moment. They come from more than 70 countries. The largest number is from Afghanistan, Syria, and also from former Soviet republics, including the Russian Federation. There are also more than 5,000 asylum seekers, who are still in the asylum process at different stages. They also come from very similar countries.

Nahaylo: Who deals with refugee status determination in the government system now? I remember it has changed over the years.

Mateu: The first instance is obviously the state migration service. They are the ones who conduct the process that will determine who is a refugee. But if the decision of the state migration service is negative, they go to different courts. So, there is an established system of checks and balances here. The state border guard services also play a role because in order to have access to the territory of Ukraine they have to go through state border guards either at the airport or land-border or land-crossing points.

Nahaylo: Returning to IDPs and UNHCR's role, I've noticed that UNHCR is leading several key clusters here, the groupings among agencies to promote synergies and cooperation. What role do you play in this regard within the UN system in partnership with NGOs here?

Mateu: I think this goes back to your earlier question. UNHCR does not have a mandate *per se* for the internally displaced; no agency or organization does. Let's keep in mind that the Internally Displaced people are citizens within their country, and they should enjoy the rights of any other Ukrainian citizen. Because of that, there's no specific agency mandated to look after the Internally Displaced.

So, the UN and other organizations, including non-governmental organizations, come together around what we call "clusters". There's an educational cluster, a health cluster, and UNHCR leads two clusters where we have experience and a certain comparative advantage.

The first one is the protection cluster. It entails legislative work, legal assistance and support for the Internally Displaced, psychosocial support, issues related to housing, land, and property, which is an issue here, and they have a significant number of entities gathered in that cluster both in Kyiv and the East.

The second cluster is dealing with shelter. Obviously, we are talking about houses and apartments that have been damaged because of the conflict. I was recently in Avdiivka and visited a family whose house was shelled for a third time. They have repaired it twice and now for a third time they need to look for support to rebuild their home. So that's the shelter cluster, which also deals with what we call "non-food items." Remember this is a country that is affected by the harsh climatic conditions, particularly in winter, and a lot of people who have been affected by the situation in Eastern Ukraine require, for example, assistance in winter. Winter support to families who live along the contact line is also something that the shelter cluster coordinates.

Nahaylo: How many people do you have for national auxiliaries here to deal with this challenge?

Mateu: In the case of UNHCR, we have eight offices in the country in the eastern provinces, two in non-government-controlled areas. We have 127 staff. A great majority of them are Ukrainian nationals, we only have 23 international staff members.

Nahaylo: Who are your main partners and main allies in this undertaking, both international and local?

Mateu: We are implementing our program through 15 partners. They are mostly non-governmental organizations. Only two are international NGOs, the rest are national entities. We are also working very closely with the newly established Ministry for Temporarily Occupied Territories and Internally Displaced Persons as well as municipalities. For example, the municipality of Mariupol is very active in trying to support and integrate internally displaced persons. Lviv has also done quite a lot of work. And also, some of the smaller municipalities, such as Irpin outside of Kyiv which has been very active in trying to support those that have decided to come from Eastern Ukraine and find a safe place.

Nahaylo: We are talking to Pablo Mateu, the UNHCR Representative in Ukraine. Let's conclude now by trying to take stock of the costs of this huge undertaking to address these humanitarian challenges, relief efforts and legal challenges. You have led the attempts to raise money from donors. What estimates have you put out most recently, and how much has the country actually received?

Mateu: This year's budget alone is 38 million US dollars. That's just for UNHCR. Imagine when you start adding up all the different UN agencies: the International Committee of the Red Cross, Caritas, the Pope had this quite generous appeal for Ukraine, and the international NGOs. And national NGOs, which have been quite efficient, I have to say, in raising funds from the Ukrainian diaspora and from supporters of Ukraine, particularly in Europe and North America. It's a lot of money, and unfortunately as the attention of the international community goes to other places like Yemen or South Sudan, the attention is no longer on Ukraine and the humanitarian support is going down.

Nahaylo: Do you sense what we used to call "compassion fatigue" for Ukraine? Because many people see it as a frozen conflict that's off the international radar screen, and which pops up from time to time, so it's not seen as something that's as acute as maybe other issues.

Mateu: Right, and unfortunately, I think this is a wrong description of the conflict. The recently appointed US Special Representative for Ukraine Kurt Volker described it not as a frozen conflict when he recently visited the contact line in Eastern Ukraine. He said this is a very hot conflict. Despite that the attention, like I said, is drifting away from Ukraine. So, part of our responsibility is to make sure that people around the world realise that there are still outstanding humanitarian needs.

Nahaylo: As a result of this, perhaps, lack of focus or attention, how much have you actually managed to raise out of the $37 million that you needed?

Mateu: Well, like I said, unfortunately the humanitarian donors are concentrating on other crises. We've managed to raise almost $12 million out of the $38 million.

Nahaylo: And who are the main donors at this stage, over the last year or two?

Mateu: The main donors are the ones who are also supporting Ukraine in other aspects, including its program of reforms. The United States, Canada, the European Union and then individual members of the European Union, such as Germany, Norway, Sweden, and Denmark. Switzerland is also a big donor, not to UNHCR, but for example to the Red Cross, and of course Japan. Japan has steadily supported, not just the humanitarian agencies but also development agencies.

Nahaylo: Pablo, we are running out time, so my last question. If you could just look into your crystal ball and look ahead. Of course, at the moment there seems to be no end in sight to this war, but one day obviously things will have to change. Will UNHCR be preparing also for contingencies for return, peace building, or rebuilding, etc. How is that already figuring in your planning?

Mateu: We have now prepared a multi-year, multi-partner protection and solutions strategy for the next five years. The solutions aspect of it is emphasized because, as you rightly said, some people are coming back and more people will probably come back in the future, even if the conflict is still ongoing. Unfortunately, there seems to be no end to the conflict for the time being. But you never know. We need to be prepared for an eventual peaceful settlement and return of the displaced.

"Wounded Warrior Now Competing in Invictus Games"

with Pavlo Mamontov
22 September 2017

https://hromadske.radio/en/podcasts/ukraine-calling/wounded-warrior-now-competing-in-invictus-games

Oksana Smerechuk: This week, the 2017 Invictus Games are starting. They will be taking place from the 23rd to the 30th of September in Toronto, Canada. This is the first time Ukraine is participating and has been invited to send a team. Lately we've been seeing lots of stories in the media about Ukraine's Invictus Warriors, as the excitement builds and Ukrainians gear up to follow the success of their men and women veterans at the Games in Toronto. This past week the whole Ukrainian Invictus Team has been to a number of send-off ceremonies. For example, there was one yesterday with representatives of Government and major sponsors coming to wish the competitors All the Best. Even the Ministry of Defence came out to congratulate and to hand out awards. And also the Vice-Premier for Euro-Atlantic Integration. So lots of media attention. Now I am speaking to someone for whom the next week will be the opportunity to show results of hard work.

With me in the studio is Pavlo Mamontov, an Invictus Games competitor. Welcome! As we know, Invictus Games competitors are all veterans of the Armed Forces or current members of the Armed Forces, who have been wounded while in the line of duty or in action.

It's not strictly this definition in your case. For one thing, Pavlo, you were a volunteer in a volunteer battalion. Also I remember when we first met you said to me, that four years ago you would have never imagined yourself as part of an army. You were just not that type of person. How did it all start?

Pavlo Mamontov: Before the war the army was something very far from me. When war came, I felt I had to go because I am Ukrainian. It's my country and I want to live here. My family lives here and I want my future kids to live here. It's like my second mother who gave me life.

Smerechuk: Did you just go and join a volunteer battalion right away? Or were you on the Maidan?

Mamontov: Yes, before the war I was on the Maidan [Euromaidan protests]. I had my first wound from the police on Maidan. After Maidan I wanted to go to the war. For me it was a big opportunity because I had some experience in the military.

Smerechuk: Did your family know that you were going to front lines?

Mamontov: I think my mother knew about this, because I had told her if war comes to our country, I would go. That was before the war.

Smerechuk: It's obviously a very emotional decision. Where did you see action? Where did you end up on the front lines?

Mamontov: I was in sector M, the Mariupol area. It was our sector, our battalion. Our regiment is still here.

Smerechuk: When was this?

Mamontov: I started in 2015.

Smerechuk: Did you continue? Were you wounded?

Mamontov: I was wounded [and after recovering] went back [to the war], but not for a long time. After that I found other opportunities, had a good opportunity to study. This was more interesting for me because after Minsk Agreements, the war was different.

Smerechuk: Tell me, where were you wounded? How did it happen?

Mamontov: It was in an artillery duel. I was with our commander and was hit by a mortar shell. It broke the bones in my hand and my arm. The bones on my finger were without flesh, skin.

Smerechuk: Was it just bone?

Mamontov: In some places, yes. I saw bones in some places.

Smerechuk: Were you conscious?

Mamontov: I did not lose consciousness. I remember I stood up.

Smerechuk: Were you taken to the hospital immediately?

Mamontov: It took a very long time, because many people near me were wounded and dead. I stood up and understood that now I should do something, because people are busy helping others. After that, I had an operation, and the same day and was moved to another hospital.

Smerechuk: All in one day?

Mamontov: Yes.

Smerechuk: Did your family know about this?

Mamontov: Yes. That day I remember I called my mother, and my mother said, "I know about your situation." I wanted to say that I just broke my hand, that it was nothing serious, but my mother knew the situation.

Smerechuk: So after this one operation, were you able then to function normally? To go back to work? You came back to Kyiv, I assume?

Mamontov: Well, after my first operation I had three months in a hospital in another city, where I had maybe six or seven operations. After three months I came back home, but was still in a hospital. In this hospital I was able to be with my girl and we thought about our marriage. And when I came back to Kyiv the day after the operation, I went to the government office and we were married!

Smerechuk: That's a nice story. So what were your plans then? Were you prepared to go back to work and back to civilian life?

Mamontov: My wife helped me with this. In all moments of life I had really good people in my life. There was an organization, it's a psychological adaptation organization, that was helping me. After that I had studied, so it was a good experience with good people and new stories.

Smerechuk: So you were able to go and study?

Mamontov: Yes. I went to the Ukrainian Catholic University for Public Administration and it was very cool. After that I started working.

Smerechuk: That's a private university that has tuition fees, it's not free. How did you manage that?

Mamontov: Yes, it's not a cheap university but it's a very cool university. I wanted to study there, and an American fund, Western NIS Enterprise Fund, helped me and my friends, also warriors, and we got to study for free at this University.

Smerechuk: How did you hear about the Invictus Games? And what made you decide to go?

Mamontov: It was before Ukraine sent in their application (to send a delegation to the games). My volunteer (friend) called me, I remember, and said, "Look at this website." It was the Invictus Games website, and I remember I saw some videos from other [previous] competitions. I remember crying at this time because it was a very emotional moment.

Smerechuk: This meant something for you.

Mamontov: Yes. It was something… I don't have words to explain it. I remember the organization said, "Write your motivation. What is Invictus for you?" And I remember I wrote the letter, and after that people said, "This is Ukraine's first time in the competition!"

Smerechuk: And you got in! Apparently 122 veterans applied to be a competitor for the Ukrainian team and only 30 were accepted. So I guess you must have proven yourself in the initial selection competition. What sports are you competing in?

Mamontov: My sports are cycling and rowing.

Smerechuk: And did you find when you started working with the coaches? Was it hard for you, or are you naturally a sporty person?

Mamontov: Well, I had some experience before. I would do skiing, Muay Thai boxing and some sort of tourism. I am a junior instructor.

Smerechuk: You would go through mountains?

Mamotov: Yes. I like that. I am a junior instructor for this. But all of these I did for myself and for fun, it was not for competition or medals.

Smerechuk: So what do the Invictus Games mean for you? What is your purpose in participating?

Mamotov: For me its emotions, new experiences, meeting new people. It's more than medals, it's higher than a piece of metal.

Smerechuk: What do you hope to do in Toronto?

Mamotov: Meet with the Ukrainian diaspora and with other participants, who have similar experiences to me. I want to know problems that they are experiencing. It is interesting for me.

Smerechuk: In your experience, do you think the Invictus Games can influence people? Do you think they can motivate?

Mamotov: Yes! For example, like for me when I was in hard times. Its hard training and you want to finish. You see other guys who are maybe without legs or hands, see their hard work, and you see for yourself that it's possible. For me, it's setting an example for people, not just being a wounded Warrior, but its an example for others.

Smerechuk: What are your plans then for the future?

Mamotov: To finish my studies and maybe find work in Public Administration. I don't know. Maybe I'll start a business with my wife, a café?

Smerechuk: That would be nice!

Mamotov: Yes very interesting.

Smerechuk: I'd like to thank you Pavlo for coming in to talk with us. I admire your spirit in going ahead and I wish you and your fellow competitors all the best of luck in the games!

Mamotov: Thank you.

"Why All the Fuss?
Ukraine's New Education Law"

with Volodymyr Kulyk
6 October 2017

https://hromadske.radio/en/podcasts/ukraine-calling/why-all-the-fuss-ukraine-s-new-education-law

Marta Dyczok: Education laws don't usually make it into the headlines. But for the past two weeks you've noticed Ukraine Calling has been reporting on the new education law that Ukraine has recently adopted. What has all this controversy been about? There's a controversial language provision in it. To explain what this is all about we have one of Ukraine's top scholars on language, media, and more, Dr. Volodymyr Kulyk. He is a Senior Research Fellow at the Institute of Political and Ethnic Studies, he has held prestigious fellowships and teaching position in the world's top universities, most recently at Yale University. He has also written and published numerous articles and books. Dr. Kulyk, thank you very much for finding the time to speak to us. Let's start with these controversies all about why is this language provision in the new law getting so much attention in Ukraine and outside its borders? What is this all about?

Volodymyr Kulyk: Frankly, it was a bit surprising even to me. But it should not be surprising, because this new law reduces the use of the minority languages throughout education rather significantly, even drastically. It makes a big change from the law which was in force until recently. Ukraine had very generous provisions for the use of minority languages in education in primary and secondary schools, even in higher education, in colleges there are languages other than Ukrainian. Mostly Russian had been used extensively.

But let me start with the levels of education. Basically for schooling, everybody had the right to choose in which language to educate their children. This was not only for people who traditionally lived in this country, or only people who belong to minority groups. Pretty much everybody could choose, even recent immigrants could decide that they want education in Russian. For example people coming from the Caucuses would want education in Russian, because they know it better than Ukrainian. That was exceptionally generous. In higher education, what was going in Eastern and Southern Ukraine, was that a professor would come into an auditorium and ask students which language they would prefer. If most of students preferred Russian, that was the chosen language of instruction.

That is now going to stop. The law clearly made Ukrainian the main language of education on all levels. It allows other languages to be used freely in pre-school and elementary school. But starting with secondary school, Ukrainian will be the only language of instruction for all subjects. Except, of course, minority languages as subjects. Crimean Tatar or the Russian language, or Hungarian language can be taught.

But there is also another provision, namely, for all official languages of the European Union. Several subjects can be taught in those languages, which also means languages of Ukraine's significant minorities such as Polish, Bulgarian, Hungarian or Romanian, but remarkably not Russian. Basically this whole change from minority languages toward Ukrainian was primarily aimed at the use of Russian in schools, because Russian was used very much in education including higher education. And the reliance on Russian meant that Ukrainian was not always at the high levels of proficiency needed as in other domains, such as the workplace. That was the main concern.

Dyczok: Sorry to interrupt! When you say "extensive provisions" what exactly were those provisions? Did this mean people could have a higher education in Romanian or in Russian? Is that what the previsions were all about?

Kulyk: Yes, that's exactly the point. The historical context is crucial. If you look at established traditional European nation states, there should not be any questions about the inadequacy or appropriateness of this law. Of course, in all these states, the titular language, the majority language is the language of all social domains and the main language of education. English is the second language used in education in all these countries rather than their minority languages. It's not about Breton in France, or Turkish in Germany. In most countries it's not about traditional minority languages, which are taught only on these very limited territories where these minorities are living. It's about a titular language plus increasing use of international languages, mainly English.

But in Ukraine the situation is different because of the post-imperial context and the legacy of the Russian and Soviet Empires, which gave the use of Russian in society incomparable dominance. Russian is still used in many regions, in many domains, more than Ukrainian. So it is not Russian that is formally a minority language. In recent legislation called the Regional Language Law, it is not Russian that is in danger or restricted, but Ukrainian.

The main goal of this legislation is to drastically extend the use of Ukrainian in education, to increase fluency and proficiency of all graduates, to make it possible to use this language in all other spheres. So graduates will not have the excuse that they have not mastered Ukrainian well enough to use it in the workplace, or in their capacity as public servants.

Here we have to distinguish between two main languages (or language categories). On the one hand, we have Russian, which formally is a minority language, but in fact is a majority language in many regions and in many domains and is anything but in danger. On the other hand, there are minority languages, which are very significant in some regions, but clearly minority languages, like Romanian in Bukovyna in the Chernivtsi region, or Hungarian in Transcarpathia. And the Crimean Tatar language.

Most notably Hungarians and Romanians had, and still have, a rather exceptional scope of education in their respective languages. They had several dozen secondary schools with education fully in Hungarian or Romanian. In pre-school, primary school and secondary school, all subjects are taught in these languages, and Ukrainian, English or German are foreign languages that are taught just as subjects.

Which means Ukrainian is taught inadequately, and the knowledge of Ukrainian which students acquire during school is not enough for them to use that language. That is one argument that the Ukrainian state is making in response to criticism on the part of Hungarian and Romanian officials. It's about your fellow Hungarians or Romanians who are citizens of Ukraine, and who need this knowledge of Ukrainian, sufficient to work, not just in these ethnic ghettos, not just to move across the border to Hungary or Romania to work there, but to be able to work in Ukraine.

In practice, they will have two languages in addition to English, or another foreign language. On the primary level they will have only Romanian or Hungarian with Ukrainian as a subject, to allow children to become proficient. From Grade five this will switch. Most of subjects will be in Ukrainian, with Hungarian and Romanian languages as subjects, and a few subjects in those languages (this could be the history of this ethnic group, or the geography of the region, literature, history, etc.). But chemistry, math, computer science should be in Ukrainian because otherwise what happens is that they are simply unable to acquire this knowledge to be able to enter university. So some of them cheated, some of them acquired some Ukrainian, then they struggled at university, or underperformed. Transcarpathia with its significant minority has the worst results in the standard independent testing across Ukraine. Very significant underperformance means they were actually discriminated against in access to higher education in Ukraine, and for getting prestigious jobs. So that should be corrected. But as I said, while this is a very important part of this problem it's not only about that, it's also about the Russian language, about making Russian speakers acquire Ukrainian and use Ukrainian much more than they have done so far.

Dyczok: The criticism that's been coming from abroad has been from Hungary and Romania, and yet you've pointed to the fact that this really, to a large degree, is about the Russian-Ukrainian conflict. Has there been criticism or commentary from Russia? How do you see the Russian language rights being protected within this Ukrainian affirmative-action language plan?

Kulyk: Of course there has been criticism from Russia. But unlike before the war, when such criticisms would be heeded and responded to, now nobody actually listens to what Russia is saying, because it is saying too many bad things about everything Ukrainian.

And that's a crucial difference. Such a law would be inconceivable before the war precisely because of Russia's predictable criticism. But now, they have a good moment because Russia is discredited. Whatever Russia is saying is not believed, even by most people speaking Russian in Ukraine. In the international arena Russia is not believed either. So it's the moment to do what Ukraine considers is right to do.

Of course there is the problem of how to treat Russian speakers in Ukraine. Not in view of what Russia is saying, but in view of what Russian speakers themselves want, what international organizations say, and what the Ukrainian state is committed to do. Legislators will have to be careful enough not to contradict directly the letter of international treaties and international documents that Ukraine entered into, such as the Convention for the Protection of National Minorities, or the European Charter for Regional Minority Languages.

Dyczok: Are those European conventions or Ukrainian conventions?

Kulyk: I mentioned both the Convention for the Protection of National Minorities and the European Charter for Regional Minority Languages, the two most important and politically relevant documents in this regard. Both mention that the state should protect national minorities. It should protect the right for a person to belong to a national minority, and the right of people speaking these minority languages. But both mention that it should not be to the detriment of the majority language, precisely because the majority language is a unifying factor in society. People could not belong together if they don't have a language in common. Many Hungarians and Romanians know very little Ukrainian, and that's the problem. They do not really belong and they cannot belong to the job market. They cannot belong significantly and adequately to the body politic. So that should be changed by means of education. But then you've got the Russian speakers. Because the languages are so close, Russian speakers understand Ukrainian. Not all of them can speak adequately for all positions but they of course understand, communicate, and there is a flow of information. So that's not a problem of understanding but that's a problem of functioning in various domains and in various capacities. They should be able to do that. Many people are now saying that cashiers at supermarkets cannot serve people in Ukrainian because they do not know it properly.

But whose fault is that? Of course it's partly the fault of those who hired them. But the problem of the workforce and the problem of employment for those people is that they are excluded from many positions because they do not know Ukrainian. So rather than discriminating against them now, something should be down at earlier levels in education to prepare them to work in various domains, for education in universities, and to enter into public service and service industries in various capacities and to be able to fully function in Ukraine.

Dyczok: Two more questions and I'll let you decide which order to answer them in: Has there been a response from the European Union and evaluation of this latest Ukrainian education law? And does this law adequately protect Russian language rights i.e. will Russians, Russian speakers, ethnic Russian who want to have the level of Russian language literacy, will that be protected under this new law?

Kulyk: The Russian language will only be taught as a subject, because Russian is not one of the official languages of the European Union. So that was a clear differentiation between the two, to exclude Russian to a greater extent than the Western European languages. Russian will still be taught as a subject so those who want it to be taught to their children will have this opportunity fully. So in addition to Russian being available through the media and throughout many domains in Ukraine, knowledge of Russian will not be a problem.

Of course I assume, that in those regions where Russian is spoken widely in the street and in the workplace, then of course Russian will be taught much more than in those regions where Russian is marginal. Ukraine will signal its change from a post-imperial context, where former colonial languages, metropolitan languages, dominate many prestigious domains. If you look at Africa and the position of French, for example, in Algeria or Morocco, and English in Malaysia or Singapore. It will be very different from those situations where the former colonial language is fully dominant long after its independence. In a more European context, languages other than the majority language are used in education in some other domains but in the limited territories where these minorities are settled and much less than the majority language. So it's a clear shift to where we belong: we do not belong to the post-colonial, post-imperial realm. We belong to Europe now. So that's also a clear political message.

Dyczok: And has Europe spoken on this? Has Europe given an evaluation?

Kulyk: Yes. Ukraine made it very clear from the beginning, a very smart move I believe, that it is willing to submit this newly adopted law to the Council of Europe to its Venice Commission, which so far has been providing its opinion about various pieces of legislation including, at some point, about the language law in 2012. So that was already done. Now Ukraine is waiting for the Council of Europe to rule and to provide its opinion.

I think it would be very important for Ukrainian authorities to follow their advice. Not just to demonstrate that we are going to listen to them, but really listen, really modify the legislation if that happens. And I believe that that would also disqualify the remarks and accusations from Budapest and Bucharest. If European legal experts decide that the legislation is in line with European standards and international commitments then that's fine. If its not, and Ukraine agrees to modify it, that will also be fine. That will clearly reveal that the criticism from Romania and Hungary is not about Ukraine's violation of international standards but is about their nationalist ambitions. They want Ukraine to do what they themselves are not doing, and they of course use this criticism, not so much just against Ukraine, but also in attempts to influence their own constituencies because the authorities are looking to the elections. They want to be more nationalist-sounding and more tough than the nationalist competitors.

Dyczok: How do you see this actually working in practice? Is this law going to be implemented? Is it going to be followed or is it just going to be on the books and people will still do things as business as usual?

Kulyk: That is part of the problem, the main issue with this law. Education is already the most Ukrainianized domain. There is a lot of Ukrainian in education, but the problem is that it is not as needed in other domains. So that's why there is this gap between what is on paper and what is in practice. And I'm afraid that if legislation for other domains is not adopted and implemented, this law will not be implemented, because there is just not enough incentive for learning Ukrainian properly.

Dyczok: So it has to be a comprehensive approach.

Kulyk: Yes. Its good that the law was adopted. Its not only about the language article. Its about education reform more generally, and it would be stupid, for example, for Poroshenko to veto this law because of this one article when, in fact, so much depends on that educational reform. But on the other hand, the timing is kind of inappropriate. I believe that a general language law should have been adopted earlier, instead of this Kivalov-Kolesnichenko proposal, and then education would have been just one part of that. Because there is no message that Ukrainian is needed in society. There is just the message that Ukrainian is needed on the radio and television and there is no message that Ukraine is needed in education. So what's new? Quotas on television existed before 2012.

A law on education with Ukrainian in there existed long before. What we need is a law that Ukrainian would be needed for services, that Ukrainian would be needed for computers, or that Ukrainian would be needed for businesses, but that's not happening so far. That's the problem.

Dyczok: So politics and language, two hot topics. Next time we have you on the show we'll talk about the language law. Thank you very much for your conversation.

"We Don't Need a New Maidan"

with Andrey Kurkov
5 January 2018

https://hromadske.radio/en/podcasts/ukraine-calling/we-don-t-need-a-new-maidan-andrey-kurkov

Bohdan Nahaylo: This week I have great pleasure to have with me a celebrated writer from Ukraine, perhaps Ukraine's best literary export of our times, Andrey Kurkov. His books are translated into numerous languages, and he has written not only novels, but books for children and film scripts. He is the only author from the former Soviet area whose books have appeared on best seller book lists in Europe. But he is exceptional not only because of his popularity in the outside world, but also because the civic position he takes, his principled stance, not extremely overt, but nevertheless in its discreet way an example of a writer pointing the way for the society in which he finds himself and which he describes. So Andrey, welcome to our program!

Andrey Kurkov: Thank you, Bohdan.

Nahaylo: Let's begin by talking about your literary output. Personally, I have lost track of all the books you have published—novels, we are not going into essays and interviews.

Kurkov: I've published 21 novels. I did not publish my first four novels and will never publish them because they were just beginner's texts. I also published some children books (about 11) and some of these children books are still in stock because I like illustrators to work on them. But generally that is my output.

Nahaylo: Is the best selling one, the best known, still the your first one you published—*Смерть постороннего* (2006), published in English in 2001 as *Death and the Penguin*?

Kurkov: It was the first to be translated. It was definitely the most successful. It was followed by *Penguin Lost*, originally published in 2005 in Russian as *Закон улитки*, then *The Penguin Novels. The President's Last Love* was very well received. And my recent English translation is one of my oldest novels, *The Bickford Fuse*, which got very good reviews in the *Financial Times* and the *Guardian*.

Nahaylo: It is really exceptional for a writer in Ukraine. And I emphasize that you are Russian-born. You are Russian by ethnicity, but I guess a Ukrainian now by adaptation, by choice and by spirit.

Kurkov: I always say that I am an ethnic Russian, but a political Ukrainian. I grew up in Ukraine. My family moved to Kyiv when I was less than two years old. So it's my country, it's my city.

Nahaylo: You are a member of the political Ukrainian nation.

Kurkov: Yes.

Nahaylo: Let's now return to your early major works, especially *Death and the Penguin*. That was such an unusual theme and approach. How did it come to your head, the imagery that you use?

Kurkov: I think it was a result of a very specific Soviet upbringing and my inborn optimism because I am still an optimist despite of all the problems the country is facing now. I was writing these novels in 1995-96, when the situation in the country was quite grave. At the same time lots of writers were writing so-called black novels which were not giving hope or even a tiny spectre of hope. They were written by depressed people who hated the subject they wrote about, they hated the country they wrote about, and they hated their characters. I would never do the same. I was trying to describe the situation in the country, which was a difficult situation, but live in hope and not forget about humour, irony as some kind of medicine against depression.

Nahaylo: Your books are both satirical and surrealistic at the same time. For me at any rate. But by the time you got to *The President's*

Last Love, I do not know why, I saw shades of Latin American writers: Márquez, or even Vargas Llosa. Were you influenced by Latin American writers?

Kurkov: I've never thought if I was influenced by them. I was actually influenced by, first and foremost, Gogol, Bulgakov, Kvitka-Osnovyanenko, Kafka, Camus and Knut Hamsun.

Nahaylo: You had "hunger" for these things... [Hamsun's most famous novel is called The Hunger)

Kurkov: Yes, exactly. I have never been crazy about Latin American literature. I like Borges but not more than that. Probably on subconscious level I could have been influenced by everything I read, of course.

Nahaylo: By who else have you been influenced by? You know English. Are you reading English authors as well?

Kurkov: I read in English, French and also in Polish and German.

Nahaylo: A "Renaissance man" born and bred in Soviet times!

Kurkov: When I wrote *The President's Last Love* I tried to create a 3D picture of human life from the 1970s to the future, and that future time for me was 2017. This is the year the novel ends and the novel was published in 2004.

Nahaylo: Amazing! Like for many of us was the case with 1984. We could not but wait with trepidation for that year to come, and then it arrived. Now we are in 2017! How have your works developed? Has the range of your interests shifted more to any specific area? Are you choosy or *ad hoc* about what turns up?

Kurkov: I get impulses from life. For example, I have a novel which is called in English *The Good Angel of Death* or *The Kind Angel of Death,* and it was written in 1997 after many discussions with Ukrainian nationalists about the role of Ukrainian language in society and about the possible, or not possible, linguistic assimilation of minorities of the country. The novel in its original is bilingual, because there are characters that speak in Ukrainian, and characters that speak in Russian. My latest novel, which I have finished now but am still editing, is called *The Grey Bees*. It is about the grey zone, Donbas, and Crimea, and about today's situation in Ukraine. So. of course. I am influenced by what has happened.

Nahaylo: You're on the cutting edge. You're staying up with current affairs and most burning issues.

Kurkov: This is a writer's role. If he is not a science fiction writer, he has to be in reality. Writing a novel like this allows you to live in two realities at the same time: your personal reality, which can be detached from the world and can be detached from politics; and, your second reality, which you fill in with what you lack in your first reality.

Nahaylo: But how hard is it to be truly honest in writing about such sensitive subjects here in this context of Ukraine, yet having publishers that want to promote the book outside of Ukraine? How do you balance your honesty with what the market expects from you?

Kurkov: I already had that situation when I was writing the book, *The Gardens of Mr. Michurin*, knowing that this book will not be translated and will not have a lot of readers, but I needed to write it. So I did. Almost nobody knows about this novel, there was only one edition in Russian, and that's all. So this time I'm not thinking about the publishers. I'm thinking about the situation I am describing, I am thinking about the local readers, and if the book will be taken on by publishers abroad it will also give them the information. Honesty is subjective. I am I'm trying to be objective in this. I went to the war zone two times, I know a lot of refugees, I talk to soldiers, I talk to people who don't want to talk to anybody in Severodonetsk. There is no fantasy there except for the plot, which I developed. It is slightly surreal sometimes, but very realistic, because everything that is described in the novel is possible.

Nahaylo: Where are your books most popular? Where are they selling best, or most read?

Kurkov: Well, in German-speaking countries, in French-speaking countries, English translations, and Japanese. And now, actually, I feel that I am more and more read in Italy and the Arab world. I have a new book in the Arab language in Egypt, and I have been invited to Dubai in March for public events.

Nahaylo: And you must obviously give a lot of interviews and are asked for your comments here and there, so that probably cuts into your writing time. And you travel a lot!

Kurkov: It does. I travel five to six months a year, and most of the interviews I give abroad are not about my books, but about Ukraine, the political situation, and the prospects of the relationship with Russia etc. So I became a sort of an expert on Ukraine after 2001 and the Gongadze case.

Nahaylo: Well you've become foremost a cultural emissary, but also a political commentator and observer. What is your typical working day when you're not travelling? How many hours on a good day do you actually put into writing?

Kurkov: Well it depends whether I am at the beginning or the end of the novel. Because when I am at the beginning of the novel, I spend more time thinking and making notes than writing, and then I can write for three or four hours. But when I am already in the process of writing the novel, the working day of writing can take up to 14 hours. When I was completing the novel *The Gardener of Ochakov*, I was writing 12-14 hours every day. Now I am writing about five, six, seven hours if I am not travelling. If I am travelling, sometimes I will write the same amount of time, but I am writing on the planes, on the trains…

Nahaylo: Do you write on a laptop or are you writing in long-hand with a pen?

Kurkov: The text, the actual text, I write on a laptop. And the notes I take on a writing pad and, actually, sometimes when the battery is flat, I start writing notes by hand.

Nahaylo: Tell us a little bit about your own personal taste, of writers that you respect, read these days, who are among your favourites?

Kurkov: Among Ukrainian writers, probably Yurko Vynnychuk. I think for me, he is one of the biggest, most important novelists in Ukraine. I very much like novels by Maria Matios. If we are talking about foreign literature, I started reading more non-fiction than fiction, and for the last five years I'm following the works of Martin Pollock, an Austrian professor of history and writer, who discovered for me a different Ukraine, a different Galicia. The first book of his I read was called *Kaiser from America (Kaiser von Amerika)*. It's the history of immigration from Bukovina and Galicia from the mid-19th century, and it turned my understanding of this history upside down, because it's a completely different from what we used to believe. So, I am reading more and more of his books now, like *The Last Train Journeys in Bukovina and Galicia (Nach Galizien: Von Chassiden, Huzulen, Polen und Ruthenen: eine imaginäre Reise durch die verschwundene Welt Ostgaliziens und der Bukowina)*, the last book which was translated in Chernivtsi into Ukrainian.

Nahaylo: That's one of the ironies and the tragedies for Ukrainians. Their history had so many blank spots, and they've been trying to recover much of this cultural and historical identity, and yet the presence of the Jews, the Russians, was also blotted out. Only now, writers like Bruno Schultz are being re-discovered and translated, or others, and the Jewish heritage in Western Ukraine, particularly we're talking about Chernivtsi and Lviv.

Kurkov: Exactly, and we are having new blank spots in Ukrainian literature now because the Crimean Tatar writers were and are ignored until today; there are no translations of their novels, or collections of their poetry. Ukrainians recently got very angry with Hungarians (over their official criticism of Ukraine's new education law with its positive affirmation as regards the Ukrainian language), but since 1991, no Hungarian-Ukrainian writer was translated into Ukrainian. Before 1991, they were always translated into Russian and Ukrainian. Now we have about 30-40 active writers living in the Ukrainian Transcarpathian region who are completely ignored, even in Uzhhorod. When I took my friends, writers in Uzhhorod, to Berehove, they were amazed to see a literary magazine in Hungarian written by Ukrainian citizens, Ukrainian writers. There are literary projects and there are many young writers who write in Hungarian, living in Ukraine, writing about their region, about Ukraine, helped by Hungarian mainland publishers or institutions, but helped like a smaller brother who cannot work properly.

Nahaylo: So, what you're saying is that Ukrainians, as the majority nation here, should not simple be preoccupied with this victim image of themselves, but should also see in their role as the strongest ethnic group how they could help others and support them?

Kurkov: Yes, they should show that they are uniting minorities around themselves. Like the British Council, or other institutions, when they bring their authors to Ukraine, for example, should look at the ethnicity of these authors. One of the previous writers who was sent by Britain to Ukraine was Tobias Fischer, a Hungarian who moved to England 20 or 30 years ago and who is now an English writer, and they are proud to show him as an English writer. We should be proud to show our writers of non-Ukrainian ethnicity as Ukrainian writers.

Nahaylo: And you obviously set a very good example of this cultural tolerance in the sphere because as mentioned earlier, you are from a Russian background, you are an ethnic Russian, yet you speak fluent Ukrainian. You do not distance yourself from Ukraine; in fact, you have become a leading representative of the modern tolerant Ukraine, this democratic Ukraine that we are building. Tell us a little bit about your role and involvement in the Ukrainian PEN Centre?

Kurkov: I am the Vice President of PEN. The president is Mykola Riabchuk. We have about 30-40 active members and this year we managed to host the International Pen Congress, the first time actually on Ukraine's territory, we received more than 150 delegates from lots of countries. And it was a success for which we have to pay now, because everybody in international PEN expects that we will be one of the leading PEN centres in Central Europe.

Nahaylo: I am talking to Andrey Kurkov, the celebrated writer, resident in Ukraine and unfortunately perhaps even better known in the outside world than among Ukrainians. Though we do have a growing reading public, particularly among the young people that are increasing more interested in reading your works and works in Ukrainian and in Russian. And Vice President of PEN Ukraine. PEN, for those who maybe are not aware, is an international writers' organization, "Poets, Essayists, Novelists," which defends freedom of speech, and writers who find themselves in trouble with authorities.

Kurkov: Actually, it is more like political literary organization which fights for human rights. And which fights for writers and journalists who are persecuted, or who are in prisons. It is very influential, because we managed, as International PEN, to get freedom for Asli Erdogan, a Turkish writer who lives in Germany. When she came to Turkey she was arrested and even her passport was returned to her. We have this situation in many countries, which is very difficult and needs international attention.

Nahaylo: This is of great interest to me, because when I was a postgraduate student at the London School of Economics my first job was with Amnesty International. But I was very closely involved with PEN, the International PEN Centre when Mario Vargas Llosa was the President. And at that time it was a major achievement for us to get Stus, Svitlychny, Sverstiuk, Chornovil, Osadchy, other Ukrainian writers (Soviet political prisoners at that time) recognised by PEN. It meant a lot and it still does.

Kurkov: You know I was not a writer at all in 1988. I was not published, but I was invited to become a member of English PEN, and my first English translation and publication was in a magazine closely aligned with Amnesty International, Index on Censorship.

Nahaylo: That is where I started. My first publication was about Ivan Svitlychny, I think, in 1980, and the second was about Ihor Kalynets in Index on Censorship. At that time, the late 1970s, George Theiner was the Deputy Editor, (he was a Czech), and Michael Scammel, who wrote the definitive biography of Solzhenitsyn, was the editor. Those were very interesting days. But Andrey, what are you working on at present?

Kurkov: I am editing the new novel, which I mentioned already *The Grey Bees,* about these grey zones, annexed Crimea and Donbas, and Ukraine. I am thinking about the next projects, which will be mostly projects organized together with PEN Ukraine and maybe PEN New York, to help young Ukrainian writers to lead public discussions on any topic. I did two projects like this last year in the Transcarpathian and Odesa regions. We involved about 25-30 young writers from all around Ukraine. We can repeat this in other areas of Ukraine, including also the Donbas, that is, the Ukrainian controlled territory of Donbas, and Bukovyna, and Slobozhanshchyna.

Nahaylo: Two final questions. Which of your books, of your many books and novels, are the most satisfactory for you? Which one do you feel is your best work? For you personally, not in term of sales.

Kurkov: Well, I mentioned already the *Bickford Fuse,* which was first self-published in 1993, but is now published in German and in

English. And among recent ones I'm very happy with the *Schengen Story*. It's called *Schengen Story*, but in French and other languages it will probably be called *Paris-London-Pienagalis* because it's about Lithuanians leaving for Europe, Western Europe, after Lithuania became a member of the European Union.

Nahaylo: Is it a sort of caveat emptor to those who see Europe as the great paradise that beckons?

Kurkov: Yes, it is. But it is a big novel, and it shows not only the situation in Lithuania, but also life in France, and life in England. So it's a big European novel, about 800 pages, four plot lines, and bits of unknown Lithuanian history, and unknown European history.

Nahaylo: Andrey, everywhere you go you are asked to comment about the situation in Ukraine, your take on what's happening. In a few sentences, where do we stand? Here we are, a few years after the Revolution of Dignity, the Maidan, which you described. Are we moving forward? Are we stagnating? Are you hopeful? Are you pessimistic?

Kurkov: I'm hopeful. I'm a great optimist. I was a black optimist in 1993, when the situation was really a bleak. I feel that the batteries are slightly flat in Ukrainian politics. The movement towards reforming the country has slowed down, and the government, the political elites, need a push. But we don't need a new Maidan. We don't need riots. We don't need pogroms. They need a push, and they need to get into real political activity. Because what we have as political activity in the country is very often fake. We have 300 political parties but we don't have daily political activities of ordinary members. We don't have offices of parties, in towns, cities, and villages. We have only so-called paid activists, who are active only before elections. So we have to change this system. Once we understand that every party has an ideology. If I'm a liberal then I want to join the liberal party, and I want to be sure that the liberal party will defend liberal values. Then political society will become much more civilized. And we won't have riots, Maidans, and pogroms, because there will be no place for them. If you are active, you can be active legally, politically, and in a civilized manner.

Nahaylo: And as a footnote, the following intrigues me. Your Russian colleagues and friends, in Russia and outside, how do they view you? They probably rate you very highly as a writer, but are they easy, comfortable, with your identification with Ukraine?

Kurkov: Such friends and colleagues, there are not many of them actually, with whom I keep in touch, they are on my side in both cases, my political statements, and my writing. I'm talking about Vladimir Sorokin, Lyudmila Ulitskaya, Boris Akunin, Tatiana Shcherbina, who lives in Moscow, and some others. But officially, for Russia I'm a traitor, and I'm a foreign writer. As I recently found out from an interview given by Dmitry Bykov in Kyiv, I'm "a French writer living in France, and not a Ukrainian writer." So there are lots of myths. But my books are not available in Russia, so I don't think anybody talks about me anymore, because I am not present there as a writer.

"Conflict Resolution in Donbas: No Magic Formula, Political Process Is Needed"

with General Sir Rupert Smith, Sir William Jeffrey and George Anderson
30 March and 6 April 2018

https://hromadske.radio/en/podcasts/ukraine-calling/conflict-resolution-in-donbas-no-magic-formula-political-process-is-needed; https://hromadske.radio/en/podcasts/ukraine-calling/conflict-resolution-in-donbas-there-has-to-be-some-sort-of-dialogue-with-the-people-who-are-causing-the-problem

Three military experts with extensive peacekeeping experience talk to Hromadske Radio Head Andiry Kulykov. General Sir Rupert Smith, expert on peacekeeping operations and security, Sir William Jeffrey, expert on post-conflict policing and DDR (disarmament, demobilisation and reintegration) with a focus on Northern Ireland, and George Anderson, expert on political reintegration and decentralization. They compare the Donbas conflict to the situations in Northern Ireland, Yemen, South Africa, and Cyprus. The interview aired in 2 parts.

Andriy Kulykov: You have vast experience in the international sphere, in different countries. We Ukrainians quite often think that people who come from abroad have solutions for our own problems. What can you say about this, General?

General Rupert Smith: I don't think we're here to offer a solution. Certainly in my experience, and I think I speak for the others, is that each problem, conflict, such as this, is unique to the circumstances they're in. There isn't a formula. You have to find the best answer in the circumstances at the time.

Kulykov: Alright, there isn't a formula, but maybe there are some rules that apply to different countries, I mean the general line of conduct. What can you say about this?

George Anderson: Well I certainly think there are lessons you can draw. And there are good lessons and bad lessons. One of the things that I worry about in this particular case is the risk that you'll end up with a frozen conflict. What we've seen in a number of countries, is that there's an inability to really engage in the issues and make the compromises that are necessary to reach an understanding. In this particular case I think both sides are hurting, but will they find a way to engage, and actually address the underlying issues, and move on to a more normal relationship? That's one of the lessons we've seen from abroad, is that there's a risk of slipping into a permanent state of confrontation.

Kulykov: You say both sides. Are there just two sides? Or maybe more?

Anderson: It's more complex than I just said. And we've seen that in a number of places. One of the issues is how many people come to the table? Or how many tables do you have? That kind of question.

Kulykov: When we speak of frozen conflicts, do we have a specific number of years after which a conflict becomes frozen?

Sir William Jeffrey: I don't think you can be as specific as that, but I think there are certainly characteristics of a conflict that has gotten to the point that nobody is really seriously expecting a resolution for a long time to come. And that's a dangerous situation. But that doesn't mean that there will always be an easy solution. The conflict I'm most familiar with is Ireland, and that rumbled on for many, many years. In a way, there was a solution waiting to be adopted, and what was needed was the political will, and the right timing, to make it successful.

Kulykov: Political will is a very popular combination of words in Ukraine. For every failure, for every drawback, we say, "We have everything but political will." I followed events in the Republic of Ireland and Northern Ireland since 1969. I lived and worked in London from 1992 to 1995, and then again from 2000. I sort of witnessed the Good Friday process and all this. Where was this political will found, after all? And why at this specific time?

Jeffrey: I think that there were two things that brought it together. One was that there was a generation of politicians in Northern Ireland who had lived through decades of fighting and were sick of it. And knew that their constituents wanted change. That was one definite factor. Another was that the security situation had reached the point where neither side could win, and they knew it. The Provisional IRA had been penetrated to the point that they knew that they were not going to win a military victory. Equally, they were strong enough that it was unlikely that British forces would do so. So in security terms, the timing was right. And then, politically, although much good work had been done by their predecessors, we had the coincidence of a British Prime Minister, in Tony Blair, and an Irish Taoiseach, in Bertie Ahearn, who formed a very close, personal, working relationship. If you add all these together, the conditions were right. But it's a combination that took a long time to come.

Kulykov: General Smith, apart from political will, and cooperation or contacts between people at the top, how important is work on the ground?

Smith: In the end, it entirely depends on the agreement to cease fire, and resolve the confrontation. And I'd like to draw a distinction between the fighting, the conflict, and the underpinning political confrontation that led to the conflict. You can only carry out your military functions according to the agreements in which you're operating. So, if we're talking of peace, there has to be an agreement to cease fire at an absolute minimum. And then you can start to contribute to developing an answer to the confrontation.

Kulykov: When I spoke to some former combatants in Northern Ireland and asked them what made them finally stop their combat activities, I was stunned by the answer. I, as a person who never took up arms militarily, heard from both sides of the conflict, "We got tired of killing." How important is this factor?

Anderson: I think it can be very important in certain circumstances. I've been doing some work on Yemen. I'm afraid they're not yet tired of killing in Yemen, and this is a country which has a plague of weapons. I referred to frozen conflicts. Sometimes the killing has stopped, but that doesn't get you to the point of addressing the underlying issues. In Cyprus now, it's been decades where they've had this frozen conflict, where the Turkish army is still on the ground in Northern Cyprus. It can get too comfortable, in a sense, even when the killing has stopped, to actually address the underlying political issues.

Kulykov: What was your major message to the Ukrainians with whom you spoke? I know that you held a seminar for the Ukrainian police.

Anderson: We met with some officials here. We had different messages. Each of us has different areas of expertise. But in my particular case it was to encourage people to start looking at the different issues, to break it up into chewable bits. And say, is there an issue around language? Is there an issue around policing? Is there an issue around security? Work your way through the list of questions and start thinking about creative responses to those questions.

Kulykov: And?

Smith: Mine I've already given. Deploying military forces into somebody else's fight must be done with a clear understanding that there is at least, as a minimum, an intention to cease fire. And then you can start to contribute to establishing the beginnings of solving the confrontation.

Kulykov: How to you find proof that there is such a wish?

Smith: The more doubtful the intentions to do what everyone is saying they're going to do in this agreement, the larger the force you're going to require. And I think there's a sort of crude correlation between the two. Secondly, you must understand that the deployment of this force is, in itself, a confidence building measure for both parties. And unless you can establish those understandings, I don't think you should deploy the force in the first place.

Jeffrey: I think my main message was to do with for the need for some kind of political settlement and overarching agreement, and in particular for some process by which such an agreement can be reached. And I agree with what Rupert said earlier, that we're not presumptuous enough to imagine that we have some magic formula that will cure the problems here, which are very deep-seated. But the only way in which there can be a solution is through a political process of some kind. We also talked about if there were such a process, and if it led to the kind of political agreement that occurred in Northern Ireland and Columbia, for example, how would one best address issues such as demilitarisation of regular armed forces, the decommissioning of weapons, and reintegration of those who have been acting as terrorists into a normal society, and changes in the police force. I think one advantage that Ukraine has, and there are not many, if one's honest about it, is that a lot of thought has been given in recent years to the question of police reform, and certainly in my experience reforming police services has been an important element in making peace.

Kulykov: You are rather cautious in assessing Ukrainian efforts because I heard you say, "A lot of thought was given." Was there a lot of action, in your opinion?

Jeffrey: I think there is evidence that things have changed, particularly in relation to community policing and patrolling. My sense is that even those responsible for these changes will acknowledge there is some way to go.

Kulykov: Before we go to questions what we got from people who live in non-government-controlled areas, one last question from me in this part of conversation. From what I hear you seem to underline, to stress, that there has to be a political will, that there have to be agreements which then will be implemented on the ground. But how important, or how probable is the process when there are initiatives that come from beneath, from the ground, when combatants or non-combatants, but who are on opposing sides, find something common to do and then this goes up and is accepted by those who work for political agreements and all this kind of stuff.

Anderson: Are you referring to things that are positive or conflictual?

Kulykov: Positive.

Anderson: That can be a useful icebreaker in the process. But one of the things that strikes me is that we have two countries here both of which have electoral systems. I mean flawed at least in one case, but nevertheless politics is real in both countries. So, when we talk about political will it's not just the leaders. The leaders are always thinking about the population. One of the problems is that if population is starting to drift apart and seeing this in very nationalistic terms, is there some space to create for leaders to find a solution? Bringing the population around to understanding the value of the solution, and the fact that the solution will require accommodation and even some painful compromises. That's a very tricky thing to manage politically. It will have to happen on both sides.

Jeffrey: I want to add to what George said on importance of the real popular view. As a follower of Northern Ireland process, you would know that we had some difficult political patches recently. Things have been set back and it is proving hard to follow through completely an agreement that was made as long as 20 years ago. I think the best chance to get it back together again lies in the public's view and public's willingness, as George said, to accept compromises.

Kulykov: General, no comment?

Smith: I would agree.

Kulykov: No comment will be accepted as an answer to following questions, but of course I am sure our listeners will appreciate at least some comments. These are questions from Ukrainian citizens who live in the non-government-controlled areas. As of now, the non-government-controlled areas are under a complete economic and social blockade. The Russian ruble is in use. We have gas and electricity from Russia. Russia pays pensions and social payments. How can a peace keeping mission have any effect, any influence on all of these? Will it have any influence on all of this?

Smith: No, it will not. As I've explained I think already that is not the purpose of the deployment of the military force.

Kulykov: All right. Anyone?

Anderson: Before peacekeepers are put on the ground, you need an agreement. Will that issue be addressed as part of the agreement, or won't it be? If it is not, then introduction of peacekeepers would not deal with that issue.

Kulykov: One SBU General (Security Service of Ukraine) made a statement all residents of non-government-controlled areas will go through filtration camps. How possible is this? Was there any experience like this in the countries that you worked in?

Jeffrey: I do not think any of us came across anything like that before. It depends on the circumstances, but I can't recall any examples in which entire populations were subject to such treatment.

Kulykov: Is full amnesty envisaged for people who carried weapons? I understand that you are not responsible for what Ukrainian authorities are planning, but what was your experience in the countries where you worked?

Jeffrey: In Northern Ireland we did not have an amnesty. We had arrangements for those who had been convicted of criminal offences associated with the troubles in Northern Ireland, which was seen by many to be very generous. But there was no question of outright amnesty. As George was implying in response to your earlier question, an awful lot of depends on what agreement is eventually reached. In each of these conflicts there is a point at which a compromise may be possible. And it is not always the same point.

Anderson: If I may add. One of the things you see in these post-conflict situations, is, first of all, how do you deal with the malefactors? Are they going to be treated as criminals? But there's the broader question of transitional justice. In some cases, like in South Africa, they had a major process just to expose what had happened during the apartheid regime and in transition to majority rule. There had been very bad things done by the ANC, and very bad things done by the apartheid regime. All of that was put out so people could see it, and it was part of coming in terms of the past so that they can move into the future. But they decided that not everything bad in the past was going to be dealt with. They were focused on the future.

Kulykov: General, what is your experience in the countries where you served?

Smith: You won't get towards some form of resolution without a degree of good-will. If one side is being thoroughly vindictive, then you're not going to get to the end. Because why would the other side then make peace? And I think the thing to hold in mind every morning, is you're making peace with your enemies, not your friends.

Kulykov: What mandate will a peace-keeping mission have, or might have? Or what mandate is feasible for Ukraine? What is a likely size of the mission, and who would be the contributing states? Or who might be, or who should be the contributing states?

Smith: The size of the mission will be dependent upon the agreement, and the confidence in the agreement. Then you have to decide, if you're going to deploy another group of people into this area, and what their purpose is. Are they merely to observe and report? Or are they at any risk, in which case, should they be able to defend themselves? Or are they to actually make the agreement happen? Now those are three stages of this thing and involve a decision of principle as to what armed forces to achieve. That will be needed to be done in the agreement.

Kulykov: How far removed from the conflict area should the contributing states be? For instance, I've heard that Canada is now discussing sending troops to Mali in Africa.

Anderson: I've heard that too. But in the Ukrainian context—Canada is a member of NATO—so would it be acceptable to have countries which are part of NATO providing troops for peacekeepers? That's a political decision. There could be a balance. Some NATO countries might be accepted in exchange for some other countries more or less on the other side, if I could put it that way. But it could be decided that no, we need to have countries that really have very little to do with this issue.

Kulykov: What will happen to current administrations and people who work for current administrations in the non-government-controlled areas? Or what happened to them in different countries where you were part of the settlement process?

Anderson: I think what we can say is, that there are people that have been involved in the current administration in the occupied areas which are playing very different roles. For example, if somebody is a nurse in a hospital, or a very low-level clerk, that's a very different kind of individual than somebody who's been one of the leaders or involved in the security apparatus in a very significant way. This is the sort of issue that will need to be broken down into its constituent pieces and presumably, the way these individuals will be treated will vary according to the kinds roles they played.

But to come back to what Bill said, which is that one should avoid an approach which is vindictive and punishing. Try to minimize the extent to which, or at least be very reasonable, in terms of the extent to which you're excluding people. Maybe redirect some people to other parts of the administration and say, "You can't work in this area any longer." A big part of what has to be done is to accommodate and bring people back in and to make them feel comfortable once again being part of the Ukrainian family.

Kulykov: I have the feeling that this question was particularly referring to some sort of punishment which may follow for these people. But I would like to ask you to extrapolate or to answer my personal question, which stems from this. How far removed or, on the other hand, how deeply involved in the future political process in terms of elections and local government, should the people who served in local administrations in the non-government-controlled areas be? Any experience from other countries?

Smith: If you look at the history of the countries that were part of the Soviet sphere in Eastern Europe, they all went through what they called these lustration exercises. And they varied a great deal in terms of how extensive it was. Czechoslovakia was probably the most rigorous. But certain people were excluded from working in government or presenting themselves for public office. These are issues of judgement, but I would expect there would be some implications for some people who'd been involved in the current regime in the Occupied Territories.

Jeffrey: In other areas, which have not been Occupied Territories as such, a similar issue arises in relation to those who were part of the insurgency. But the Northern Ireland experience, and the experience in Columbia as well, although it's different in character, is that part of the settlement is that a place in found in political life for those, at least the political representatives of those, who have been part of the insurgency.

Kulykov: I think that we also have a very interesting example of Nicaragua, which we now tend to forget, where although the Sandinistas effectively won, the Contras were allowed to take part in democratic elections. And although the Sandinistas won the first election, the next election brought victory to the Contras. And then it changed again. How relevant is this to the Ukrainian, or European experience?

Jeffrey: It has some relevance, I think. There's no easy answer to any of this. And the recent Columbian experience, for example, which was intended to provide a political path for FARC, I wouldn't say it backfired, but it's certainly the case that in the recent elections in Columbia, FARC's political representatives, were remarkably unsuccessful. I think the main point is that a peace deal can be capable of accommodating as an essential element, a political role for those who have been combatants in the past.

Kulykov: Sometimes Ukrainians ask very straight-forward questions to which there are no straight-forward answers. Now we go to such a question. Who will fund the restoration of Donbas?

(silence and chuckling)

Kulykov: No comment?

Jeffrey: I think we know who will be expected to.

Kulykov: Alright. How would people's civil rights be observed? Is it only the responsibility of the local administration, or national government, or is there a place for an international mission in this as well?

Smith: We'll go back to two things we've already said. The nature of the agreement that is being put into effect, and in particular, the transitional justice arrangements that get you from A to B in this journey. The more it is done correctly by the people who are going to do it, or the organizations or institutions that are going to do this in the future, as soon as possible, the better. Putting in an international body to do these things and then replace it by something only delays the process from beginning, let alone developing.

Anderson: I would add on this that Ukraine is party to a whole number of international conventions on human rights, as well as having human rights provisions within its domestic constitution and what have you. Really, it's a case of respecting those provisions that Ukraine has already committed itself to.

Kulykov: To your mind, how are the Western partners of Ukraine prepared to control the Ukrainian authorities in keeping and observing those human rights, or will they say, "Well this is Ukraine, they are basically in their right."

Anderson: It's possible that one of the mechanisms that could be introduced into a case like this would be international observers and certainly there's experience of that within Europe, with the organizations that exist within Europe. They will not assume the powers of the sovereign country, they will be reporting, monitoring, etc.

Jeffrey: The best guarantor of human and civil rights is an agreement that protects them, and national institutions that operate legally and consistently with that.

Anderson: But a strong message from the Ukrainian government that understands its commitments in this area could be a very powerful communication with the populations that might have concerns.

Kulykov: Alright, again, proceeding from your experience in other countries, what will be the status of this territory of the non-government-controlled areas? How reliable is decentralization? And which documents will fix this? Were there cases in other countries where the conflict inside, if they were territorial, got a special level of autonomy within the state? Where these constitutional arrangements changed as a result of the settlement process?

Anderson: Any number of cases internationally, some of them following conflicts, like the Province of Aceh in Indonesia. There was a very bloody conflict there, but eventually it led to an agreement in Aceh has a particular status within Indonesia. In North Eastern India there have been a number of conflicts which led to creating special states that resolved the issue. And there have been arrangements out of peaceful situations such as South Tyrol in northern Italy, the Aland Islands in Finland, there are a number of models for this type of thing. And certainly, a central issue when you look at the negotiations in Cyprus, they're talking about a bi-zonal structure, where the Turks and the Greeks would have very large elements of autonomy as well as a common government. So, these things exist, but the issue for Ukraine is to what extent would there be a real demand in interest in having some particular arrangements for the Donbas area, or the so-called "particular districts" within the Donbas area.

Kulykov: Now a specific question. I think that our British participants have very good knowledge of this process: how can disarmament of a population be conducted peacefully? Well maybe, in your case, not of the population but still you have in Northern Ireland a huge experience of decommissioning weapons.

Jeffrey: It was a huge issue, as you say, in Northern Ireland, and it held up the implementing of the 1998 agreement for almost ten years. The problem being that the IRA was very reluctant to give up arms. The agreement was clear about the commitment that the political parties were making to decommissioning within two years, including the Sinn Fein, which represents the IRA, but it didn't commit the armed organizations themselves. That meant there was a long period of further negotiations before arms could be put beyond use. And this held up the establishment of political institutions, because Unionists were reluctant to sit in government with representatives of an organization that was still fully armed. So, it can be a very problematic issue. And one of the things that one can learn from that is, to the extent that it is possible, and it may not be, it's wise to be clear in any peace agreement, exactly how this issue is going to be dealt with.

Kulykov: General, from your experience, how can the disarmament of peaceful residents be conducted, and is there a place for a peacekeeping mission in this?

Smith: The peacekeeping mission can become involved in the collection of weapons, the certification that this force isn't there, doesn't have its weapons or whatever is required. But this requires this fundamental agreement to start with.

Kulykov: My last question is, again from myself, and it also leans on the Northern Ireland experience. In Ukraine we often hear the statement that you don't negotiate with terrorists. Now, not putting this stamp of terrorist to any participants in the Northern Ireland conflict, but I think that it was a very interesting and useful mechanism whereby some armed groups that had their political wings which could be involved in the negotiation process, thus bypassing the need to talk to those who had arms directly. What can you say, any other experiences in other countries? And how workable was this?

Jeffrey: I agree with you that the existence of a political wing and political representatives who are already taking part in elections is an advantage. It is still necessary to be clear about the terms in which they can be involved in discussions about a future peace settlement. But in my view, the settlement we eventually reached in Northern Ireland is much the stronger for having had Sinn Féin as the political representatives of the IRA involved in its negotiation.

Anderson: But there are cases, for example in the island of Mindanao in southern Philippines; the Philippine government worked directly with the Moro Islamic Liberation Front. There was no fig leaf about a political organization—these were the rebels. The same with Aceh; the Indonesian people were dealing directly with the rebels. And some of the issues you're talking about, like getting people to lay down their arms, you really have to have a way of engaging the people who have the arms one way or another. Maybe there's a fig leaf, maybe there isn't, but you do have to engage those people if they're going to comply with that part of an agreement—come to that kind of agreement and then comply with it.

Jeffrey: I think having said that, it is a very emotionally charged and difficult issue because the terrorists have caused great pain, great harm, great damage, and suffering. And the simple statement, "We mustn't negotiate with terrorists" is a powerful reason. I think nevertheless that eventually, there has to be, however indirectly, some sort of dialogue with the people who are causing the problem.

Anderson: And that doesn't mean they're absolved of everything they've done.

Jeffrey: No not at all.

Anderson: And, so, one of the issues that does arise, is an issue of how to go into the agreement, how will things like past crimes be dealt with?

Kulykov: General Smith, when you were commanding and taking part in peacekeeping missions, when there was a need to assess the situation on the ground and apply certain measures or to resort to some actions, who had the right of the ultimate decision? The military or the international officials? And how was this solved?

Smith: Well, it depends on the circumstances. There are three cases in the 1990s when I was in the UN, I was a General in Northern Ireland, and in NATO. In each case, there is a political authority to which I am answerable: The Security Council, the North Atlantic Council in the case of NATO, and my own government in the case of Northern Ireland. And it's here that, as I said at the beginning, it's helpful to distinguish between those things to do with the conflict—the actual acts of fighting and so forth—and those to do with the confrontation, the political underpinning of the whole business that you're engaged in. Now as a General you stand with a foot on both of those issues. But if you analyze it that way, it becomes clear whether your weight is on the conflictual one or is this a confrontational matter. And you start to make the judgement accordingly.

"There Has to Be an 'or Else.' Washington Analyst Whitmore on War, Ukraine, Russia, Hybrid Containment, and More"

with Brian Whitmore
5 May 2018

https://hromadske.radio/en/podcasts/ukraine-calling/there-has-to-be-an-or-else-washington-analyst-whitmore-on-war-ukraine-russia-hybrid-containment-and-more

Marta Dyczok: This Monday, on the 30th of April, President Poroshenko announced that the Anti-Terrorist Operation was over, and Ukraine was starting a new Joint Forces Operation. On the same day the first US Javelin missile launch units arrived in Ukraine. To explain what is this all about we have with us Brian Whitmore, Senior Fellow and Director of the Russia Program at the Washington Centre for European Policy Analysis.

Some of our listeners remember Mr. Whitmore was Senior Analyst at *Radio Liberty/ Radio Free Europe* in Prague where he gave us an excellent interview about a year ago. Thank you very much for finding time to speak to us again. Let's start with the what and why. What does this mean? For four years Ukraine has been on the receiving end of a war and defending itself. Suddenly it changed the name. What does this mean?

Brian Whitmore: That's a very good question, which a lot of us are trying to answer, and to be quite honest with you, Marta, I am having trouble figuring out what it means myself. It's hard to figure if it's simply a rebranding, or there is something significant here. There are couple of important points. The fact that the Law designates Russia as an aggressor country and establishes the territory of Donetsk and Luhansk oblast as temporarily occupied by Russia and uncontrolled by Kyiv and therefore Russia is held responsible for moral and material losses inflicted on Ukraine in these territories. This strengthens Ukraine's position in international courts. It also effectively rules out Russian peacekeepers ever being deployed in Donbas. It also appears to increase the power of the President who has now an authority to use Armed Forces without declaring martial law. The authority of the operation moves from SBU, Security Service of Ukraine, to the Joint Operational Headquarters of the Armed Forces. But beyond this, the proof is going to be in the pudding. We have to see how this plays out, whether it is going to spell a significant change in Ukraine's strategy in the war or not. I know some Parliamentarians are worried about the lack of Parliamentary oversight in the conduct of the war. So I think we have to see going forward. I know what everybody else knows from reading what's been written about this in the media and by talking to people in Ukraine about it. But I really don't know if this is going to change anything, if it's a rebranding or if it's a really significant change.

Dyczok: Well that's actually exactly what I was thinking. Is this going to be an escalation? Is it possible that we'll just have to wait and see? The other thing that caught my attention yesterday was the fact that the US is finally sending offensive, lethal weapons to Ukraine. The delivery happened on the same day as the announcement of this rebranding. That may or may not have been a coincidence. But the fact is that Ukraine has been asking for help. They have been saying, "We can't fight this war by ourselves, we signed the Budapest memorandum, the US guaranteed our security, now we are being attacked, please help us, give us weapons, let us buy weapons." Under Obama the answer was, "No." And now Trump is in the White House and the answer somehow became, "Yes." What do you make of that?

Whitmore: You mean the Obama Administration, and the personalities, who were much more cautious on this issue. The Trump Administration is a little bit more open to this. I think the atmosphere in Washington toward Russia has changed dramatically, for reasons that should require little elaboration since the last election in the United States. I think you do have an increasing bi-partisan consensus moving in favor of this. That just tipped it. This is one of those issues where there are compelling arguments on both sides. The argument against sending defensive lethal weapons to Ukraine was that (I've heard this argument made by very "Hawkish" military people) effectively, Russia has escalation dominance in Ukraine vis-à-vis the United States, and vis-à-vis the West in general because, let's face it, Russia is going to be willing to escalate more in Ukraine.

Dyczok: Right.

Whitmore: So, if the US sends anti-tank missiles, Russia will send stronger offensive weapons, so on and so forth. The argument against sending lethal weapons to Ukraine had nothing to do with not supporting Ukraine. It was about not wanting to escalate in a theatre in which the West does not have escalation dominance. Now that is a compelling argument.

Dyczok: Now what's changed?

Whitmore: Now there's another argument that Ukraine is not the only theatre of operation. In other words, for example, the Soviet Union had escalation dominance in Afghanistan. Not saying that Afghanistan was the same as Ukraine, but just looking at these two theatres. The Soviet Union supplied weapons, but the US supply of Stinger missiles to the Afghan Mujahedeen, leaving aside all the problems created later, did inflict a lot of damage on USSR, despite the fact that the Soviet Union had escalation dominance. So, the idea here is that if you raise the cost in Ukraine for Russia, Ukraine is not the only theater of operations that the Russian Armed Forces operating. So, if you raise the cost there, you raise the cost everywhere. There are compelling arguments on both sides of this debate, and I think that the changing attitudes towards Russia in Washington are due to the fact that the current administration is a lot less cautious. Making no value judgments about which of those things is better. We are seeing a change in attitude towards the conflict. We will see how this plays out. How Russia's going to respond.

Dyczok: Well that's my next question. You're a Russia expert, you've been watching Russia very carefully for a very long time. You're one of the top analysts. So, what do you think? How is Russia going to respond to this?

Whitmore: Russia is not going to let Ukraine go. This is seen in Putin's Kremlin as an existential threat: the emergence of a democratic Ukraine, the emergence of a European Ukraine, the emergence of a Western, successful Ukraine. Something we all want to see, is seen by this Kremlin as an existential threat. Any Russian imperial project begins and ends with Ukraine. The Putin regime understands that to see a democratic Ukraine turn West would mean the end of this regime. So, I think they're going to stop at nothing, which is why I believe the war in Ukraine is about actually much more than Ukraine. It's basically about the future of Western civilization, to be honest.

Dyczok: Well, starting with Putin and then the rest of the world, what you've just said makes me a little worried. Because if you're right, that Putin is not going to give up, and Ukraine is now saying OK, we are intent on de-occupying the Donbas, which basically means kicking Russia out, and we're launching this new operation, and there's this new weaponry appearing from the United States—to me that looks like an escalation.

Whitmore: It could be interpreted as such, for sure. I painted this very bleak picture, but if the West loses Ukraine, it's an even bleaker picture. Because Ukraine is not the end game here.

Dyczok: No.

Whitmore: Ukraine is the beginning. Because while there's a reason why a successful democratic Ukraine is an existential threat to this Kremlin, it's the same reason that the European Union, a successful, unified, strong Europe, is an existential threat to this Kremlin in its view. It's the same reason why a strong trans-Atlantic relationship is viewed in this Kremlin as an existential threat. The way I like to put it is that Putin's regime is not threatened by anything the West is doing; it's threatened by what the West is.

There is an assault going on against Western civilization right now. All these things are part and parcel of something larger. I'm working on what I hope to turn into a book about the key to understanding Putin is to understand the ideological part, and the kind of mafia part. It's kind of like the spook meets the godfather. The kleptocrat meets the ideologue. And how these two things operate together. And this is a larger view of Russia, where it's not just an ideological state, and it's not just a kleptocratic state, it's an ideological kleptocracy. It's both. It's a hybrid state. Putin's a hybrid man. He's waging a hybrid war. And we have to respond with hybrid containment.

It's hard not to get pessimistic about the situation now. But that's why Ukraine is so interesting in my opinion. So many times there's been dark history, and it looks pessimistic, and bleak. And then something happens and it just spins it the other way and makes it positive. Even in the past 25-30 years. We saw the Kuchma dark days, and then that changes. And then we saw the Yanukovych kleptocracy. And he got booted out. So, watching Ukraine's recent history, and longer history, it doesn't stay in those dark places. And I'm also still optimistic that Russia will find that spark, and change things.

There was a point in the Cold War when everything looked very bleak. We thought that the Soviet military was stronger than ours [US]. They were kicking our asses in the espionage game. But yet, we won. Why did we win? Because our model was superior. It's simply that simple.

Dyczok: Or, perhaps, their model wasn't working.

Whitmore: Well, because our model was superior. There was an effective alternative out there that was working and working very well. So, I think in the long run we're going to win this. In the short run, yes, we're going to see a continuation of the war in the Donbas. There's no question about that.

Dyczok: And that's so depressing. I have a friend from Mariupol and her parents still live there. And they say, "How much more of this are we supposed to endure?"

Whitmore: Oh I know.

Dyczok: How many more people have to be killed before this is all over?

Whitmore: It's not going to be over as long as this regime [Putin] is in power. It's not going to be over until they calculate that the costs of it outweigh the potential benefits. And again, they are looking at something that they see as existential. They don't see Ukraine as a separate country.

Dyczok: But I would isolate Putin from the rest of Russia's elite and society.

Whitmore: I would, but I would not isolate it too much. You would be surprised how many Russians do not view Ukraine as a real country.

Dyczok: That part I wouldn't disagree with. But, I believe that a lot of people around Putin like having power and wealth, but they also like to be part of the world. I think they like to be isolated. I think they want to send their kids to Oxford and buy property in Vienna.

Whitmore: This is where we beat them. This is their Achilles heel. Kleptocratic Russia needs engagement with the world. Ideological Russia can deal with isolation.

Dyczok: But the people with the power and money, they don't want the isolation. They don't want to vacation in Sochi (a resort town on Russia's Black Sea coast, site of 2014 Winter Olympics) and send their kids to MGU (Moscow State University), right? They want to be part of the world, for lots of reasons, including making money, but also being part of a cosmopolitan society. And Putin's actions are limiting their ability to do that.

Whitmore: This is our ace in the hole. We just need to learn to use it more effectively. I want sanctions to be made permanent. Another element of my hybrid containment policy is something that I call exclusion. Because for decades now, Russia has been able to have it both ways.

Dyczok: That's right.

Whitmore: They've been able to earn their money in a kleptocracy and stash it under the rule of law. They've been able to try and undermine the Western system while…

Dyczok: Using it to their advantage.

Whitmore: Right. So, we have to send the message to them that it's one or the other. You want to be North Korea, be North Korea. You want to be part of the West, abide by the West's rules. We can do that. There were things during the Cold War, like this institution called CoCoM that forbade the sale of any dual use technology to the Soviet Union and its allies. Let's deprive them of their iPads! Let them buy Chinese knock offs. Silicon Valley would scream bloody murder because they'd lose that market.

Dyczok: It's not such a huge market.

Whitmore: It's a pretty big market. But they're going to scream bloody murder over losing any market! But let's start thinking about things like export restrictions. Let's start thinking seriously about a SWIFT ban. Cutting them off from the world financial system.

Dyczok: That would work in an instant!

Whitmore: But that would harm our (US) European allies, and that's what gives me pause about that. It would be so disruptive to Europe's economy. The SWIFT ban is the financial equivalent of a nuclear weapon. Because it's going to hurt us too. But export restrictions. Let them choose. If you want to be North Korea, be North Korea.

Dyczok: They won't choose that. North Korea doesn't even want to be North Korea anymore!

Whitmore: This is our ace in the hole. I don't think we can win this on the battlefield in Ukraine. I think the best we can do is what the Ukrainian Armed Forces are doing right now. Fight Russia to a draw. And raise the cost. But in the broader war, we have escalation dominance.

Dyczok: There's been talk about peacekeeping as a strategy to end this conflict in a way that's face-saving and will prevent further killing.

Whitmore: That began to get some traction late last year. Putin surprised everybody by this, a lot of people were suspicious about what this would actually mean in practice, because let's say we get the peacekeepers in. The first question is, who are they going to be?

Dyczok: Who's going to qualify?

Whitmore: Who's going to qualify? Russians are of course off the table. CIS peacekeepers in general, are off the table, that's unacceptable to Ukraine. But any peacekeepers from any NATO countries are going to be off the board from Russia's perspective. So what kind of peacekeepers are we going to get in Ukraine? I don't know how we square that circle. I mean what are we really going to be talking about here? But let's say we get over that hurdle right, and you get some peacekeepers in Ukraine. Those who are suspicious of this will say OK, now we have a ceasefire in the Donbas, we're complying with Minsk, now Ukraine has to comply with its part of Minsk and that is effectively decentralizing itself to the point of dysfunction, right? So, I think there's a lot of fears that this would be a clever ruse on the part of Moscow. Quite frankly, what worries me, is that Russia's going to return to its old tricks in Ukraine, and rely on the political system being dysfunctional, that it will continue to try to exert its power through the oligarchs, and over time just wear Ukraine down that way. That's also a risk. We have to pay attention to the non-kinetic part of Russia's war as much as to the kinetic part. Because Russia is weaponizing things like corruption, and finance, and organized crime, and cyber space, and all sorts of other tools…

Dyczok: Effectively.

Whitmore: Very effectively. I think much more effectively than they are using their kinetic tools, to be honest. We have to be paying as much attention to this. One of the things I'm working on here at CEPA is to come up with what I call a hybrid containment strategy.

Dyczok: Tell us about it!

Whitmore: We're facing a hybrid war.

Dyczok: Yes.

Whitmore: This term has been used very loosely. We want to be careful about what we mean by this. I see two types of hybrid war. One is using non-kinetic means to prepare the battlefield for kinetic action. This is something Russia did in Georgia and this is something they did in Ukraine. But we also see Russia using non-kinetic means in Germany, the United States, in France, throughout Western Europe, in Canada. And I think I can reasonably assume that Russia is not planning to start a kinetic war with Canada or the United States anytime in the near future. This is something that we have to me a lot more mindful about containing. We need to have a coordinated, multi-lateral, coherent approach to this. Just like in 1947 we had a containment policy of the Soviet Union in a military sense. We have to start thinking about, how do you contain weaponized corruption? How do you contain weaponized organized crime? How do you contain weaponized finance? Because these are the tools, in addition to the military tools that Russia is using against Ukraine, they're going to be using against Ukraine across the board. And they're going to be using these tools against the West in general. The goal here is to, I think, not just subjugate Ukraine, but to destroy the European Union, to destroy trans-Atlantic unity. And we have to wrap our heads around this fact and be very mindful. The fact that we're in a war. Outside of Ukraine we're not shooting at each other…

Dyczok: Not with guns.

Whitmore: Not with guns. But that doesn't mean that we're not at war. So, we have to start thinking about that. Part of this is resilience. Part of this is reforming our own institutions. Vladimir Putin did not invent offshore. But he's using it very effectively, to spread corruption in Western society. To create networks of influence. He didn't invent money laundering. He didn't invent shell companies. Right? But he's using these things really, really effectively. He didn't create the polarization in our societies. But he's exploiting it. So, part of this is taking a good look at ourselves, and becoming more resilient. It's funny, the further east you move, you hear that term used more and more often. You hear it in Ukraine, you hear it in Georgia, you hear it in the Baltic States, you hear it in Poland. But as you move West and you say resilience, people kind of look at you like, huh? What are you talking about?

And this is what I mean. We have to look at our institutions, look at ourselves very clearly. And plug these holes. Because these things are becoming national security threats. Deterrence has to be an element of containment. There has to be an "or else." It was the lack of an "or else" that allowed Kremlin-backed hackers, before they even thought about hacking the National Democratic Committee of the United States, that led to the hacking of Estonian banks and government institutions in 2007.

Dyczok: And Georgia.

Whitmore: And Georgia in 2008. And later, where did they move on to? Well, they hacked the Bundestag. They hacked the Polish Stock Exchange. They hacked a French television station, posing as ISIS terrorists, to spread fear in France about migrants. They hacked a German steel maker. They hacked the US State Department.

So, the lack of an "or else," and they got away with it in Estonia. They got away with it in Georgia. They got away with it in Ukraine. They got away with it in Germany. They got away with it in France. They're going to keep going. There has to be an "or else."

It was the lack of an "or else" that allowed Putin's agents to assassinate Alexander Litvinenko in the UK. And to attempt to assassinate Sergei Skripal in the UK. Both of whom are UK citizens, by the way. It was the lack of an "or else" that allowed Russia to kidnap Eston Kohver, a law enforcement officer, from Estonian territory. And drag him back to Russia and put him on a show trial for espionage. For doing his job as a law enforcement officer inside Estonia.

Incidentally, very interestingly enough, what Mr. Kohver was investigating at that time, was a cigarette smuggling ring, run out of eastern Estonia, by Russian organized crime groups, and the FSB (Russian Secret Service) working in collusion with each other. And the deeper you dig into this, the more and more interesting it gets. Because this wasn't just a case of corruption with the FSB taking a cut from the cigarette smuggling ring and lining their own pockets. They were taking a cut to create what the Russian call a "chornaia kasa," a black cash box. And suddenly you have all this unaccountable black cash, that you can use for all sorts of other active measures, across Europe, and beyond.

So, this is an example how organized crime is being weaponized. There has to be an "or else." You have to have deterrence. And then the West has to be ready to retaliate.

Dyczok: So. Deterrence. This is a good phrase you've been using. I thought it went out of favour after the Cold War.

Whitmore: Yes.

Dyczok: But to wrap things back to supplying Ukraine with weapons, is that possibly part of that deterrence thinking, that perhaps Washington is coming around to?

Whitmore: Yes. I think the thinking here is that the West can inflict as high a cost as possible on Moscow in Ukraine, even given the fact that Russia has escalation dominance in that theatre, that this will raise the costs for Russia. And anything that raises the costs, will raise the likelihood that they will eventually have to sue for peace and back off. I think that's the logic there. My thinking is that, the thinking we're using in these hard security situations, we also have to be using in these non-kinetic situations. Where things like corruption and organized crime are being weaponized.

The Former US Deputy Assistant Secretary of Defence, Michael Carpenter, had a very, very good article in, I believe it was in *Foreign Policy*, right after the decision was made to supply Ukraine with the Javelins. He said this great. Now we have to help Ukraine defend itself against weaponized corruption. Because all the Javelins in the world aren't going to defend Ukraine if Moscow is able to continue to create networks of influence inside of Ukraine.

Dyczok: Inside Ukraine and in other countries.

Whitmore: And beyond!

Dyczok: I think the really interesting point you made is that Ukraine is not the "end game," Ukraine is really just Moscow probing.

Whitmore: No, it's not, it's the front line. Ukraine is West Germany. And I've made this argument before that the security of Ukraine is no less important than the security of West Germany was in the Cold War. That's the unhappy role that Ukraine has to play right now, along with Georgia. But these are the frontline states right now. This is the battle between two normative systems. One to the West that's based on all these things we hold near and dear: the rule of law, the rights of the individual, the sanctity of contracts. And one to the East that's based on cronyism, corruption, and the subordination of the law to power. The stakes are very high here, and the stakes are high not just for Ukraine, but for all of us. And these are our institutions that are at stake right now and these are the institutions that gave us everything we have that's good. So, I can't over-estimate how important this is and yes, Ukraine's the beginning, it's not the end.

Dyczok: You made the point that Ukraine has fought Russia to a draw, which I think is an excellent point. How do they get out of this situation militarily though? Because I hate to keep coming back to it because, you're right, the corruption and all those things are part of the war, but it seems to me that Ukraine is now thinking about what to do on the military front and I don't see any good answers there.

Whitmore: I don't see any good answers either. I don't see any good answers at all. As long as Russia insists on continuing this kinetic assault on Ukraine, the only thing Ukraine can do right now is to continue to fight them to a draw. And the West can continue to raise the costs with things like sanctions. We have to get away from this fixation that both sides need to implement the Minsk Agreement. I have a big problem with that. I had a problem with the Minsk Agreement when it was signed it, because effectively, Russia was allowed to participate as somebody who is helping resolve a conflict when in fact they were the aggressor. And they're very good at this. They create conflicts and then they present themselves as a broker or an honest mediator in a conflict that they created. They're probably not going to stop doing this, but we in the West can at least stop falling for it. I think we have to get away from this notion that both sides need to implement the Minsk Agreement and get away from that mantra. And this is where I think that new law is a very positive thing, where it basically designates Russia as the aggressor. This is self-evident and obvious to anybody that's been watching this conflict, but I like the fact that it is now part of a normative act passed by the Ukrainian Parliament. The territories of Donetsk and Luhansk are occupied. I'm surprised it took this long to get that in black and white in a normative act, but we're there, and that's good. That part of this I think is good, and a lot was made of the fact that this law doesn't say a lot about Minsk.

Dyczok: I think that was very deliberate.

Whitmore: I also think that was deliberate and I think that I actually like that. I think it's a very positive thing, because I think we have to call things as they are. Russia invaded Ukraine. Full stop. The responsibility for ending this war lies with Russia and Russia alone. Full stop. Ukraine has a right to defend itself. Full stop. I think we have to change the way we talk and think about this war. Full stop.

Dyczok: Thank you very much Brian, I think that's a really nice place to stop. The way we think about this war, and that leads perhaps to new approaches and new solutions.

Whitmore: Lets hope so.

"Was It All Worth It? Babchenko's Case and the Credibility of Ukrainian Authorities"

with Michael Bociurkiw and Kateryna Kruk
2 June 2018

https://hromadske.radio/en/podcasts/ukraine-calling/was-it-all-worth-it-babchenko-s-case-and-credibility-of-ukrainian-authorities

Kyrylo Loukerenko: This week the media reported that on the 29th of May, Russian journalist and Putin critic Arkadiy Babchenko had been gunned down in his Kyiv apartment. The next day, at a press conference we learned that Arkadiy Bachenko was in fact alive and well, and that the murder had been staged by the SBU, the Ukrainian Security Service, as a sting operation.

Today our first guest is Michael Bociurkiw, Canada-based journalist, global political analyst, and formerly spokesperson for the OSCE Monitoring Mission in Ukraine (2014–2016). We reached Mr. Bociurkiw on Skype. Michael, what is your personal feeling towards what happened?

Michael Bociurkiw: Thanks for having me. First of all, let's go back a little bit and talk about where we stood before all of these came out. What I mean is the reputation of Ukrainian Security Service. As many listeners I am sure know, they have quite bad reputation for botching investigations, for not following on leads. I am also thinking about a grizzly murder in broad daylight in Kyiv of journalist Pavel Sheremet two years ago, which still has not been solved. In fact, some of the Ukrainian journalists have come up with more evidence than investigators have. And there are other cases which have not been solved. Not one big fish, so to speak, from the previous administration has been put behind the bars.

So when they come out in a press conference that is broadcasted around the world in prime time and say, "We have foiled the plot and the journalist is alive; we have evidence." Well, I think number one it is great that the journalist Babchenko is alive.

But secondly, I think the honours fall on them very hard, and now it up to the President Poroshenko Administration to come up with the evidence why this was necessary. Why this was necessary to fake the murder, broadcast it around the world? There are a lot of questions that need to be answered. The Committee to Protect the Journalists in the past few hours has come out with an urgent request to President Poroshenko to answer many questions, including how imminently credible was the alleged threat to Babchenko? What evidence do they have, and why did SBU need to go extreme measures of announcing Babchenko's murder in order to stop the alleged plot and arrest the alleged organizer? Finally, the big question is, "Was it all worth it?" To fake the murder at a time when there is so much fake news going on. Russia is the biggest source of fake news in the world. It looks to some that Ukraine is taking a page out of that playbook.

Loukerenko: Actually, my question was what is your personal feeling about it? How did you receive the news and what was your second impression after his "resurrection?"

Bociurkiw: I was very saddened, because I practiced many years as a journalist, and still consider myself a writer. Whenever a person like this, who has such a distinguished record and who is so brave to criticize Putin, and who dies. We were all saddened. I started writing and tweeting about it. My good friend Zhanna Nemtsova, who knew Babchenko, wrote a very painful piece saying this is such a tragedy. Many other journalists wrote similarly about it. And then 24 hours later we woke up with breaking news that he is actually alive. I felt almost a sense of betrayal. On one hand, we are totally happy that he is alive. But secondly, could this really had happened? We, actually many of us, thought its fake news. I think many of us feel a dangerous line has been crossed and I will tell you why. When SBU or Presidential Administration or Yury Lutsenko (Ukraine's General Prosecutor) come up again with big news, we would feel that we need to double or triple check it. That is not a reputation any government or any person really wants.

Loukerenko: The SBU, the General Prosecutor and President Poroshenko himself claim that a plot was found and they averted at least one death, of Babchenko obviously, and also they say that about three dozen journalists are in danger. They called at least two names of people who may have ordered (contracted) it on Moscow's request.

Bociurkiw: I'll go back to what I said at the beginning. These very same people have a reputation for deceit or fabricating evidence. The President, and our memories are still very fresh, of his deception over the Christmas holidays—taking a secret vacation to the Maldives, and then having to say later on that he did do it. You can do this when you come from a platform or position of moral authority and you have this reputation for being honest.

If you look at the shoddy, embarrassing, I would say, performance of Lutsenko on Amanpour (CNN) the other night, when he was asked direct questions of what evidence do you actually have, he could hardly answer. So when you go to these extremes, to actually stage or fabricate a murder, and then you come out to the world and say sorry, it actually didn't happen. We did it because we wanted to save someone's life. You have to come out very quickly with some kind of answers and evidence as the Committee to Protect Journalists is demanding right now.

Loukerenko: Why do you think the Ukrainian authorities did this?

Bociurkiw: As I wrote in my *CNN.com* piece, I think they were desperate for some kind of "win." That having not solved many other cases, including involving journalists, they needed to come out and prove that they are capable of breaking a case. I hate to sound overly cynical, but as I've said in the international media in the past few days, one can't help but think that there is also an election around the corner. Poroshenko's popularity rating is in the single digits. They might have felt that they needed to prove they are capable of this big "win."

But I'll go back to what I've said in several panels in Ukraine over the past few months, is that reputation takes a long time to build up. And I do believe that in its arguments against Russia, in its statements on the hybrid war being played out in Eastern Ukraine, that up until now Ukraine has held the moral high ground. That its been believed. That the well of sympathy and support has been absolutely incredible. But then they go and within a few minutes I think they've caused a lot of damage to themselves. And that actually makes me very sad.

Loukerenko: So what about the international implications for this situation?

Bociurkiw: I've followed international media very closely, and I think it's almost a universal feeling: the international media feels it's been played. Actually a lot of the feeling is this is absurdity, and it's going to be a lot more difficult to believe the Ukrainian government henceforth. Now I think that sentiment also extends to many foreign governments. They're just in shock because a lot of them did issue statements of sympathy when they heard that Babchenko was killed. And then I have to add too, that monitoring the discussions on social media, especially among members of the Ukrainian diaspora, this has had the unintended and unfortunate consequence of dividing the community. I can't remember seeing as many heated arguments about whether this was feasible or not, whether it was a good idea or not. I'm hoping this will only be a temporary kind of flare up, but there are a lot of arguments taking place among members of the diaspora on social media on this one.

Loukerenko: And what do you think about domestic implications? Will it eventually actually help Poroshenko to succeed in the future Presidential elections?

Bociurkiw: I doubt it. If I read the poll correctly, yesterday when I was on Zik TV, they were polling Ukrainians on whether they thought this caused positive or negative impact on the country's image. And it looks like the majority said it caused a negative image to Ukraine. And you know I've been speaking to many of my former colleagues in Ukraine, and many of them actually support my position, that this perhaps was not a good idea. I think a lot of people feel that it could have been done another way. Don't forget the SBU is one of the best-resourced arms of the government, tens of thousands of employees. And I think this incident also raised questions about where are we with the reform processes? Especially with the SBU—it was supposed to have been broken up a long time ago, international donors are demanding that—and turned into a leaner organization that is focused on one or two main areas.

I think that the kind of negative sentiment towards Poroshenko is quite high, because I don't think that people feel like their lives are getting better. I don't think that people feel the safety factor, for example, in big metropolises like Kyiv, is getting better either. So this is happening actually relatively soon to the election season, and I think it could backfire on them.

Now, one quick thought: maybe they're going to surprise us. Maybe they're going to come out with a press conference and say, "Look this is what we have, there is no other way." And they need to say that this was an extreme measure, that we fake something, and that it's not going to happen again. Because that's why I use the term, "It's playing with fire."

Loukerenko: But this is, actually, what is happening. They are claiming that actually it was an extreme situation, and they are on the way to find how Russia is trying to influence the situation in this country.

Bociurkiw: I've listened to Babchenko as well, and I think I'm hearing things that he hasn't necessarily said publicly. But it does seem more and more that he might have been played to a certain extent. That the evidence that he was shown was very flimsy, and that out of fear, I think he agreed to take part in this. And I feel very badly for him, of course, having to go through this, and having to even deceive his family, friends, and colleagues. But you know given the very poor, acrimonious relationship between the security services and journalists, and him being forced in a way to collaborate with them, I think it could be very difficult for him to go about his job. Of course he's probably going to need 24/7 protection. It's very difficult to do journalism when you're protected by policemen all the time. And I'm also hearing from journalists and colleagues, what kind of credibility will he have as well. Again, maybe he had no choice. But this is a very, very serious step to take, for a journalist to collaborate with the state security services and be complicit in an operation that was staged, that was faked.

Our second guest is Kateryna Kruk, a journalist and political analyst. She is working with StopFake and is a Fellow with the European Values Think Tank in Prague.

Loukerenko: So, what's your personal feeling about what happened with Arkadiy Babchenko?

Kateryna Kruk: First of all, thank you very much for having me here, and having this discussion in English, for an international audience. For me, for a person who is working in English, on Twitter for years, it was a huge surprise to witness the reaction of foreigners to the case of Babchenko. And how at some point, everything became more about the Security Service of Ukraine, about Ukraine, and not about Babchenko himself. That is why I think it is very important to have more voices from Ukraine explaining our perspective, from people who are walking the same streets, and, obviously, living in the same country.

Getting back to your question about my personal reaction. I remember that at the moment I learned about the assassination of Babchenko, it was Tuesday evening, if I'm not mistaken, and I was with friends who knew him personally, who have worked with him. And immediately it became very personal for all of us. Because anyone working in the public sphere, in journalism, providing commentary, being a vocal critic of Putin, of Russia, of what they have done in Ukraine, and continue doing in Ukraine, and Syria, and other countries, we do understand that we are targets. Either on Twitter, by bots, or trolls, or threatening e-mails, but also even personally.

For me, personally, the most shocking detail was that he was shot at his home, in his own apartment. Meaning that there is no refuge, there is no place where you can feel safe. So the entire evening and then the next morning were very tragic, I think for many people in Ukraine, especially those who are involved in journalism, or the public sphere. It was mostly about self-reflecting, how the balance and peace that we see around us, we go to the city centre of Kyiv and everyone is smiling, singing, sitting on the grass, drinking coffee. And how this peace is so fragile. It takes just one shot to realise that our reality is very drastic. That we are at war. And we have a terrorist state, the biggest one in the world, against us.

But the moment I learned that he is actually alive, I felt nothing but pure joy. That he's alive! That we didn't lose yet another friend, yet another good friend of Ukraine, a good journalist whose work is brilliant. He's really worth reading.

Loukerenko: Basically, I felt the same. I felt this pure joy, but some people also felt different feelings. They felt that betrayal, I would say. This always happens, when you learn that there are lies. And you feel a little bit, or not just a little bit, betrayed.

Kruk: I was asking myself this question. And this is something that I would like to have more information on from the SBU. Did we really have to go through this emotional roller coaster? Because that was hard for everyone. Because at the very beginning we felt that we lost a dear friend of ours. And then the next day he's alive. And you ask yourself the question, what about all this pain, that was very much real, the mourning, the condolences that we shared with his family? And the memories that we revived about him. It was all very real. And I think that we shouldn't be ashamed of that.

We should question SBU whether it was really the best scenario possible. So far we do not have enough information. That is why I don't have a tendency (inclination) to say that it could have been done differently. I'm not an intelligence officer. I'm a journalist. I'm a political scientist. So, I can comment on the things that I am aware of and know about. We don't have all the details of this operation. Therefore, I think it's going to great lengths (going too far) to say, "You should have done it differently," based on the information we have so far, first of all on the interview that Babchenko himself gave yesterday, when he answered this precise question.

And he is the person who is in the very centre of the entire operation. He said that he didn't trust SBU at the very beginning, so it took some time for trust building, credibility building between themselves. But that when he saw the professionalism of the people who were working with him, then he trusted them that he could be part of this operation. And then they described all of the different points, all of the different stages of the operation, and he agreed to them.

And no matter how harsh our emotions were, just try to imagine for one second what he, his family, his wife, his daughter, his mother, and obviously all his close relatives had to go through. So, I think we shouldn't be too egoistic when it comes to this case. And remember all the time that it was, first of all about, saving a human life, a great human life. Secondly, it was an intelligence operation, which wasn't about faking something, about creating fake news. I'm really very much against using these words. Because that takes out of context only one aspect of the operation. And operation that was saving a human life. Uncovering an entire network that was planning assassinations of roughly 30 people. And obviously shaking the entire network. To prevent them from doing things like that in future. This is what it is about. Looking at the entire picture. And, obviously, asking whether it was worth it. But not in the context that I was personally very much involved, and was it worth it or not, but looking at the results, and the entire operation.

Loukerenko: Are you satisfied with the information published by the Security Service of Ukraine about the person who ordered this assassination? And also about the person on the Russian side? What is your opinion of the quality of the information released by the SBU?

Kruk: First of all, there is a specific style of the *modus operandi* of the SBU, which is giving information piece by piece. This is what we saw yesterday, for example, or during the past few days. That almost every two or three hours there was a new statement, a new piece of information, from the Ukrainian SBU. This is how they work. They don't give you the entire picture from the very beginning, or all at once. Also, I think to some extent, it may be the case that the operation is still going on. We're aware of the most public aspect. Because, obviously, taking into account Babchenko's popularity, it would be impossible, it would be simply impossible, to stage this sort of thing and not have a very big public reaction, both in Ukraine and abroad.

So far, what I find really appealing, and what I find really professionally done, are the video and audio recordings. Where you can see the suspects. Where you can hear their voices. This is very strong, solid evidence. Because if you have something just printed on paper, or if you have only the words of the SBU themselves, you know perfectly well that its not the most trusted institution in Ukraine. Then there could be room for speculation. Video and audio recordings of certain people—this is evidence which is much harder to shake. I'm still waiting for more details, because it was really confusing when Mr. Herman started answering questions yesterday at the courthouse, when they were deciding what was the degree of punishment for him.

Loukerenko: Mr. Herman is the suspect.

Kruk: Yes. Exactly. He is the first suspect who was detained by SBU.

Loukerenko: For ordering the murder, not perpetrating it.

Kruk: In fact, what he was describing himself as, is that he was a contact person between Russia and people who were to be the assassins. And this is the moment when it became confusing. Because he started saying that he is counter-intelligence. And in this case, you see the conflict between two institutions. To be honest, I think, so far, I'm not really convinced that he is counter-intelligence. Obviously, it might be the case that certain intelligence institutions haven't been closely in touch with each other, because there is this tendency towards internal conflicts. But I don't think this is the case right now. I think this is really wise advice that he got from someone, how to use the public reaction to the entire situation, of the entire operation, and picking up on this very weak point.

Loukerenko: Some international journalists, and some opponents of the Ukrainian President, and Ukrainian authorities, Michael Bociurkiw mentioned this in his interview, say that basically it was a special operation which was invented in order to help Poroshenko to win his presidential elections, which will be in a year.

Kruk: Well, first of all, in a year's time, no one will remember this situation. Because the intensity of life, of events in Ukraine is so incredible. You mentioned that I also work in Prague and many European capitals. I always have the feeling that the number of events that happen in Ukraine in one day, would happen in a month in a normal, calm European country. So, talking now about elections which will be a year from now is too far reaching. Definitely, based on the intensity of Ukrainian events, of political life in Ukraine, this is not something that can be remembered. We don't have this situation (election) immediately. I wouldn't say that this plays directly into the hands of Poroshenko. If solid evidence is presented by the SBU, it would rather have the effect of increasing the trust of Ukrainian society in the SBU itself but also in intelligence institutions more generally. I don't see that there is a direct link going directly to Poroshenko.

The second aspect, the reaction of foreign journalists and commentators on Ukraine. This was a very sad situation for me. Because, to be honest, we weren't only criticized by people who are always against Ukraine, like Russia, or some Russian puppets in Western countries, but also so-called "friends of Ukraine." And for me personally, people with whom I worked for the past four years on an almost daily basis since the Euromaidan. And I saw a very critical stance, a very critical assessment of the situation from them, and I was very surprised how, I don't want to use the word egotistical, but very much egocentric it was.

There was a nice blog written yesterday, published in the *Washington Post*, written by a Ukrainian journalist Maxim Eristavi, who is now a non-resident Fellow at the Atlantic Council. And I never use such words on my Twitter. But he very sharply said, "Dear Western journalists this situation is not about you, and it's not about how you felt about it but it was about saving a human life."

For me personally, the statement of an organization called Reporters Without Borders was a huge disappointment. Its one of the largest organizations which is aimed at protecting the rights of journalists. They are saying that nothing can justify faking a journalists' death. And I was asking myself, and also my readers, even saving someone's life? I think there is a great deal of not understanding the reality in Ukraine. That Russia has not only occupied Crimea, and is waging war against us in the Donbas, but it is also terrorizing Ukraine on different levels.

Many people have mentioned assassinations of Ukrainian journalists. But two years ago, there was a very prominent case, a very important one, when a high-ranking Ukrainian intelligence officer was killed. It was also a car bombing. His name was Maksym Shapoval. This was the person who was responsible for the work of the team that was collecting evidence of crimes against humanity, and war crimes by Russia in Ukraine. Evidence that was later used in international courts against Russia. This is a hybrid war. And when someone is talking about hybrid war, this is precisely the description. Not only media, not only fake news but also eliminating people who are key, who might show to the world, and to Ukrainians, obviously, that Russia is an aggressor.

Loukerenko: What do you think about this stance, this position of Western media, and some journalistic organizations? Will it eventually be transformed to a change of policies and attitudes of Western governments towards the Ukrainian government?

Kruk: I don't think so, judging by official reactions of governments, ambassadors, institutions, not journalists themselves or their personal opinions and journalistic organizations. There was a statement by the European Delegation in Ukraine, the EU commented that Ukraine has the right to protect people on its territory using whatever means. Once again, there are certain things that are getting out of focus. There are three things that I would like to mention. For me we are very critical, and this is something that I was also pointing out to my foreign friends (I work very closely with foreign journalists, and politicians, and think-tankers). First of all, it was not an operation aimed at lying to the Western audience, or lying to Ukrainians. It wasn't about ridiculing media as such. It is really very wrong to take just one aspect, one dimension of the entire operation out of context. Obviously, there was a very strong media element, the publicity element, but the entire operation wasn't about that. It wasn't about faking Babchenko's death and then showing that the SBU has resurrected him. It was something more. That is why we have to look at the entire picture, not only focusing on our own perceptions.

Secondly, I think, this situation is a very serious test for Ukrainians, but also for foreign journalists, and editors working with Ukrainian issues. Showing that there is a certain bias when it comes to covering Ukraine. This is something that was really widely commented among my network of friends on Twitter, for example. When we compared the perception of media and journalists when it came to the assassination attempt of the Skripals [former Russian spy poisoned in England], and also the victims of the use of the nerve agent, dozens of UK citizens in Salisbury. And back then no one, literally no one, I didn't see any articles, not even a tweet, that questioned the qualification and professionalism of MI6, the Security Service of Great Britain. No one was saying that UK is a fallen state, that they weren't able to protect their own citizens. And the damage is much greater that in the case with Babchenko. When it came to Ukraine, even before he was resurrected, a few hours after the information that he was killed, immediately people started criticizing SBU. Saying that it's so deeply infiltrated by Russian agents, that it's absolutely impotent, that it's not able to protect key figures when it comes to the Russian war. But then, the moment that we learned that actually SBU did something, SBU became an even bigger victim. It shows a certain bias that there is a critical stance towards Ukraine, and no matter what our institutions are doing, whether we are doing something, or whether we aren't doing anything, there is always criticism. So, I think this is the moment for many journalists and experts in Western countries to look in the mirror. And really think, do they have an objective stance when it comes to commenting on Ukraine.

And the last point that I would like to make in this regard is that it really shows, once again, that Ukrainians and our friends are repeating at every single occasion, that we have war in our country. That this is real. The West still thinks that you can deal with Russia in white gloves. That they don't like the entire operation because it was inelegant. Because it had an element of really staging someone's death, and making it public information, and so on. And I really have a feeling that the West still hasn't left its comfort zone, and still hasn't realised how serious it is for Ukraine. Because we have war going on. Almost every single day we receive news that someone was killed at the frontline. And the numbers of victims are thousands of people killed. And we have millions of IDPs, internal refugees. So, for us it's not about looking nice. And I do believe that based on the information that I have so far, and obviously not being a great fan of Ukrainian security services, but in this situation, in the Babchenko case, with what we know so far, I think it was worth going to these lengths to save a human life and to uncover the entire network. It was worth it.

"Everything Was Agreed in Advance"

with Oleksandr Danyliuk
16 June 2018

https://hromadske.radio/en/podcasts/ukraine-calling/everything-was-agreed-in-advance-ex-finance-minister-oleksandr-Danyliuk-on-his-dismissal-by-rada

Bohdan Nahaylo: I am delighted to welcome you to our latest edition of Ukraine Calling on *Hromadske Radio* here in Kyiv. We are very fortunate to have as our guest this week Oleksandr Danyliuk. Until a few days ago he was the prominent Minister of Finance of the country, but suddenly had to leave, was "dismissed." I hope that today we can shed some more light on the actual circumstances in which the departure of this key reformer in the government of Ukraine happened and allow us to draw certain conclusions. Welcome! Shall I address you as you as Mr. Minister, Mr. Ex-Minister, or simply Oleksandr.

Oleksandr Danyliuk: Oleksandr is much better.

Nahaylo: Thank you, Oleksandr! Let me begin by saying that I looked at your biography to prepare for this interview. It's very impressive. You come across as one of the younger generation of people who inspired hope after the Revolution of Dignity. Hope that finally professionals and reformers had come to the helm. How did you move form the private sector, from academia, from your impressive background to become a minister? Was it out of sense of duty, or simply because the job was there?

Danyliuk: Clearly, it was something inside me, something was calling me to come and work for the country at this important moment.

Nahaylo: And this was in 2016.

Danyliuk: Yes. Actually, prior to that I worked as Deputy-Head of the Presidential Administration. I worked on the reform agenda. I was the President's representative in the Cabinet of Ministers supporting the team of reformers in the government at that time.

Nahaylo: So, you were very much an insider.

Danyliuk: Yes. Not only professionally, but I also had very close, friendly, links to them because we shared the same values, goals. Naturally when the new government was formed, I informed the President that I do not see myself anymore with the Presidential Administration because it's good to be a part of the team, but if I want to do something, I have to be where things are happening. That is how I was offered a position as Minister of Finance. Actually, originally it was Minister of Economy, but then Minister of Finance. I realised that this was my opportunity because I think the position of Minister of Finance is where if you do your job properly you can move reforms forward very quickly.

Nahaylo: As an individual, you have ideas, and you have your ideals. The Ministry that you headed, was it still a kind of old regime, conservative body? Or was it already in the process of change in terms of mindsets and how things get done?

Danyliuk: It is somehow stuck in the middle. I cannot say that is an "old" organization, but there were people who had worked in it worked for 20-25 years.

Nahaylo: Have they adapted to the challenges of new times?

Danyliuk: They did very quickly. Why? Because one of the important roles of the Minister is to motivate people properly. Except if they are totally corrupt, whom you cannot motivate... The Ministry is a very professional ministry. Even if people have different views, if you work with them, you tell what you want, you give them responsibly, and they deliver. I created a motto, "The Ministry of Finance is a driver of reforms," and they started to believe in this. Which means, for example, if we have education reform and it requires some money, do not say just "no."

Nahaylo: Or medical reform…

Danyliuk: Yes, or medical reform. We just say "yes" and we help to launch it, to provide financial support, to think it through. And that would motivate people, because they would see the results, they are not just crunching numbers.

Nahaylo: Did you have the support that you expected? After six months, a year of doing your job, did you feel you had sufficient support from the Presidential Administration, from the government itself? Or at some stage, did you feel you had got stranded?

Danyliuk: When I came to my position as a Minister, I had realistic expectations. I did not have rose-tinted glasses.

Nahaylo: You were realistic?

Danyliuk: I was very realistic. And it was very important not to have naïve expectations. We were planning reforms. In Ukraine, it's not going ideally, not the way you wanted it to happen. So, when you plan something, you also plan how to ensure nobody will stop the reform. It's not like you have a wonderful idea of doing it, and you create a perfect model for the health care, education, or budget reform. It's not how it works. You need to have a perfect model, but you also need to think how to preserve it, how to implement it, and you know that almost everyone will be working against you. That's a typical model in Ukraine, unfortunately. This is not just about being smart. It's about being a fighter in moving things forward and having your team, your colleagues, near you, so you will be like an icebreaker to move things forward.

Nahaylo: Is this because of the mentality inherited form the Soviet period? Is this because of the vested interests and corruption? Wanting a piece of the cake before anything is done? Greasing the palms, as the Americans say? What is at the bottom of these obstacles to reforms?

Danyliuk: All of that. It's clearly vested interests. That's one of the biggest obstacles. Second is absence of desire to actually do things.

Nahaylo: Political will?

Danyliuk: Yes, political will. Sometimes what is claimed is not what you see in reality. And obviously another issue, which is very difficult to tackle even if you have political will, is the weak institutional capacity to implement things. We were moving on several reforms at the same time. And clearly, we don't have that many people capable of doing that successfully.

Nahaylo: And we are losing a lot of people because of the brain drain, or not?

Danyliuk: Brain drain from Ukraine is happening. But if you look at the state sector, this is where it's especially painful. Because you see people who can actually do things are losing their motivation. And this is very painful, because you need to have a critical mass of people to move ahead. That's why I was very sad to see people from the previous government, reformers, are leaving. And they don't want to return. This is a very bad message. When I was sacked last week, for me it's also very important not to send a message that that's it. Because there are still people around who are doing things. Yes, we work together, we were helping each other, but they need to move on. Otherwise it's a full stop, if not reverse.

Nahaylo: That's a very generous and principled position, and that's been noticeable in your behavior. Tell us about the importance of external motivation, the conditionality that has been built into providing credits and political support. To what extend was that a driving force rather than political will?

Danyliuk: Very good question. Short answer: that's what drives changes in the country. It's a short answer, but if you look at how things evolved in the last four years for example, initially if anybody like the, IMF or World Bank said something, it meant that it had to be done. Then approximately two years later, in 2016 when our government was formed, the public got tired. They said, "Why do we want a government if they do what others tell us to do?" And even if we understand it's the right thing to do, publicly we couldn't communicate this because people are just tired.

Nahaylo: It's not just, "We're tired," we have very widespread populism as a political weapon, and it's very easy to dump on, to criticize, without providing alternatives.

Danyliuk: This is very true, but it is two different things. Populism, you're absolutely right, I should have mentioned it first. But secondly, Ukrainians want to have a government that is capable of doing things without outside pressure. So obviously we're changing the rhetoric, we're saying we're doing it for Ukrainians. But I can tell you as an insider, yes, that's how we're communicating, but if it wasn't for the external pressure, those reforms would remain only in words. Conditionality really works. The Anti-corruption court, the law on it last week, happened only because it's a condition for the next IMF tranche. Period.

Nahaylo: OK, but for our listeners to understand, and some of them listen in Ukraine too, the proposals, the reform agenda that is given to Ukraine from outside, is it one that serves one hundred percent the interests of the Ukrainian people and the state for the future? Or is it self-serving to some extent in terms of what is expected of Ukraine, in terms of its resources, in terms of where it's seen to fit in to the economic model of relations? In other words, is the support that is given as altruistic, as generous as it seems? Or are there some, shall we say more sinister elements connected to the conditionality? I'm asking this because you often hear this in the streets, people say, "Oh yes, they're giving us loans but we'll be paying for twenty years or thirty years, and they just want to use us as a base for getting resources out of, etc." What would you say about this?

Danyliuk: Again, a very valid question. Based on my experience, obviously, there is a genuine desire to support Ukraine. And especially the package of support, financial support that we are currently using was formed at the most difficult time in our recent history. It was 2014-2015. As a result of the war, the economic, military aggression, as a consequence of the Revolution, we obviously needed support. And a package was put in place, there was a genuine desire to support the country. So, I understand where all these messages come from, but they have no grounds.

But what should be expected from every government official who works with these organizations is to protect the interests of the country. I wasn't an easy person (for them deal with). I have excellent relationship with IMF, with the World Bank, with EBRD, but each of these institutions had a very strong stance on some issues. I said no, that's not going to work, we're against that. Because we treat your money as money of our taxpayers. We should not waste money of our taxpayers, we should not waste your money, right? If it's loan, so what? We're going to repay it. So, with them I was a very tough negotiator sometimes. But actually, that attitude, that approach, builds trust. Because they see on the other side it's not just weak people who are desperate...

Nahaylo: They see us as partners.

Danyliuk: And that's important. The people you respect in life, in professional life, are the people who actually partner with you.

Nahaylo: But critics would say, and they do say, why have we not seen substantial, deep, radical reforms? What we've seen are either a kind of lip service paid to external creditors and donors, or cosmetic changes. Or changes that have the guts taken out at the last minute by people who are supposed to run the institutions that are created in the so-called reforms. This may be an exaggeration, but how do you see this?

Danyliuk: Another very good question. I was asking this question all the time, how to break this vicious circle. Well, the reality is that we didn't have a radical change of elite as a result of revolution, right? We have people who have been before and didn't deliver. So, if it's the same old people linked with each other, to the business elites. Some people are slightly younger, but their mentality is similar. Obviously, there are some exceptions of ministers who come out of the blue as technocrats, and they really were committed to carrying out the changes. So that's one explanation. The second is, that those people like the balance. Ukraine is, I call it, a perfectly balanced country. Where it's so difficult to change something because if you change something, immediately you pull the string that touches other people and they are trying to pull it back, to keep the balance.

Nahaylo: Some would say that "balance" equates "status quo."

Danyliuk: Yes, so difficult to break, so you need to be, how can I call it, a destroyer. But in a constructive sense. Because those links need to be broken, there are still monopolies with oligarchs impacting on politics, having an influence on the media.

Nahaylo: Are they as powerful as they were three or four years ago?

Danyliuk: They are less powerful…

Nahaylo: Particularly in the energy sector, or where are they less powerful?

Danyliuk: Overall, they are less powerful, but they're still very powerful. If you look at, for example, what is important for elections, right? It is financing, access to media…

Nahaylo: Control of the banks?

Danyliuk: Control of the banks… Yes, we're past this. I know what you are hinting at, but I think we resolved that issue. But look, the main media are owned by oligarchs and you can see how they position themselves, who they support. This is clearly a biased approach, and new people will not have access.

Nahaylo: So when was the moment that you realised that you could not put up with it anymore, that you had to speak out?

Danyliuk: Well, actually, I was quite vocal throughout my tenure. On the first day I said that ,"I will be fighting very hard, no one will stop me on state fiscal service reform, on the tax police reform." I was vocal, but at that time people thought I was not serious. When it comes to decisions, I was the first to attack the corrupt Head of State Fiscal Services, Roman Nasirov. So many state officials said, "Don't do it, that violates the balance," "Why are you doing it? Do you want him imprisoned?" And I thought, this is a club and I am not a member of this club. I am the Minister of Finance and this guy is the head of an important state organization that collects taxes. He should not be a member of the club he needs to work for people. He should not be corrupt, he should be professional.

Nahaylo: Club? More of a cartel than a club?

Danyliuk: Exactly. And it was a similar situation with the Prosecutor General. Nobody ever, ever had conflicts with the Prosecutor General in this country, because he is very powerful. Well, I don't care, because I believe it is an outdated institution that keeps Ukraine moving slowly. It suppresses businesses, civil society. That's what people are talking about, what I experienced in my job. So I would never accept just closing my eyes and keeping my position, and thinking about the security of my position, and ignoring things—no!

Nahaylo: You obviously weighed the risks and political price that you would probably have to pay for appealing to the G7 ambassadors and voicing your concerns. Was that to be interpreted as a plea for support and understanding from outside, or was it a broader signal, for society and people of your generation and reformers, "Look what's happening, help, SOS, let's try to mobilize and do something about the situation," or am I reading too much into it?

Danyliuk: You know, actually, there is a lot of background, but we don't have time to cover it. I don't want to oversimplify, but I will give you some insights. First, all of the ambassadors had a direct relationship to the reform of the state fiscal services. This is where I was moving forward and was being pushed back, blocked from all sides. They, being members of the supervisory board for that reform, knew how I fought for it, how critical it was for me, and we used the money of those countries, donor money and technical support, loans, to reform the state fiscal service. So, it was my duty, first of all, to tell them what is happening. That is A.

And B. I also have a very good relationship with the ambassadors, and they know how difficult it was for me. They would tell me, "You need to stick around and push things forward." And obviously when they got the news that there could be a resignation, they were concerned. I wanted them to understand the real reason because we had trust, so I had to do it. It was maybe a last resort because I had exhausted all other options. Okay, that was done, and I think it was the right thing to do.

Nahaylo: And you also said publicly, "I will not resign."

Danyliuk: I will not resign, because I will never give up. If someone wants to get rid of me then good luck, do it, but it is not because I am weak. I will fight to the end. Why? Because I believe that what I was doing, my team, my colleagues were doing, is very important for our country.

Nahaylo: Were you disappointed by the vote to dismiss you? The Prime Minister submitted the proposal to fire you on the same day that the law on the anti-corruption court was passed on its second reading. You were, kind of, slipped in through the back door. One issue went through, but the more contentious one remained with us. What did you feel? Were you disappointed that so many deputies actually voted for your dismissal, knowing your record?

Danyliuk: I looked around the Parliament, and I know all of them. I know who is good, I know who is bad, and I wasn't disappointed, no. Everyone reacted in the way I expected they would, and that reflects the quality of the Parliament and their principles.

Nahaylo: Did they react as per a scenario that was worked out for the voting?

Danyliuk: Everything was agreed in advance. That's how the Parliament works. No surprises. Everything is pre-agreed. Deals were done. If you vote for the resignation of the Minister of Finance, you will get such and such, either financial support, or something else, we will give you such and such a position. Unfortunately, it was like a bazaar. And I know how this type of market works. I want the Parliament to be different. So, I'm looking forward to the next election. That's why I was blocking the use of state money to make the elections unfair. We have to do a lot as a country, to change the quality of our institutions, including the parliament, including the government. The country deserves better.

Nahaylo: Are you prepared to go into politics yourself to make the country better?

Danyliuk: Look, I have my rules, right? I know that when I'm tired, I shouldn't make any decisions. For many years I was thinking about returning to the private sector. That's still an option. At the end of the day, I paid a very serious price and also my family. But I am also committed to work for the country. So, I need to have a rest. I need to rethink everything. And then I will make a decision. I'm not evading the answer.

Nahaylo: Now looking back. It's only been a few days since you left your Ministerial post. What do you see as your main legacy in those years that you were there? From April 2016 till June 2018, those two years. When you look back, say in five years time, what will you be proud of?

Danyliuk: We did a lot in terms of reforms. Mid-term budgeting. We fought corruption in the VAT refund area. We nationalized PrivatBank. That was a very dangerous and very complex move that everyone was shying away from, because it was so risky. But I also understand that the question is, "Where will Ukraine be in five years?" Because if there will be a reversal, I will not consider this as a legacy. So, for me now, the real legacy is two things. First, it is that the Minister and the team learned how to work together, how to be motivated, how to change the country. This is now inside them. Nobody will take it away from them.

And second, I was from day one actively and vocally working against the system. And that actually motivates other people to do the same. And this is also, I believe, a legacy. I'm sure there will be more people like me. And there are people like me. We need to fight till the end. You cannot be loyal to everything and expect the country to change. You need to break the rules.

Nahaylo: What do you feel personally, looking ahead as an economist, three, five years down the road, will Ukraine sustain this, even if it's not a full-fledged, movement towards transformation, towards modernization, towards democratization? Will it stay on that trajectory? Or will it meander off somehow?

Danyliuk: I think even if we stay on this trajectory, and move slowly, as we are moving now, we are destroying our country. We are destroying the future. Even if its a case that we reverse now, but later there will be a new momentum to go much faster it may be better than just moving slowly and telling people, "We're doing reforms." Because that is what people hate us for. They want to see results.

Nahaylo: And two percent, or three percent growth.

Danyliuk: Yes, exactly. Because we started at the same level as Poland, and now Poland's GDP per capita is way ahead of us.

Nahaylo: Are there any obvious models for Ukraine to look at? Or should it just go its own way.

Danyliuk: I've been involved in reforms for many years. I can tell you that solutions are important, models are important. But much more important is actual, real desire, and commitment to change the country. That's it. Because you realise that there are other models. But you do it for the benefit of the country. Not to keep your position. Not to keep your wealth. Not to secure your future. With that attitude no model will help. I think the commitment, and sincere desire to change Ukraine, to have the institutional capacity to do that, that's what will change the country. And we need to move very, very quickly. Our people deserve it.

Nahaylo: And as a parting message, it can be to your listeners, it can be to your staff that you've left behind, what is your parting thought, or whatever you want to say?

Danyliuk: [Pause] You got me on this.

Nahaylo: It's tough. I ask all my guests this.

Danyliuk: All I can say, is this is only the beginning. For all of us. It's only the beginning.

"The Good, the Bad, and the Very Ugly. Michel Terestchenko on Ukraine Regional Politics"

15 September 2018

https://hromadske.radio/en/podcasts/ukraine-calling/the-good-the-bad-and-the-very-ugly-michel-terestchenko-on-ukraine-regional-politics

Bohdan Nahaylo: It's my very great pleasure to invite a very special guest today to Ukraine Calling. It's Michel Terestchenko, who comes from the celebrated Terestchenko family, particularly famous at the end of the 19th and beginning of 20th centuries. He's their direct descendant, and he took a very conscious political, cultural, economic choice, which he'll explain to us a bit later, to leave France where he grew up, and where he was educated. And, as a French citizen, he came to Ukraine, and now is the mayor of Hlukhiv, the famous old Ukrainian Cossack city, which is situated in the East of Ukraine. So Bienvenu Michel.

Michel Terestchenko: Glad to be with you Bohdan.

Nahaylo: Michel, let's start with more of a philosophical, or historical, question. This year, 2018, is a hundred years since Ukraine attempted to establish itself as an independent state. Now we know that one of the Terestchenkos was a key figure in the Russian Provisional Government, and that Terestchenkos had been very active in promoting cultural and public life in Ukraine when it was part of the Russian Empire. What do you feel 100 years later as their descendant?

Terestchenko: Well, I think we all agree that the last 100 years, and especially the Soviet period, were particularly cruel, particularly tough for Ukraine. And my feeling now when I come back to Ukraine is basically that I find it more or less at the point where my grandfather left it in 1917. My grandfather, also Michel (Mykhailo) Terestchenko, was the last Minister of Foreign Affairs of Russia [before the Bolsheviks seized power]. But he was a Ukrainian, and as a Minister he took several (important) decisions. One of them was to give his own house where he was born—he was born in 1886 in a house which is located on 36 Taras Shevchenko street (this house right now is collapsing, being demolished unfortunately, although we tried to protect it), but he gave his house to the UNR.

Nahaylo: The government of the Ukrainian National Republic (UNR).

Terestchenko: Yes. And the first members of the UNR Directory were chosen in this house. It is an historical house, I would say. Secondly, as Minister of Foreign Affairs of the Provisional Government of Russia, he gave five oblasts (regions) of what were then called by the name Southern Russia to Ukraine, to the UNR. That was on 30 June 1917. It caused a shock. He had been in Kyiv with Alexander Kerensky and Irakli Tsereteli, at the negotiations with the young UNR, and it was such a shock that when they came back to Petersburg it brought down the government. The Cadets (Constitutional Democrats) left. Prince Lvov (then Prime Minister) decided to leave the Provisional Government, and that was when Kerensky took over. Basically, all because of my grandfather. So yes, he was important. He left the Russian government at the point when very serious questions about the independence of Ukraine, and the future of Ukraine, and about friendship or war with Russia, were still to be discussed and to be decided. And those questions are still relevant today.

Nahaylo: Now, less than 100 years later, you took a very conscious decision to return to your roots, to your family's roots. Was that out of nostalgia? Was it a sense of being Ukrainian? In fact, I wanted to ask you, when you were growing up in France, the Russian émigré community, "the white emigration" is very strong there. Were you not primarily influenced by them?

Terestchenko: No. I was not part of the Russian diaspora in France. My grandfather was considered a devil. I remember when I was seven years old and I was in school in France, Patrick Golitzin, he was the descendent of the very noble Russian family—

Nahaylo: The Golitzins.

Terestchenko: And I remember when I came to his house (I was only seven years old) and we wanted to play together. I met his father, Prince Golitzin, and then Patrick told him this his friend was Michel Terestchenko. I was ready to shake his hand, but Prince Galitzin refused to give me his hand. So no, my family has always been a little bit apart. My grandfather lived between London and Monte Carlo, also Portugal and Paris, but we were not part of the Russian emigration.

We were not really part of the Ukrainian diaspora because my grandfather decided to build a new life. He was still young in 1917, he was only 30 years old, and he decided that we will be French, and we will speak either French or English. So, I did not have any base in France that tied me to Ukraine.

Just after the collapse of the Soviet Union I decided to come to Ukraine, and here the genes did their thing. I mean it was extremely pleasant to be on Tereshchenkivska Street where all my family had lived. Extremely pleasant to see the very good memories that people of Ukraine kept of my family. People were extremely friendly. I had been in the United States and I had found the same enthusiasm, the same entrepreneurship in Ukraine as in the States, and I liked it very much. So, I tried to help.

Nahaylo: Why Hlukhiv?

Terestchenko: Why Hlukhiv? That's a big question. It's the homeland of my family (батьківщина моїх батьків). That's where all my ancestors are buried. But it seems to me that that all came after Maidan.

Before Maidan I was like an expat. I was like a tourist. It was pleasant in Ukraine, I took in the best of it and I didn't care much for the bad part of it, because I didn't feel myself as a Ukrainian but as a French expat.

But after Maidan it changed. On 20 February 2014 I was in Hotel Ukraina and I saw 14 bodies, 14 members of the Nebesna Sotnia [Heavenly Hundred] who had been killed. They were there in Hotel Ukraina and I saw them. And this moment was a very strong shock for me and for many people. And I said: "Well, I have to help."

Those guys, mostly young guys, will not have died for nothing. We have to realise their hopes and ideals concrete. We have to turn this page. We have to end 350 years of Russian colonization and start a new life for Ukraine: European, Western, civilized, democratic, and if possible, without corruption.

So, I believed in this dream. But I found myself unable to help in Kyiv, because Kyiv has so much. There was Klychko here, Poroshenko, and all the guys who were on the scene during the Maidan... (and I believed) they would take the helm and everything would be okay.

But I could probably help the people of Hlukhiv, because Hlukhiv is on the border with Russia, 300 kilometres east of Kyiv, and there people are not ready. For them Maidan was something you watch on TV. But they were not ready to turn the page. So, I tried to help.

Nahaylo: I'm talking to Michel Terestchenko from the famous Terestchenko family, who's currently the Mayor of Hlukhiv. So, you arrived in Hlukhiv. How were you received? As a stranger?

Terestchenko: Well I couldn't be a stranger in the city where my family built ten historical and still active buildings: the university, agricultural college, the bank, two schools, two hospitals, and their own residence, which is now the Institute of Flax and Hemp. So, no, I couldn't be anonymous in Hlukhiv.

But it was a surprise for me when people asked me to be the Mayor. I was not really ready to be a mayor, especially a mayor in Ukraine. I told them I was ready to help. I already had a small investment there, a small scutching mill for flax and I was helping the Institute for Flax and Hemp, which is in the former residence of my family in Hlukhiv. I was helping them, to work in cooperation with French people who do the flax and the hemp, and to develop their assets, to develop all the new patents that they had for selection, and so on.

So, I was already working a little bit in Hlukhiv, but I did not know anyone particularly. And then people said, we want things to change also in Hlukhiv. We don't want to be a no-man's land between Russia and the European Union. And you know that the plan of Putin is that between the Russian Federation and Europe there would be some kind of…

Nahaylo: No-man's land, buffer zone, cordon sanitaire…

Terestchenko: …zone of no law, of contraband, where barons are just controlling everything. And the people of Hlukhiv said, "We were the capital of the Ukrainian Cossack State, the Hetmanate, for almost 100 years. We were very civilized. We have a very high-level university. And the many of the people have received a very high education. We want to be Ukrainian, and don't want to be Russian, or to live in a no-man's land."

Nahaylo: The Wild East?

Terestchenko: The Wild East, but basically without Rule of Law, and banditism, etc. And people say that for the past 20 years, this oblast, especially the northern part where Hlukhiv is, has been controlled by a mafia. And this mafia came from Dnipropetrovsk (called Dnipro now) 20 years ago and tried to control everything. Every director of every school, university, college, every chief doctor, every chief of the Pension Fund. Every chief of whatever institution from the budget that you can name, is a member of the clan of Andriy Derkach, who is our Member of Parliament, representing Hlukhiv.

So, it was a totally ideal situation for Putin and his wish to make this a no-man's land. But it is also a big risk for Ukraine, because all those people are pro-Russian and the Russkiy Mir is very strong in Hlukhiv. We have a monopoly of the Patriarchate of Moscow, there is no Patriarchate of Kyiv. Until now, even after three years, I still couldn't give any plot of land to the Kyiv Patriarchate to build their church, because nobody wanted to take the risk to vote for it. Immediately Derkach would be applying some kind of repression against those people. I am a free man, but unfortunately the people of Hlukhiv are totally under stress and pressure…

Nahaylo: Michel, you've shown courage, you've shown leadership. You've come up against some very fierce and nasty resistance. Have you feared for your life?

Tereschenko: No, I've never feared for my life. I understand that if I am the Mayor of Hlukhiv, like the grandfather of my grandfather, Mykola Tereschenko, who was Mayor for 22 years. I feel he was willing me to do that and he's protecting me. I do not fear for my life, at all. But I fear a lot for the quality of life of the people that are helping me.

Nahaylo: We've read a lot about the problems that you encounter from the mafia, the attempts to besmirch you, to denigrate your reputation, to destroy you in effect. Where do things stand now? Have you somehow managed to find a position where you feel more comfortable, where you see progress?

Tereschenko: Unfortunately, not at all. The situation is getting worse and worse. I think the deal with the President is such… When I started, when I ran for mayor, I was willing to help the President [Petro Poroshenko]. And the first time I met him, on 15 November, right after my inauguration, he was very warm, very supportive; he spoke very nicely about this challenge and said that he will help, and he will come himself to Hlukhiv. Not only did he never come to Hlukhiv, but he did all the contrary. For me, it's just… I do not understand. If there is someone who betrayed me most in my life, it is Poroshenko. And I think he betrayed not only me, but basically all of Ukraine. I trusted him, but now for me…

Nahaylo: What's happening now?

Tershchenko: He basically gave the oblast to Derkach. Even if he said he would do the contrary. I think for some business reasons, or maybe because of some kompromat (compromising material) that they have on him. I don't know why he was obliged to give the oblast to Derkach. I think the only thing he (Poroshenko) said, and that is why I don't fear for my life, "You can do anything you want, you can get rid of this French guy if he is bothering you, but I don't want any scandal. Especially not international scandal." So very strangely, I feel very safe. But everything else is possible. Which means the Protocol Against Corruption, forty lawsuits, three Protocols against Corruption, nine criminal cases. I have to fight in the courts all the time. They are trying to get me out by all possible means: falsification, provocation. They buy my deputies.

The prosecutor is against me all the time. It's not even persecution. It's sadism against me. You cannot even believe what's happening and what's happened to me. It's started at the demand of the governor. He is a total bandit. He is my main enemy in the Sumy oblast. It's like Chicago now at the time of prohibition. This governor is taking all possible means including very illegal means to get me out because he is Derkach's man.

Nahaylo: So they launched a war of attrition against you, trying to grind you down and force you to leave.

Terestchenko: This is a David against Goliath battle. Unfortunately, I am not as strong as David.

Nahaylo: Michel, obviously this conversation has gone somewhat differently than I had planned. I thought we would talk more optimistically, about a family tradition. Let's look ahead. We have elections coming up. Of course, there are a lot of people who say that without fundamental change…

Terestchenko: There is no change in Ukraine right now, no decentralisation.

Nahaylo: So, we can only foresee stagnation? So, you are not feeling any impact of de-centralization, no control of budgets locally?

Terestchenko: Right now, it's not decentralization. Everything is in the hands of the governor. The governor is basically acting on political instructions of the President or members of Parliament that have leverage on him.

We did not see decentralisation in Hlukhiv. We are totally deprived of any financing for infrastructure, regional development, ecology, social-economic development.

I do not see anything good right now. I can see grants are available, but they are all given to grant–eaters. The corruption has never been as high as today. Much higher than at the time of Yanukovych, at least in the Sumy oblast. The reforms are just an imitation of reforms. In Sumy region we still do not have medical reform going. Everything is zero. This government is a total failure. It has betrayed the people of Ukraine, especially the people of Hlukhiv. Yes, we need to prepare for elections, but unfortunately, I do not see a light at the end of the tunnel. In Sumy oblast now we are preparing for the Parliamentary elections.

Nahaylo: In October 2019.

Terestchenko: If I am still mayor of Hlukhiv. Probably, I now have to consider doing something else. I understand that decentralization is not working. That the governor is just a political instrument of the President, unfortunately, against the people and not for the people of Ukraine. There is no other presidential candidate in my eyes that can change the system. The system now is not working for people that were on Maidan. They (the leaders) did not destroy the old system, they made it work for them. All the candidates that I see will do the same thing, so the system will continue. So, we have to start the fight on another level. I will probably enter the battle for the Parliamentary elections in order to fight in the Parliament. It's basically the only place where you can do something.

Nahaylo: Looking forward let's hope that changes do occur, that civil society will reawaken again, lesson are drawn, and mistakes are not repeated. It's been a great pleasure to talk to you. I wish you strength, endurance and I hope your message will get across and people will pay attention not only to politics in the capital but also to the very serious challenges that more remote communities face.

Terestchenko: Thank you, Bohdan. Just to finish. You started by reminding us of an experiment by my grandfather, who was a Minister of the Provisional Government. You know our descendants. I am very scared now. The period of reforms, the provisional situation... I am very scared that it will end up the same way it happened in 1917. We have people dying at the front everyday to give us time and possibility for reforms but unfortunately, we have lost four years of reforms. Everything is going wrong. The police are more corrupt than before. The justice system is more corrupt more than before. The Presidential Administration is just a nest of corruption.

"Resurrection of Christianity in Ukraine. Prof. Jaroslav Skira on Religion and Politics, and Newly Created Orthodox Church of Ukraine"

23 December 2018

https://hromadske.radio/en/podcasts/ukraine-calling/resurrection-of-christianity-in-ukraine-prof-jaroslav-skira-on-religion-and-politics-and-newly-created-orthodox-church-of-ukraine

Marta Dyczok: Ukraine hit the international headlines again, but with a good news story. It created an independent Orthodox Church on Sunday, the 15th of December. To explain how this happened and what it means, we have with us Professor Jaroslav Skira. He's a leading expert on Eastern Christianity. He's the Acting Director of the Metropolitan Andrey Sheptytsky Institute of Eastern Christian Studies, at the Faculty of Theology at St. Michael's College at the University of Toronto. And he's also Associate Professor of Historical Theology at Regis College. Thank you very much for finding the time to speak to us, Professor Skira.

Jaroslav Skira: Thank you very much. I'm glad to be on the radio with you and to make your acquaintance.

Dyczok: Let's start with the "What." An event happened in Kyiv last Sunday that some are calling historic. Can you remind our listeners of *Hromadske Radio's* Ukraine Calling exactly what happened?

Skira: On December the 15th in St. Sophia church in Ukraine, a unifying Sobor, or council happened that brought together a number of Ukrainian Orthodox bishops, clergy, and laity, toward the healing of schisms that have been plaguing the Ukrainian Orthodox Churches over the last 100 years. And this essentially was an attempt to bring these various Churches and clergy and laity into a unified structure. And here when I talk about a unifying council, I'm referring to three major jurisdictions in Ukraine, which were: the Ukrainian Orthodox Church of the so-called Moscow Patriarchate, and two other Churches, called the Ukrainian Orthodox Church of the Kyivan Patriarchate, and the Ukrainian Autocephalous Orthodox Church. And those last two were seen as being in schism by global Orthodox Christianity for many years.

Dyczok: Can you explain to our listeners why there were three Orthodox Churches in Ukraine until now? And what schism is?

Skira: Certainly. Ukraine had been attempting for many years to establish nationhood, and with that nationhood was an attempt to establish a singular Ukrainian Orthodox Church on the territories of Ukraine. These attempts date back from the 1920s right up to today. And what had happened in most recent times, is that because of the Soviet revolution and the rise of communism in the Soviet Union, the Ukrainian Churches, both the Orthodox and the Eastern Catholics, were suppressed and subsumed under the Russian Orthodox Church. And it was only when Ukraine declared independence in 1991, that there emerged a Ukrainian Orthodox Church that would be proper to Ukraine. And that Church began to seek independence from the Russian Orthodox Church. And through various attempts at independence, or what we would call autocephaly, that is, self-governance, there were disagreements amongst some of the clergy and with Moscow, which led to a schism, which basically means a division within a Church. Part of that group remained faithful to being in communion with the Russian Orthodox Church, and part of the group formed what is known as the Ukrainian Orthodox Church under the Kyivan Metropolitanate, or the Ukrainian Autocephalous Orthodox Church. And it's those last two Churches that were considered to be out of communion, or in schism with the rest of Orthodoxy.

Dyczok: They're out of communion, in schism, does that mean they're illegal, illegitimate? And again, why is there the Russian

Orthodox Church, and then there's these Ukrainian Orthodox Churches that are in schism. What does that actually mean?

Skira: The basic principle of unity within Orthodox Christianity is that a Church is canonical. By canonical I mean it is recognised by the other Churches and recognised in its celebration of sacraments. You can go from one Church to another Church and take the Eucharist and pray with them. Being in schism, or division, means that you are not recognised by these other Churches. And so it's a form of disunity. If you use a modern analogy from politics, it's like one state not recognizing the existence of another country; not recognizing its borders or its government, and that's what effectively happened to a significant portion of the Ukrainian Orthodox faithful in Ukraine.

Dyczok: Thank you, that actually explains things really clearly. So why did it take so long for this to happen? Ukraine declared independence in 1991, and this unification happens in 2018. What were some of the obstacles?

Skira: Part of the issue has to do with Ukraine as an emerging state or country after the fall of the Soviet Union. In many ways it was still under the control of the colonial imperial powers of Russia. It was still learning to walk on its own feet. You also had the same thing within the Church structures. In the 1990s there were attempts to establish an independent Orthodox Church, and those attempts failed. And that's kind of where we are today. You didn't have unanimity among the various Orthodox clergy and bishops; you didn't have the goodwill amongst those who are in the Russian Orthodox Church and the Ukrainian Orthodox Church to establish a distinct structure. So really, the process that we see today is the process of maturation, where you have not only the state reaching a point where it recognises it wants to affirm its membership within a European Union; it wants to rid itself of corruption; it wants to function in democratic means; it also wants to shake off the tutelage of any influence from Russia. And with that comes the maturation also in the consciousness of its believers, who have been seeking for many years to regain this kind of canonical status, where they would enter into unity with other Christians.

From the Christian perspective, the problem is really a sin of Christian division, where you do not recognise a fellow Christian as being a part of your Church, or not fully part of your Church. There are many layers to why this has happened, and this just seems to be a time where you have the alignment of the stars, so to speak, that provided an opportune situation. And part of the opportunity is really something that had backfired for Russia and for the Russian Orthodox Church. In wanting to still continue to keep the Ukrainian Church under its tutelage, the war in Eastern Ukraine and Crimea has effectively put a wedge between any goodwill or symbiosis that Ukrainians would have had in Russians. And that has further pushed Ukraine into developing this consciousness, akin to what happened during the Euromaidan movement, where you had people wanting to affirm their own dignity, they wanted to affirm their independence, they wanted to affirm their freedom. And again, coming with that also includes the idea of the Church. Wanting to affirm that it is a Church that is meant to minister to the people on the territories of Ukraine.

Dyczok: Well, politics and religion have a very close relationship, as you've just been saying. To what degree is the decision that was reached in the unification of the Church is this a political decision? Is this a religious decision? Is it a little bit of both? And is the significance more political or religious?

Skira: I think you have to recognise that this is primarily an issue based within the Church and the faithful. Here you have the Churches wishing to affirm that they are a distinct entity within global Christianity; that they want to minister to their own faithful; that they want to be in unity with other Christians. This is part of a broader movement within global Orthodoxy. It's also a political issue because this is a way where the Ukrainian Orthodox Church and Ukraine itself will see itself as casting off any vestiges of soft power influence that the Russian government and the Russian Church would have in Ukraine. And so, this unifying Sobor was held in St. Sophia, which is a very symbolic place because in Constantinople, or Istanbul, there is this major church also called Hagia (St.) Sophia, which was traditionally the centre of the Ecumenical Patriarchate. And the Ecumenical Patriarch exercises a leadership role within all of the independent Orthodox Churches, and he's recognised as an elder among the Orthodox Churches.

And this was also recognition on the Ecumenical Patriarch's side that he must do something to heal this schism and division within global Orthodoxy and Christianity. And I think when you look at the videos and the images from the actual Sobor itself, in answer to your question, you'll look at the head table of all the delegates, and in the centre is the Metropolitan Emmanuel of France, who is representative of the Ecumenical Patriarchate, who is chairing this session. To his left is Patriarch or Metropolitan Filaret, who was the leader of the major Ukrainian Orthodox Church, the Kyivan Patriarchate. And sitting to the Chair's right, was the President of Ukraine, Poroshenko.

And when they announced later on who the new Patriarch or Metropolitan of the newly established Ukrainian Church would be, and his name is (Metropolitan) Epiphaniy, on stage were two representatives of the Ukrainian government. In answer to your question, is it primarily a religious or ecclesial issue? That is tied very closely, obviously, within these Eastern bloc countries, to nationhood and statehood, and part of the culture and identity of a particular people.

Dyczok: There's also a historical dimension to this. You're a professor of historical theology and you mentioned St. Sophia and Constantinople. The actual announcement of the Sobor happened in front of St. Sophia in Kyiv. This is a symbolic historical spot for Ukraine. If you could again just explain the ancient history of all of this. The separation from the Russian Church. The Orthodox Church in Ukraine, is it not older than the Russian Orthodox Church? And what is the symbolic significance of this separation, if you will.

Skira: Certainly. 988 is traditionally taken to be the year in which Ukraine accepted Christianity from Byzantium. And Ukraine at that time was known as Kyivan Rus. And Byzantium was the major Empire at the time, and had its capital city in Constantinople, which is modern-day Istanbul. And in that city the major church was called Hagia Sophia, or St. Sophia. And so the ancient Ukrainian state and communities received Christianity from Byzantium. And eventually they built their own St. Sophia Church in Kyiv in the 11th century. And that is the inheritor of that Church that we're talking about today. And in a sense, that transplantation of Christianity, the inheritance of Christianity from the Byzantine Empire into the Slavic lands, really has its roots within Kyiv, within ancient Ukraine.

And it begins this process of development and expansion through Ukraine and north and north-eastwards, towards Belarus as well as the Principalities of Muscovy, which eventually turned into this kingdom of Tsars and eventually modern-day Russia. And so this historic development, which is in part contested by Russian Orthodoxy and some of the ideology of the Russkiy Mir within Russian Orthodoxy, and even within President Putin's mythology of the Russian State, emerged out of this 988 event. In reality, the historical origins of Christianity in Ukraine, Russia and Belarus have their roots in Kyiv in Ukraine.

Dyczok: If I could summarize what you said, Christianity comes to Kyiv in 988 and in 2018 Ukraine reclaims its mantle as its own Church. So perhaps it's not a schism, but it's a reclaiming. How will this all affect individual believers? We talk about churches and history and politics, but it's really about people who go to church and worship. This big decision was taken, this big change happened at the highest levels. Will this affect the way people are worshipping in Orthodox parishes?

Skira: I think the primary reason for any attempts to heal disunity or schisms in a church are so that one can be in unity with other Christians. You have these multiple jurisdictions, villages which had two or three churches, and even families that were split among various jurisdictions. And formally, they could not participate in each other's weddings, be baptized by their priests, or intermarry or receive the Eucharist. And for Christianity, these are important markers of Christian unity. So at that level, believers will begin to see that there is this unified Church, which restores these dimensions of communion.

As a caveat to that, the Ukrainian Orthodox Church of the Moscow Patriarchy, the Russian Orthodox Church, has formally broken off Communion with the Ecumenical Patriarchate and anybody associated with the Ecumenical Patriarchate.

Dyczok: This was in Constantinople?

Skira: In effect, the Russian Orthodox Church has introduced a formal break in Communion or Schism as a result of these unifying attempts by Constantinople and Kyiv to heal the Schism.

The other dimension of this unity is that you will have a parallel jurisdiction in some places, where people will want to maintain their own ecclesial affiliation, whether that be Russian Orthodox, whether that be Ukrainian Orthodox, but at least they will have these options for this one unified church.

They may notice some differences in the commemoration, of which bishops get commemorated in the liturgy. Some of the churches will be adopting the modern Ukrainian vernacular, and some will retain the older Church Slavonic, which was used in parts of the Ukrainian Orthodox Churches. And some may actually use Russian.

But the whole point of all of this, is to say that there will be perceived differences amongst these believers. But as with any major changes like this, this may take some time to really trickle down in the consciousness of individual believers. There's a lot of disinformation going on in Ukraine. There's some mistrust based upon the past historical period of Ukraine being under the Soviet regime. And so, this will be a slow transformation. Some parishes have already signalled their move over. And for some it may take a little bit of time. Some may delay.

But I think over time you will begin to see this larger one unified structure of the Ukrainian Orthodox Church in Ukraine, which will presumably also respect religious pluralism of other Christian traditions within Ukraine, like the Ukrainian Eastern Catholics and the Roman Catholics. The Russian Orthodox Church will still be there, as well as other non-Christian faith traditions.

Dyczok: Professor Skira, you have been organizing a very interesting series of talks at the University of Toronto on this issue of Orthodoxy and the Ukrainian Orthodox Church. One thing I learned is that orthodox church parishes have decision-making power that perhaps other churches like the Catholic Church have less of. Can you talk a little bit about what was happening at the parish level in the lead-up to this unifying gathering or Sobor, and if you have a sense of how many parishes were in favour of this unification and what we actually saw at the Sobor? How many parishes from the Church that was loyal to the Moscow Patriarchate joined this unified Ukrainian Church?

Skira: I think that's a very good question, and the short and quick answer is, some parishes were quick to signal their intent to join the new Church or want to be part of the unified Church. Some may have split. There are examples where you have the church doors locked and the community barred access to all the buildings on the church property because of such a division. And some will remain in the Church of their origin for now. In terms of history, one must recognise that what has happened and now up until recently, has been happening fairly quickly in terms of historical time. We're looking at a period that began in April this year, which reached a climax in September and then formally reached clarity with a Unifying Council in December.

Dyczok: Quite amazing for an Orthodox Church, for any Church, to move that quickly.

Skira: It certainly is. But it's too difficult to say at this point. We need more information. I think some churches will wait still to move over. It's important to remember here that this Unifying Council has not quite finished its work. December 15th (2018) was the council that elected Metropolitan Epiphaniy as its Primate. The Primate had a speech where he welcomed others to join in Christian union within this newly erected church, the Orthodox Church of Ukraine, which is its formal title. But there is still a process, where the church has been told that on January 6th they must visit the Ecumenical Patriarch in Constantinople to receive the final statutes, the declaration. It's called the Tomos. This will declare this church as being self-governed, or autocephalous. That will really be the final step in this process. I think some churches may be sitting on the sidelines, waiting to see what happens, and whether this church will be recognised fully as an autocephalous church. Then, I think, you'll have a slow migration of churches (parishes) to this newly created church. Certainly, a majority of people in the Church have come from the Ukrainian Orthodox Church of the Kyivan Patriarchate. The statistics from not long ago placed that Church [Kyivan] as having over eight and a half million believers, whereas the Ukrainian Orthodox Church of the Moscow Partiarchate had just under four million. So the larger church, the one that actually was considered to be in division (schism) is the one that wanted to move towards unity.

Dyczok: Do we have a sense of how many parishes from the Moscow Patriarchate joined this newly created Church? Or is it too early to tell?

Skira: We do have some indications. When you look at some of the news reports, the reporting has been somewhat scant about who attended, the names of people, the total number of delegates. I did find a source that spoke about there being about 190 delegates to the Sobor. And if you think that every bishop was allowed to bring a representative from the clergy or the laity, so that roughly puts it at about 60 bishops, maybe even more, who attended this unifying Sobor. The majority would have been from the Ukrainian Orthodox Church of the Kyivan Patriarchate. The next largest group would have been from the Ukrainian Orthodox Autocephalous Church.

And based upon some recent condemnations by the Russian Orthodox Church and the Ukrainian Orthodox Church-Moscow Patriarchate, we do know that two bishops were formally condemned and removed from their ministries. So, we know that at least two Ukrainian Orthodox Church—Moscow Patriarchate were at this Sobor. I suspect there may be more, but this is only a few days after the Sobor and some of the details of the attendees have not been released just yet.

Dyczok: Interesting. So a very important step has been taken, but there are other steps to be taken. What do you see as potential obstacles to this process, if there are any? Or at this point is it just a matter of sorting out the details?

Skira: Well, if you look at institutional renewal, and here I'm talking in purely secular terms, if you want some change from an existing leadership, you appoint somebody new. And that's what happened with the appointment of Metropolitan Epiphaniy. He was a candidate who would have been widely acceptable to a majority of the bishops who voted in favour of him. There were two rounds of voting and he clearly came out at the top. So as a unifying factor he may be able to give this church a fresh start, a centre of unity. Some of the obstacles, though, will be if internal conflicts will continue to exist among the bishops over jurisdiction, over territory. The question will be who owns which property? There are a lot of church properties and associated buildings and monasteries, so there might be some conflicts that may arise. We also have to deal with the threat of localized acts of violence, from subtle coercion to actual physical violence. And, of course, what worries all Ukrainians, is the increasing military build-up on its borders by the Russian government, which has shown that it is not afraid to intervene and disrupt not only other democracies, but particularly Ukraine.

And the final (possible) obstacle, Ukraine hopes that other Orthodox churches will recognise the existence of this new Ukrainian Orthodox Church and will acknowledge the efforts of the Ecumenical Patriarch to bring about Christian unity within

Ukraine. This is a very important issue, that the other orthodox churches recognise this new Ukrainian church. Because in many ways they are all independent entities, they function in this communion which is led by the Ecumenical Patriarch. So this process of recognition and not rejection of this new Ukrainian Orthodox Church will be important.

Dyczok: When is that going to happen?

Skira: This usually is a process, and it takes time. But it has already begun, because some of the Synods have been meeting. They have been saying, "We need more dialogue between the Ecumenical Patriarch and the Russians and Ukrainians. Don't introduce further divisions." And I think it's too far along to turn back. There may be a process, where a number of the orthodox churches will say, "Yes, we recognise the Ukrainian Orthodox Church, we bring them back into communion, we wish to celebrate Christian unity and unity in the faith with these other groups." Churches like the Romanians – it will be important to hear what they say, the Church of Antioch. We do know that some of the churches will side with the Russian Orthodox Church, like the Belarusian Church, perhaps even the Serbian Church. And again, I go back to my analogy of political states. The existence of a government requires recognition by other entities. And once you're recognised, you can start functioning, being invited to councils. You can pray together, and you can exist in harmony. If you would pardon me bringing in this secular analogy. This will be a process.

Dyczok: Thank you for that analogy, that of a new state declaring independence requiring recognition. I think that clarifies things for people who are not religious experts. I have three more questions for you, but I don't know if we'll have time for all of them, so I'll throw the questions at you and you answer whichever ones you want. I'm very curious what your assessment is of the newly elected head of this newly created Ukrainian Orthodox Church. This is a young man, who has a lot of energy, but perhaps unknown to many listeners. The other this is, what do you think will happen with the Monastery of the Caves, the jewel of the crown of Ukrainian Orthodoxy, the Orthodox world. And thirdly, what, if any, actions do you expect from the Russian side?

Skira: Well, from the Russian side, the reaction has already come. They have had their own Sobor, or Council, and they've condemned the activities in Ukraine. They won't recognise the Ukrainian Orthodox Church. They have already effectively said that they're breaking communion with the Ecumenical Patriarch and everyone who is associated with him. So this shows the disagreement, or conflict, between the Ecumenical Patriarchate and Russia. I've already alluded to the fact that the threat of violence from Russia is very much a reality for the Ukrainians.

As for the newly elected Metropolitan Epiphaniy, he comes from a church that's in an area that's not too far from Kyiv. He's the Metropolitan of Pereiaslav and Bila Tserkva…

Dyczok: Historical sites!

Skira: This is an episcopal area where he would reside and have ministry. But he was also a member and Abbot in the monastery there. And Rector of the Kyiv Theological Academy. He has leadership qualities, as others have recognised that he should be the Patriarch of the Church. It's also a somewhat risky move, given his relative youth. (Metropolitan Epiphaniy is thirty-nine years old.)

Dyczok: Oh, I think it's a great move! Do you remember how old Filaret was when he was appointed (head of the Orthodox Church in Ukraine)? Thirty-Seven! He (newly elected Metropolitan Epiphaniy) is older than Filaret was when he was appointed!

Skira: Indeed! So there will be many years of him being at the helm of the Church. Hopefully that energy that he has, and his relative youth will translate into an energy that will reinvigorate the Ukrainian Orthodox Church. And you had a third question?

Dyczok: About the Monastery of the Caves, Pecherska Lavra. If you have a crystal ball, what do you see happening with that?

Skira: Pochaiivska and Pecherska Lavra are the two holy sites within Ukraine. And currently they have been delegated to the Ukrainian Orthodox Church Moscow Patriarchate, which, I think, for the interim will continue to exercise their stewardship over those areas. Some of the buildings on those two sites, however, are not in the possession of the church, and they are state-owned. What I think the Ukrainian government and Ukrainian church will probably do is affirm their right to these sites. And, I think, over time, the churches that are not directly part of the Ukrainian Orthodox Church will be slowly asked to move elsewhere.

Dyczok: Let's hope that all happens peacefully. Is there anything you would like to add?

Skira: Again, this is a very historic moment that has happened very quickly. I think this is a very positive moment. It's part of the maturation of the Ukrainian state. But more importantly, it's part of the unifying attempts to bring the church in Ukraine into one body, after years of divisions, after years of persecution and repression. This is a moment, in a sense, of resurrection of Christianity in Ukraine. And I hope that it will continue to spur a further renaissance within Ukraine, of the historical Kyivan-Rus, of Christianity, for many centuries to come.

"Ukraine 2019 Rada Election. Olga Onuch on Results and Implications"

26 July 2019

https://hromadske.radio/en/podcasts/ukraine-calling/ukraine-2019-rada-election-olga-onuch-on-results-and-implications

Marta Dyczok: Hello, and welcome to a special election episode of Ukraine Calling. I'm Marta Dyczok for *Hromadske Radio* in Kyiv. There's been a snap election in Ukraine for Parliament. To explain what the results are, and what this will mean for Ukraine, we have in studio Professor Olga Onuch. She is a political scientist based at Manchester University, England. She's also a fellow at the Davis Centre at Harvard University, author of many publications. She's in Kyiv on a research trip, has been watching the election campaign and now the results. We're very lucky to catch her here. Thank you very much for finding the time to join us Dr. Onuch.

Olga Onuch: Marta, thank you very much for having me.

Dyczok: So. A snap election. What are the results? And what does this mean for Ukraine? You've been watching this carefully and you have some interesting analysis.

Onuch: Well, first of all, I think, we're all really pleased to see that this was the freest, the fairest parliamentary election that we've seen in Ukraine. But this is also a seismic shift.

Dyczok: Explain.

Onuch: When I say that I get shivers because we have never seen something like this, where the President will have a party in Parliament that has a majority. They can pass laws without going into any coalitions. This was what the sociological survey data was showing us, but it was hard to believe. And sure enough, they will have a majority and they will be able to pass many things. Constitutional majority, no. They will have to go into coalitions for that, but they will get a lot of things through without going to anyone else in Parliament.

Dyczok: So, let's back up a little bit. A few months ago, a new President was elected by a landslide. A few days ago, a new Parliament was elected, and the President's party has won the majority. So, concentration of power.

Onuch: It is a risk. Those of us, like yourself, who are watching and observing Ukrainian politics, we are looking at this wondering, will hubris win out in the end? Will they take this as a mandate to do absolutely anything and not consult with others? Or will they in fact be a technocratic government as they are promising us to be. We can't be certain. We don't know this President, we don't know Zelensky as a politician at all. The unknowns around him, his team, this brand-new party, are huge. So, we don't know what to expect. There is a serious risk of that if the wrong people are in power, if the wrong politicians are in Parliament, if his [Zelensky's] team is poor, if they do not want to have compromises, they'll go it alone and yes, maybe concentrate power in the hands of one or two or few people, yes.

Dyczok: Well, we don't know a lot about the President and his party, but what do we know? He came to power on this slogan of change, new faces. We have new faces in the President's office and now in Parliament. What do we know about these people?

Onuch: Well, we're getting to know these people slowly and surely. Some of these people are in fact very experienced in various industries, some were in civil society, some were in journalism. There are also some very suspicious faces, no need to highlight them here, that should worry some people. But this is across the board in various parties, in European Solidarity, which is Petro Poroshenko's party.

Dyczok: They didn't do so well.

Onuch: No, they did not do well at all. But it's as if they didn't learn their lessons. These campaigns were not, "Let's go out into the field, into the regions, listen to people and then form a campaign around that," they were just, "This is what we think we should be campaigning on," and going forward. But in his party there are some old faces that should worry us, certainly. We know they have complicated histories, and some of them may or may not have legal issues pending. And there are new faces in all parties, whether it's in European Solidarity or in Holos.

Dyczok: Let's talk about Holos. Holos is a new party that appeared, led by rock star Sviatoslav Vakarchuk of Okean Elzy, and they ran for office. How did they do? Where do you place these people? How do you see their future?

Onuch: Great music. Absolutely. I loved all of their different albums. Maybe not the best political strategy and strategists involved in that campaign. "Divided we fall, united we conquer" should have been the strategy for European Solidarity, for Holos, another party, Samopomich, and maybe the former Prime Minister's, Groysman's party. If they had united, they actually would have done much better. It is important to note that around 2017 Holos signed an agreement with these other parties, that they would head into the elections together. When the President disbanded Parliament, Holos did a U-turn and said, "We're only going to take new faces." Of course, Sviatoslav Vakarchuk is not a new face because he...

Dyczok: He has been in Parliament.

Onuch: Yes. He was in politics, and surely that's an interesting contradiction. Their mistake was not taking some of the good MPs and reformers from the last Parliament, people like Svitlana Zalishchuk, Hanna Hopko, others, who learned the hard lessons when you first enter a Parliament. They didn't do this, so that strategy was not to say it was... bad is not the word, it was...

Dyczok: Not as effective as it could have been.

Onuch: I think not effective at all. When people that I work with were going around the country and asking people, "Are you going to vote for this party or that party?" in the west of Ukraine people were saying that they were going to vote for Holos. They were also saying, "Well, who else can I vote for? I want new faces in Parliament." But he (Vakarchuk) really shouldn't have gone into politics, he should have stayed in music, or been a moral figure outside of Parliament.

Dyczok: You mentioned a number of women's names. The gender issue in Parliament is something that international observers have been noticing more than Ukrainian observers. From what we know of the results, are we seeing a bit of a shift in the gender balance? Are there more women that have been elected this time?

Onuch: There are more women. We will have the largest number of women in Ukrainian Parliament than we have had to date. I believe it's around twenty percent. I think previously it was around eight percent.

Dyczok: That's more than twice as much as last time, so that's an improvement.

Onuch: Absolutely. And I think the new faces story helped in that way. When you are looking for new people to join Parliament, all of a sudden you find lawyers, professionals, NGO workers, and so forth. And many of these are women in their thirties, maybe even a little bit younger, who are already achieving amazing things professionally. I think that Holos was quite good at this. So, perhaps in that light, it's a shame that they didn't get more support because there could have been even more women in Parliament. But yes, that's an interesting shift, and I think that's positive.

Although, in the individual ridings, where people ran in the first-past-the-post part of the election, there was a really gendered campaign. Female candidates were criticized on several occasions, and even attacked. Their opponents were very much targeting them. Someone even coined the term, "ostannya majoritarka," [reference to the last barricade] playing on the Ukrainian term "majoritarka" [the individual candidates running not on party lists]. In other words, the last female candidate remaining. It was much more difficult for women. Generally, in those constituencies, that's where all those bad things happened, not quite fraud but...

Dyczok: Sort of, mild violations?

Onuch: Mild, but also not so mild violations. People being offered things like tickets to concerts, a bag of apples, or a variety of different things. A bag of apples doesn't sound like it's a big deal. But one person in Eastern Ukraine told us, "in the summer it's not so bad because you don't need to turn on the light the whole day, so I'm saving a lot of money and I can eat properly." People are telling you this, and Holos, and certainly European Solidarity did not get that message. There was no talk about the daily struggle that the average voter faces in Ukraine. And that is a tragedy. And even after this dramatic loss by the President, losing by 73%, his campaign's not reacting to this.

Dyczok: Let's talk about the other party that did well, the Opposition Platform. Describe who these people are, how they did, and what this means.

Onuch: The Opposition Platform for Life is what Western observers would call the "pro-Russian party." I think it's a particularly interesting party this time around because they were previously in a coalition with another party, the Opposition Bloc. Essentially, these two different political clans, political networks in Ukraine, divided and formed two parties for this election.

Dyczok: And these are people who come out of the old Regions Party.

Onuch: The old Regions Party. As you know, in the 2000s, the Regions Party was an amalgamation of different Eastern Ukrainian parties, and they fell apart practically after the Euromaidan in 2014. But then they formed around this Opposition Bloc, and then they split up again. And the shocking thing about the Opposition Platform for Life is Viktor Medvedchuk. I don't even know how you describe this character in Ukrainian politics.

Dyczok: Well, he's a lawyer by training, has a long political history, and he is a brother-in-law or something like that with President Putin.

Onuch: That's a very light-touch description of who this person is. He's essentially a major political kingmaker in Ukraine, especially the Eastern region. In terms of manipulations and falsifications in the past, this man has been involved in various things. And so again, this is a Wikipedia moment for your listeners, but that fact that he is now going to be in Parliament in Ukraine is shocking to me. And I think a lot of people are shocked by that as well.

Dyczok: And how well they did.

Onuch: There's always a portion of Ukrainian voters, thirteen percent or so, that will vote for this party. They see it as *their* party, representing *their* interests. We have those people in our surveys, those people are a little bit different, and they certainly belong to the various clientelistic networks, specifically in Luhansk and Donetsk provinces or oblasts. So I don't think it's surprising that they got that much of the vote. If they got more than that, it would be much more surprising.

Dyczok: So, what you're saying is that their result shows that support for those views is stable?

Onuch: Yes.

Dyczok: Another point is this Parliament will be smaller. There will be a fewer number of seats. There are 450 seats in Ukraine's Parliament, but there will be fewer actual members of Parliament this time. Could you speak to that a little bit?

Onuch: Yes, I believe it's 423. And it's the same as the last Parliament, because of the occupied territories of Ukraine, in Luhansk and Donetsk Oblast. And Crimea. Because the government is unable to run elections there.

Dyczok: Let's step back and take another big picture look. We've got pretty much a clear idea of what this Parliament will look like. We have a majority, we have a clear outlier, the Opposition Platform, they have very different views. We have a few other parties. So, what do you see this Parliament doing? Are there going to be any coalitions? There's no need for a coalition when you have a majority, so what will be the dynamic with the other parties? Or is it too early to tell?

Onuch: I think it is in some ways too early to tell. But we can say if Sluha Narodu, the President's party, goes it alone, which they can do, they will have to find allies should they ever want to do anything that will require a constitutional change (which requires 2/3 of the votes).

So, who knows what's going to happen. But they will be the only ones left to blame for when things don't work out, and it's impossible that everything will work out. So that's a risky strategy. The inverse, if they really want a technocratic government, experts, an economist as prime minister to pass reforms policies, then it would actually be very smart of them to extend an olive branch to a party like Holos. And I know that Holos' leader is open to working with Sluha Narodu.

That would be an interesting moment to, first off, show unity, and I think this country would like to see that. I'm sure some of the voters would see that as a positive thing. Also, I think international partners would see that as a positive thing. Secondly, I think it would surprise their critics, because their critics are expecting them to now go it alone. I think that could be an interesting strategy, this olive branch scenario, and a lot advisors are saying this.

Dyczok: Well, it would make for good optics if nothing else.

Onuch: And I think Zelensky is about good optics in some ways. But also, I think strategically you can get other things done faster with the support of, for instance, Holos' leader Svyatoslav Vakarchuk. He has a lot of support from Western partners, including people in the U.S., several political scientists in the U.S. Not all of them are experts on Ukraine and that kind of came through in how his campaign was guided throughout this process. The rumour mill in Kyiv spread the message that his advisors didn't understand what hybrid war was in Ukraine. I'm sure that's not all of them. But nonetheless, there is a lot of investment from other foreign partners, international experts, that are very much respected around the world. He also has that capital that he can bring to Sluha Narodu. We'll see.

Dyczok: So, we've got new faces, new parties, Zelensky, Vakarchuk. What about the old players? What's going to happen to them? Have they been swept off the political map? Do they have a political future? They're going to be in Parliament, but they won't have very much power: the Opposition Platform (former Regions Party), Yulia Tymoshenko's Batkivshchyna Party, former President Poroshenko?

Onuch: I'm glad you mentioned this, because no one's talking about Batkivshchyna, Yulia Tymoshenko's party. This party has staying power.

Dyczok: They're the only party that we can say has lasted since they were created. All the others have fallen apart.

Onuch: Yes. Very few people have been focusing on Yulia Tymoshenko's staying power, and in a sense, the only real party in Ukraine. This is not someone you can get rid of in Ukraine, and even though her support has dwindled, she still did a lot better than expected, considering how few places they actively campaigned in. For instance, in Kyiv's city centre there were very few campaign posters, but in the suburbs, there were many. In regions where they knew they weren't going to win, they didn't campaign very much.

So, considering what result they still got with having this very targeted campaign, about eight percent, that means they have a real base that is very dedicated to them.

Dyczok: It's not shrinking, but it's not growing.

Onuch: Which just means that this is a party you will have to deal with if you are in power, in some way, shape, or form. I think, being in the opposition really suits Yulia Tymoshenko and Batkivshchyna in terms of their rhetoric and style of politics. But, yes, she and her party are not going anywhere anytime soon.

Dyczok: Let's talk about who didn't make it, those who've been swept off the political map.

Onuch: For now. For instance, the far-right parties, or right-wing parties, united for this particular election and did not make it. Those observers who think Ukraine has been inundated with far-right politics and far-right politicians consistently miss the point. This is yet another clear demonstration that there is no right-wing party that can win anywhere near the number of votes that they need to get into Parliament.

Dyczok: They got something like two percent or three percent of the vote, right?

Onuch: Yes. I believe they are still within the two percent range and they're going to receive state funds.

Dyczok: So, the right-wing nationalists are not quite off the map but they're not in Parliament. Who else didn't make it?

Onuch: There are three that are perhaps the most surprising for people who have been observing politics for a long time. One is Groysman's party. He really didn't have a chance with this party. The former Prime Minister and this party just came together very quickly, and it was just because there was no way that he could go into the former President's party, into European Solidarity, because they had this quite open conflict. By many accounts he was quite a good Prime Minister, he's a very good technocrat.

Dyczok: Is there a possible role for him in the new constellation of forces? He's not a new face but he's competent with a proven track record.

Onuch: He's very competent it seems in recent years and has been able to align himself with all the different parties in power when need be, certainly has proven his competence. But because Sluha Narodu and Zelensky keep saying no previous politicians….

Dyczok: The other party that didn't make it, the Radical Party…

Onuch: Liashko's party, yes.

Dyczok: I think it'll be a lot less dramatic and comedic in Parliament without that character, but I think also, that shows something about political attitudes.

Onuch: Hopefully fewer fist fights, yes.

Dyczok: Is there anything else looking forward that I haven't asked you that you think is important?

Onuch: Well we haven't talked about the low turnout. Everyone's saying, "oh, it's the vacation." Well then that should be spread across evenly, across the country, right.

Dyczok: Remind our listeners what the voter turnout was.

Onuch: It's the lowest in Ukraine's history, about forty-nine point something percent. When conflict was brewing in 2014 and Ukraine held its Parliamentary election it was nearly three percent higher, and that vote was severely depressed by the conflict. So, we see a drop in turnout in two ways. We see a record low turnout in places like Lviv, in Western Ukraine. So that's one thing that needs to be addressed. The other thing we also see is a massive decline in turnout between the presidential and parliamentary elections in Luhansk, Donetsk, Kharkiv, Kyiv, and, I believe, Zaporizhzhia.

Dyczok: So that is the East, Centre, and South. What does that mean?

Onuch: We're talking double-digit difference of turnout between presidential and parliamentary elections. Some say it was the vacation period, but why those places and not others? I think it was the places that Sluha Narodu was going to win comfortably some voters decided not to turn out. That's one hypothesis.

Dyczok: So, disengagement with the political process?

Onuch: Disengagement, yes. Potentially, if those people were voters for Holos and European Solidarity, they didn't turn out because they didn't think their party could possibly win. We don't know that, but I don't buy the vacation story because it's just not spread out evenly enough.

The other thing is the lower turnout in Western Ukraine. Everyone is saying it's the migrants. I just ran an analysis last night with our project Mobilize, to test whether those who intended to vote for Sluha Narodu and those who intended to vote for Holos and European Solidarity were more likely to also migrate, or have friends and family abroad, therefore be connected to an already migrated network. And this did not correlate in any way to support for European Solidarity or Holos, but it did to Sluha Narodu.

Dyczok: That's interesting.

Onuch: So, if you said in surveys prior to the election, "I am planning on voting for Sluha Narodu," you were more likely to want to leave the country. You also were five percent more likely to have family and friends already living abroad, and out of that batch you were also more likely to be from Western Ukraine. So, there is an interesting story there.

Dyczok: For our listeners, Professor Onuch has started at this new research project which is going to be three years long, looking at precisely these issues. So, we'll have to have you back on the show. But we're going to have to wrap up now so thank you very much. Lots of interesting things. Seismic shift, is that what you called this election?

Onuch: Yes.

Dyczok: So, fasten your seatbelts and let's see what will come next.

UKRAINIAN VOICES

Collected by Andreas Umland

1 *Mychailo Wynnyckyj*
Ukraine's Maidan, Russia's War
A Chronicle and Analysis of the Revolution of Dignity
With a foreword by Serhii Plokhy
ISBN 978-3-8382-1327-9

2 *Olexander Hryb*
Understanding Contemporary Ukrainian and Russian Nationalism
The Post-Soviet Cossack Revival and Ukraine's National Security
With a foreword by Vitali Vitaliev
ISBN 978-3-8382-1377-4

3 *Marko Bojcun*
Towards a Political Economy of Ukraine
Selected Essays 1990–2015
With a foreword by John-Paul Himka
ISBN 978-3-8382-1368-2

4 *Volodymyr Yermolenko (ed.)*
Ukraine in Histories and Stories
Essays by Ukrainian Intellectuals
With a preface by Peter Pomerantsev
ISBN 978-3-8382-1456-6

5 *Mykola Riabchuk*
At the Fence of Metternich's Garden
Essays on Europe, Ukraine, and Europeanization
ISBN 978-3-8382-1484-9

6 *Marta Dyczok*
Ukraine Calling
A Kaleidoscope from Hromadske Radio 2016–2019
With a foreword by Andriy Kulykov
ISBN 978-3-8382-1472-6

7 *Olexander Scherba*
Ukraine vs. Darkness
Undiplomatic Thoughts
With a foreword by Adrian Karatnycky
ISBN 978-3-8382-1501-3

8 *Olesya Yaremchuk*
Our Others
Stories of Ukrainian Diversity
With a foreword by Ostap Slyvynsky
Translated from the Ukrainian by Zenia Tompkins and Hanna Leliv
ISBN 978-3-8382-1475-7

9 *Nataliya Gumenyuk*
Die verlorene Insel
Geschichten von der besetzten Krim
Mit einem Vorwort von Alice Bota
Aus dem Ukrainischen übersetzt von Johann Zajaczkowski
ISBN 978-3-8382-1499-3

10 *Olena Stiazhkina*
Zero Point Ukraine
Four Essays on World War II
Translated from Ukrainian by Svitlana Kulinska
ISBN 978-3-8382-1550-1

11 *Oleksii Sinchenko, Dmytro Stus, Leonid Finberg (compilers)*
Ukrainian Dissidents
An Anthology of Texts
ISBN 978-3-8382-1551-8